1 50

All Flags Flying!

Illustrated by Robert Reedy

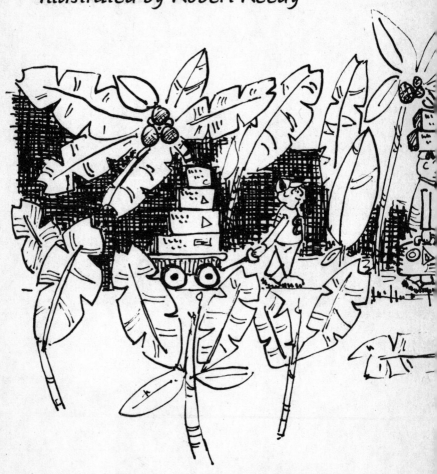

The National Spiritual Assembly of the Bahá'ís
of South and West Africa, Johannesburg

All Flags Flying!

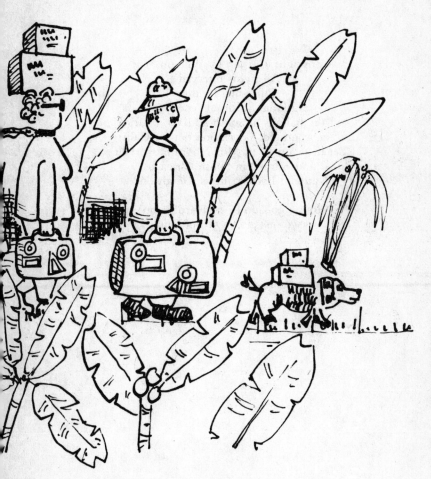

by William Sears

Contents

CONTENTS

THE SHIP IS LAUNCHED

"That way lies madness"

1

She was very nice. A lovely Bahá'í girl. Her name was Marguerite Reimer.

I was a fairly decent, somewhat devout, Christian boy. A Catholic named William Sears.

When I told my close friends the two of us planned to marry, they all disapproved. Immediately. Vocally. Every last one of them. Together. In unison. Like a Greek Chorus.

"That way," they warned, "lies madness." They added, "Inter-racial marriages are seldom—"

I objected. "It's hardly an inter-racial—"

"Madness!" they cried. "Madness!"

One was a Jew, one a Baptist, three were Catholics, one an agnostic, one an atheist, and one a very delightful variety of mixed nothings.

All were prejudiced.

Against marriage.

Quite obviously and unreasonably.

Marguerite and I were married anyway, in spite of them and their warnings. They were right, of course. It was madness.

That's what this book is all about.

2

You probably know all there is to know about Christian marriage: "Do you, William, take Marguerite to be your lawfully wedded wife?" And leave out the obey.

Elimination of the word "obey", of course, was Marguerite's contribution.

I know it's quite a commonplace deletion nowadays. Today, no one wants to obey anyone about anything. Above all, not during such a tentative thing as a marriage. This deletion of Marguerite's, remember, was way back in those long-ago days of the dominant husband: "Do this! Do that! Don't just stand there! Hop to it, sister!"

It was during that glorious, lost-forever heyday of him who unfortunately has come to be called a "male chauvinistic pig". Long before this wonderful male creature came to be called that by "female chauvinists"—I really don't want to become involved in that aspect of marriage.

Not at this late hour. "Late" as in "her late husband".

The point I'm making is that Marguerite was far ahead of her time. She broke early ground for women's rights. Not about *Women's Lib*. Bahá'ís believe in, and courageously teach, the complete equality of the sexes. Members of the Bahá'í Faith, men and women alike, have always worked together like the two wings of one bird. It's part of their Religion.

Forget that. I am not talking about religion. I'm talking about way back in those halcyon days when *ERA* meant "Earned Run Average". Those hazy happy days when women knew their place and nothing about baseball.

Okay, so I think somewhat differently now. Don't blame me, blame the Bahá'í Faith. If you insist on blaming some person, blame Marguerite. She gradually changed me over the years. I don't say it was for the better. Not at first anyway. What I actually said was: "Over my dead body!"

Marguerite took it in good spirit. Smiled her warm smile and said: "If necessary."

There is something you must understand at the outset if you are to appreciate this book.

Bahá'ís are obedient to their Spiritual Assemblies, both National and Local. They are obedient to the duly constituted Authorities of the States, Provinces, and Countries in which they live. They are loyal, law-abiding, peace-loving, non-violent, fierce upholders of law and order.

But when it comes to Marriage:

"Charge!"

3

Some people feel that Marriage today is gravely ill, almost "terminal". This once-proud family institution, they say, is succumbing to frequent spells of Cheyne-Stokes breathing. In fact, if you listened to the opinions of the world in general, you'd believe that Marriage was now approaching its death-throes and final jerks.

Not so with the Bahá'ís.

To them, Marriage is still spelled with a capital letter M. Marriage as an Institution is alive and well in all parts of the world. Improving every year. Not weakening, *strengthening*.

Can you believe that?

Bahá'ís do.

I mean, how out of tune with the times can you get?

Don't become nervous. I'm not going to lean too heavily on marriage here, knowing the dangerous state your own is in.

All you need to know, as Marguerite and I launch off toward our Fiftieth Wedding Anniversary described as "golden", is this: With the Bahá'ís, all that permissive free and easy attitude toward Marriage, that, "Don't call me and I won't call you"; "Goodbye, Baby, it was fun, and what was your name again?" is out the window. The Bahá'ís have exchanged "live-in" boy friends and girl friends for a "live-in" Religion.

If you do marry a Bahá'í, it's supposed to be for keeps. Not only "until death do us part", but far beyond that.

"Until eternity do us part" would be more like it.

All attempts to minimize the importance of Marriage, or to belittle or ridicule it as an Institution, are resisted strongly. The Bahá'í Faith considers marriage, children and the family to be the basic unit of all society. And get this, the Bahá'ís themselves really believe it.

Talk about swimming against the popular current.

6

More, these Bahá'ís plan to change the direction of the stream. Are you getting all of this down?

Of course, I'm enchanted! Otherwise why would I be saying these darned fool things?

With these Bahá'ís, it's not good enough to have merely the "milk of human kindness" running through your veins. I could stand that. It's the "*cream* of human kindness" they expect from you.

Of course I'm bewitched!

Otherwise why would I be trying to become a better person than the fine one I am right now? Tell me that.

I keep telling Marguerite that it's all part of a subversive Bahá'í plot. She just laughs and says, "Every Bahá'í is supposed to try and become a better person, a finer human being. It's part of our Religion. Yours, too, now."

It's not just a theory, they work at it each day. Some more successfully than others, but they all try. It's expected of them. Every Bahá'í marriage and Bahá'í home is supposed to strive to achieve this same excellence and became a haven of love.

It can warp your judgement.

Why else would I give away free blood transfusions? And my last good Hart-Schaefner and Marx suit and my newest beige sports jacket? Cashmere. Bill Blass. And, if that weren't enough, with glazed eyes, I even threw in a pair of my best Bally sports shoes. To benefit and comfort some poor suffering beggar whose name I didn't even know last week.

Mind you, I'm giving these clothes away, free. Outright. In cold blood. Not selling them at a garage sale, or a flea market, for a little decent profit.

Do you suppose this is all a secret religious post-hypnotic command that Marguerite gave to me while I was asleep?

Hypnotized is not strong enough for the way I feel about it now that I'm awake.

I'm mesmerized!

"Don't call my lawyer.
Call my friends!"

4

A very close friend of mine, Robert Quigley, is fond of saying, "Don't fool around with City Hall."

These Bahá'ís *are* City Hall. They're also the Governor's Mansion, the White House, the Houston Space Centre, the Mayo Clinic, and the United Nations. All rolled into one. I mean when it comes to Marriage. And that's only for starters!

Bahá'ís have the strange idea of bringing back the popularity and dependability of the home, the family, children—and get this—Marriage!

Is that a laugh?

In today's permissive society?

Really!

If I started in on how Bahá'ís feel about divorce, it would blow you right out of the water. I mean *out*. Capitalized, underlined, with an exclamation point: OUT!

It's far too early in the book for you to undergo that kind of a traumatic shock, so I'm sparing you.

Oh yes, Bahá'ís accept divorce. If it's either that or the electric chair. Meaning that divorce is permissible in their Religion, but only in extreme circumstances.*

You don't break up one of the best things in life merely because it's inconvenient or was based upon the flimsiest of pretexts in the first place. What you do instead, is spend a little time learning about each other before marriage. Not after casually bumping into each other at the Boat Show.

Marguerite said that, I didn't.

---

*You notice I keep saying *their* Religion, not *my* Religion although I am a Bahá'í myself. To be honest, it's so doggone decent and good that I keep feeling it's just too good to be true, and I keep looking for something wrong and I don't find it. I'd better straighten up and fly right myself.

Bahá'ís figure that Marriage is such an overwhelmingly "good thing" that once the true value of Marriage is properly understood, divorce will become as rare as icebergs outside Mombasa.

I swallow all this about Marriage because of that special spirit that surrounds me when I'm with Marguerite and the Bahá'ís. It's enrapturing. No exaggeration. It's so simple and sweet to the taste that I keep asking myself: "Can anything be that wonderful?"

Before this gets too saccharine, let me hasten to add that I don't think it can be the people. When I meet them outside of those Bahá'í meetings, I wouldn't have most of them on a stick. But *inside*, there really is something working. Marguerite says it's the Bahá'í spirit of love and unity.

It must be something because most of these individuals couldn't carry a single precinct in a local election. But get them all together in one room—Run for the hills!

Sometimes when I get home after one of those delightful Bahá'í Fireside meetings, I look in the mirror and say to myself, "Was it really that good? Or are you under some kind of a spell? Watch your step, Billy boy! They may nail your hide to the fence."

They did.

There were times in the beginning when I feared that it might already be too late for me to escape. Or for anybody to come to my rescue. I wasn't sure I wanted them to. That's how grave and dangerous my position became. Worse, I was even thinking of marrying one.

My friends who called my marriage "madness" also warned me to beware of this very early stage of allurement. One of them, an historian, told me about the bewitchment that took place when the Founder of the Bahá'í Faith, Bahá'u'lláh, had been exiled to the Holy Land which became the World Centre of the Bahá'í Faith. People who were not Bahá'ís warned their friends to be careful when visiting Bahá'u'lláh or having tea with Him. It could be dangerous, they said. They accused the Bahá'ís of putting something in the visitors' tea because it had been noticed that those visitors after tea-time, invariably came out of Bahá'u'lláh's Presence in a state of exhilarated joy and happiness with unusually radiant faces. They seemed to be transformed into different people entirely.

Enemies of the Bahá'í Faith said that.

9

The world-renowned Orientalist and Christian scholar, Professor Edward Granville Browne of Cambridge University, said that ridiculous as these false charges were, a special "spirit" did seem to pervade all those who came into the Presence of Bahá'u'lláh and His followers. It "most powerfully" affected "all subjected to its influence", Browne declared.

Browne added: "Let those who have not seen disbelieve me if they will, but, should that spirit once reveal itself to them, they will experience an emotion which they are not likely to forget."

"See," Marguerite said, after she had shared these words with me, "I told you it was the spirit."

Was that what was happening to me?

I couldn't take a chance, so I called for help. This, of course, was before I became a Bahá'í.

"Don't call my lawyer", I warned my potential rescuers. "He's a Bahá'í now, too. He ignored all my warnings. Call my close personal friends who are not yet Bahá'ís. Move very carefully on this. But fast. I'm told that a lot of people are going down like tenpins."

It was partly my fault. I shouldn't have raved so enthusiastically about the "fringe benefits" of becoming a Bahá'í. I hoped I still had a few hard-nosed friends left who were not yet Bahá'ís.

"Tell them to get me out of this," I urged, "while they still can."

The truth is, I could feel myself slipping away. I was going down for the third time, and the only word I could think of was:
"Help!"

"Hurry! I'm being hooked on goodness!"

5

Make no mistake. I thought the Bahá'í Faith was wonderful even when I was treading water. I just wanted more time to think it over. No one likes to be "steamrollered". Even by love and kindness and logic.

Of course, I was worried. No one had a right to feel this splendid without feeling guilty. It felt so good it had to be illegal. But I knew that if by some miracle it was okay, I wanted in. All the way. I just needed more time to make certain.

"Make it plain to my hard-nosed friends when you call them", I urged, "that these Bahá'ís nearly have me hooked on 'goodness'. Also on 'sacrifice'."

Everyone knows that's not the Bill Sears style.

Unfortunately, as my rebellion and resistance became more feeble, I suspected that the Bahá'í Faith was gradually becoming habit-forming. Without drugs, but with some astonishing side-effects. For example: Almost overnight I was becoming a do-gooder. Something I'd always hated. Worse, I was becoming a do-gooder's do-gooder.

Me!

I used to be such a nice normal self-centred person. I was one of the very first ones to say, "I gave at the office" even when I didn't. I lived a happy-go-lucky trouble-free life on Saturday nights rolling the dice at Eddie Mandick's Twin Lanes Tavern to see who would pay for the sloe-gin fizzes and the boiler-makers. I didn't give a charitable hoot about my fellow man. Live and let live. Everything was simple.

Now, look at me, since this Bahá'í girl led me inside the enchanted woodcutter's cottage. I've stopped drinking. Entirely. Except for Perrier Water and Moni's Grape Juice. I'm spending my nights and weekends supplying milk to the underprivileged. And bringing it there in person. And paying for it. I'm cheering the disconsolate. I'm visiting the ill, the halt and the blind. I'm spending half my income on strangers. On people I never even heard about before the Bahá'í Local Spiritual Assembly decided to launch an "Operation Befriend" programme and enlisted my help. Be kind to your neighbours in need, they said.

Do you wonder I'm worried about myself?

It's a crisis!

6

Psst!

Another word of caution to those who are going to try and "spring" me. If a Bahá'í—any Bahá'í—young, old, male or female, beautiful or ugly, stranger or friend, asks you if you'd like to attend a Bahá'í "Fireside Meeting", set your inner warning alarm to go off instantly, flashing the one word: "Danger!"

The answer to that question is a loud resounding "No!" You may even want to throw in a "Never!" But remember your survival as a "non-involved" rugged outsider depends upon your replying with an immediate, absolute, firm and unwavering: "No! I do not want to go to a Bahá'í Fireside Meeting!"

Tell them you have an appointment to see your psychiatrist.*

Here are a few additional self-preserving security aids: Keep away at all times not only from Bahá'í Firesides, but also from all Bahá'í Pot-Luck Dinners, Dawn Prayers, and Deepening Classes. They are all booby-trapped.

Be warned. You have seen for yourself what they have done to me.

"Befriend everybody", the Bahá'ís told me. "Make it a way of life."

That included being kind to people who a year ago, I didn't know existed. And certainly didn't care.

One night, after our Bahá'í marriage, just as I was about to put out the light and go to sleep, Marguerite put her hand on my arm. She wanted me to appreciate how sweet my work would be on the

---

* You may want to arrange such an appointment anyway, if you are still reading this book.

Befriend Committee, to which I had just been appointed. She read to me a particularly tender passage from the Bahá'í Writings about such an "Operation Befriend"!

> "Let each one of God's loved ones . . . do some good to every person whose path he crosseth, . . ." "Think ye at all times of rendering some service to every member of the human race."

Gently I removed her hand.

"Marvellous!" I told her. "Now can we let the other better-persons and finer-human-beings do all that grand work on behalf of their fellow man? And let this self-loving, earth-bound, still happily undeveloped Bahá'í put out the light and go to sleep?"

Of course I'm alarmed. Suddenly, every person who's in trouble, or feeling depressed has become my personal responsibility. Sure, other members of the Committee are doing the same work. That's not the point. The point is, *I'm* doing it! I'm encouraging and comforting total strangers simply because they're underprivileged. Far worse, I'm getting to care about them. I worry and can't sleep wondering if they're cold or ill. Me, old "non-involved".

Is that spooky?

Are you getting all this down? Like I suggested?

We're talking about me: William Bernard Patrick Michael Terence Sears, the Seventh. *I'm* the one who's doing these crazy things. Voluntarily. I'm taking baskets of fruit and groceries to the poor. I'm feeding the hungry. Not only on my own time, but on my own budget. I'm cheering and uplifting the "shut-ins" of life. Even on my Saturdays, Sundays and holidays. And my days off. Even on those precious days when the Dodgers are in town, playing their bitter enemies the San Francisco Giants.

What a rotten way to spend your weekends.

I'm even baby-sitting senior citizens. I'm taking the neighbourhood children to the zoo. Letting them bowl me over and tramp on me as they rush through the gate when it's opened, and head for monkey island, singing at the top of their voices: "Happy days are here again!"

They aren't.

Not for me, Bill Sears. Father Christmas in July!

The most sickening thing of all is, I volunteered to do all this. Volunteered!

If I don't get some outside help soon, I'm going to become noble. Me! Noble!

Ha!

Is that humiliating?

I used to be such a splendid, egotistical, worldly, fun-loving, materialistic rotten egg.*

How the mighty have fallen!

I'm going to take down that huge billboard on top of the downtown Bank of America, and put up a sign reading:

"BEWARE OF BAHÁ'Í MARRIAGE!"

And that's only the tip of the iceberg.

---

* You may want to use far stronger language here. I once would have myself, but no longer find I can. Weep for me.

ON YOUR MARKS!

GET SET!

"Off in a cloud of dedicated dust!"

7

Once you are safely wed, one of the first things you learn about your new Bahá'í marriage partner is this: They all want to pioneer.

Almost without exception.

I won't say they're fanatic, but the urge to pioneer does burn deep down inside every Bahá'í heart. Like a smouldering, inactive volcano.

Inactive volcano is what you, the innocent new marriage partner, are led to think it is.

Just poke around inside that apparently "inactive" pioneering crater, and pow!

There is no end on your stick.

And the part that is left, is a smouldering Mt St Helen's.

Or worse.

Krakatoa!

There are no sweeter or more gentle people on the face of the earth than the Bahá'ís. However, once their pioneering torches are ignited, they become a menace—to their families, to their friends, and to themselves. It's a spiritual Jekyll-and-Hyde syndrome. Unintentional. Unexpected. Irreversible.

Only one thing can cure them. Release them into the pioneering field.

Immediately.

It's one of the best ways to preserve your marriage. Let alone your sanity.

This is the iceberg.

Once the word "pioneering" is mentioned in their presence, especially in connection with such motivating and inflaming phrases as "virgin territory", "open countries", "unclaimed areas", or "arise", Bahá'ís tend to "self-destruct". In an incredibly short time. Unless they can be freed to pioneer to a goal city.

You see them today, they are gone tomorrow.

Phhfffttt!

Off in a cloud of dedicated dust!

Bahá'ís are drawn to pioneering "posts" as steel filings are drawn to a magnet.

Plunk! Ping! Bong!

The next time you meet them, they are tanned from the tropics or sallow from the frozen north. They are talking Senegalese, Gikuyu, or Urdu. They have come back home only to arrange their final affairs before flying back to their true home, their new adored pioneering post.

"The sooner I can get back where I belong," they tell you, "and away from this soul-deadening decadent Western materialism, the better I'll like it."

When these restless, temporarily-back-home, pioneers walk by you at the Bahá'í Nineteen Day Feast, you can feel the heat radiating from their departing exhaust pipes.

These visiting Bahá'ís would rather land a new "overseas" pioneer to take back with them to their newly adopted homeland than a thirty pound muskellunge or a blue marlin. As an innocent bystander not yet swept into the vortex of this swirling, all-consuming pioneer blaze, it appeared to me that next to becoming a Bahá'í, the greatest excitement in any Bahá'í life apparently is to pioneer. It is a sudden uncontrollable urge on the part of every Bahá'í, male or female, young or old, newly-enrolled or veteran, to arise, to volunteer, and to rush off to some far away goal city or country. The farther away, the better. The more primitive and untouched the post, the more meritorious.

It is called: *Pioneering*.

It is also catching. Even if you are not yet a Bahá'í.

In fact, if you stand, only by accident, a little too near this infectious pioneering fire, look out! Or we two may next meet in American Samoa at Pago Pago on the way to your new pioneering post in the South Pacific as fellow-Bahá'ís.

But you can't say I didn't warn you.

I cite the story of the two Arabs fighting with scimitars. One went "Whoosh!" with his blade. The second Arab laughed and said, "You missed me!". "Did I?" said the first. "Just shake your head." He did, and his head fell off.

The Bahá'ís, of course, are non-warlike and are not violent. They use only the gentle, loving sword of their tongue to capture the hearts of their listeners.

Even so, you can lose your head to the Bahá'í Faith just as easily through this eloquent blade of love. You can also lose your heart to the Bahá'í Faith equally as easily and especially to pioneering.

So I suggest: "En garde!"

"Cairo, Egypt! I thought you said Cairo, Illinois!"

8

It is difficult to explain the magnetic attraction of pioneering unless you're a Bahá'í. Or married to one. Especially if like myself you are inordinately attached to this old materialistic world of shopping malls, discount houses, freeways, Bullock's, health food stores, pineapple yoghurt, television, the Dodgers, the Angels, the Forty-Niners, the UCLA Bruins, the Trojans, the Kings, Santa Anita, Hollywood Park, Baskin-Robbins and Hormel's Chili.

I was once asked by a renowned Bahá'í, "Bill, how can you stand this materialistic West?"

"I can't", I admitted, frankly. "Not unless it's really decadent."

That's why I was telling the truth when I kept saying to a restless, eager "on your marks!" Marguerite, "I'm not ready to pioneer yet."

She replied, with that sweet angelic smile which frequently unsettles me:

"You *will* be."

It sounded quite ominous.

My personal and intimate contact with every variety of Bahá'í pioneer over the years, has enabled me to place all of this in a useful perspective for you. I use a basic formula from comparative religion:

1 Becoming a Bahá'í is heaven.
2 Pioneering for the Bahá'í Faith is
  the next best thing, purgatory.
3 All else is hell.

I learned these truths about Bahá'í pioneering on my way to Reno, Nevada, with Marguerite. We went there on our Bahá'í honeymoon.

No, you heard it right.

Reno. On our honeymoon.

Divorceville on the Truckee River.

The grass-widows in Reno toss their wedding-rings into the Truckee River from their hotel-room windows, or from nearby bridges. This symbolizes the end of their unhappy marriages.

Of course, if their wedding rings are studded with real diamonds, emeralds and rubies, they throw in a back-up ring from Woolworth's instead. They then tell their husbands they threw the real thing into the stream, and that it is lost forever.

It is, too. At roulette, blackjack and the slot machines.

Yes, I can't deny it, Marguerite and I went to Reno on our honeymoon. This was the beginning of the "madness" referred to by my friends.

Marguerite and I were being caught up in this "pioneering fire". We were on our way to Sacramento, California.

Once this "blaze" is ignited, the Bahá'ís take off like Olympic torch-bearers racing for their pioneering posts. They are eager to light other torches in far-off countries whose names they cannot yet properly pronounce. They are radiant. Tingling with anticipation. Zealous to reach whatever part of the world has taken their fancy or the fancy of the Pioneering Committee.

It is essential that you consult with your wife or husband in the greatest detail before leaving for, or arriving at your new pioneering post. Leave nothing to chance. Otherwise, the results can be both surprising and disastrous.

I remember vividly the husband who had left his wife home to baby-sit the children while he attended the first two days of a National Bahá'í Convention. He became so inflamed with the idea of pioneering that he volunteerd both himself and his wife for Africa. He admitted to the packed Convention that his wife didn't know about these plans yet, but he was confident that when he went home to baby-sit the children for the last two days of the Convention so she could attend, she would be overjoyed at the news.

He didn't tell her. He couldn't work himself up to it. When his wife arrived at Foundation Hall, she, too, in her turn was so ignited by this same thrill of pioneering that she volunteered the services of both herself and her husband for Latin America. She admitted that her husband didn't know anything about these plans yet, but she felt sure he would understand and accept when she told him. She couldn't understand why the Convention broke out into uproarious laughter followed by spontaneous thunderous applause. A standing ovation.

Our illustrator, Robert Reedy, has captured for us the excitement as well as the danger involved in such a moment. He has also captured the possible shocking consequences of failing to consult thoroughly and in detail with your spouse before launching upon these vital, life-changing decisions.

SIBERIA?! I THOUGHT YOU SAID LIBERIA!*

* If you do not respond to the above "Siberia–Liberia" caption, perhaps you might prefer: "Athens, Greece! I thought you meant Athens, Georgia!" Or "Lebanon, Beirut! I thought you meant Lebanon, Missouri!" et cetera.

23

Ego—blasted to smithereens!

9

Some of my Bahá'í friends may feel that I have been too impertinent in my comments about pioneering, and even about the Bahá'í Faith itself. The purpose, of course, is to take you with me on these pioneering journeys as I made them, so that you may see the changes that took place in my own thinking as the years passed; and hopefully in my own life as I gradually deepened my knowledge and appreciation of the Bahá'í Faith in that never-ending struggle to become a better person and a finer human being.

I was in love with both the Faith and Marguerite. In fact, I kept a personal record of the progress of our married life so that I could properly evaluate what was happening to us.

I made a chart and listed the protagonists. I used three columns:

TIME FACTOR   MARGUERITE   THE BAHÁ'Í FAITH

You are about to see the copies from my original statistics. I kept them in a private file away from prying eyes during those early years. The figures show clearly who had captured the greater part of my heart, my head and my devotion as time went by.

It developed into quite a pitcher's duel.

The statistics helped me to become much more sympathetic with what Marguerite was trying to do with her own Bahá'í life than I had been at the outset of our marriage. She had bowled me over with those film-test teeth, that warm demolishing smile, and all that honeycomb Bahá'í love. It snowed me under. Until I settled down.

I was very suspicious of anything so wonderful. I kept asking myself, where is the stinger? When will I feel the pain?*

---

* I know I said something similar before, but when you go down to the stream to wash your tin breakfast plates just to clean them for lunch, and you come up with a pan full of gold nuggets, that's Religion!

That's why I made the chart, I decided to analyse our married life together as Bahá'ís. I charted it as follows:

TIME FACTOR	MARGUERITE	THE BAHÁ'Í FAITH
First 5 years	95%	5%
10 years	80%	20%
20 years	70%	30%
30 years	60%	40%
40 years	50%	50%

"Fifty-fifty is not bad", I told Marguerite.

To tell you the truth, right now, *45 years* later, as I stand on Table Mountain, looking down upon Cape Town and the spot where the Indian Ocean and the Atlantic meet, creating the mighty "Cape Rollers", I have to admit that Marguerite is now losing 75 to 25.

She doesn't know that. When she fell below fifty per cent, I hid the charts and refused to comment on them.

"What are the current percentages?" Marguerite would ask me from time to time, unable to curb her curiosity.

"It's touch and go", I'd tell her vaguely.

Marguerite blasted my ego to smithereens one day, saying, "What we really want to see on your chart, Bill, is one hundred percent for the Bahá'í Faith and zero for me."

"Zilch!"

"With a capital Z."

"Really?"

"Of course."

Marguerite smiled her enigmatic beatific Bahá'í smile, the one I find so maddening and so beautiful. She kissed me gently on the cheek.*

"You see," Marguerite explained, sounding exactly like her father, Charlie Reimer, "whenever anyone puts the Bahá'í Faith first in their lives, everybody associated with them is a winner. I think what you're doing is simply wonderful. Go for the shut-out!"

Marguerite gave me a big hug and another kiss. She had successfully pulled all my claws.

* Have I said this before about Marguerite's smile? Repeatedly? Well, after all it *is* a love story: Maiden against Messenger of God. I'd better up her percentage figures at least ten points. Make that fifteen. Because obviously she's a goner in the long run.

As soon as Marguerite left the room, I dug my charts out of the secret compartment and changed the odds.

Not ten percent but fifteen.

TIME FACTOR	MARGUERITE	THE BAHÁ'Í FAITH
Right now	40%	60%

She deserved it. Temporarily at least.

The "lead", as you can see, still remained where it belonged, and where my heart told me it would stay forever, with the Bahá'í Faith. Besides, I had learned long ago that it was impossible to compare the two, and my chart was merely for fun.

Both were heavenly, but One was incomparable.

Perhaps I was growing up. Spiritually speaking.

A fairly holy soul arises

10

The warm spirit which Marguerite generated in our home inspired me to suggest we should go pioneering wherever she wanted. This is a brief flash-back to the days before I became a Bahá'í. I not only went pioneering before I was a Bahá'í, but kept the Bahá'í Fast before I was a Bahá'í, too. Not because of my own deep spiritual nature, but because there was no food on the table between sunrise and sunset for nineteen days.

The story of our pioneering journeys begins here. All before was only preamble. The size of the book grew so alarmingly that I was thinking of renaming it "The Decline and Fall of the 'Roaming' Empire".

Fortunately, I didn't. Marguerite wisely pointed out that it was not decline but flourish, and not fall but rise.

One morning in Sacramento, Marguerite showed me a cablegram that had just arrived from the World Centre of the Bahá'í Faith in the Holy Land. It called for "nine holy souls" to arise and pioneer to the nine States in America where there were still no Bahá'ís. Utah was among them.

I stepped back a pace from Marguerite as I read the cablegram. She was incandescent, and I knew where her heart had suddenly gone.

"Isn't it exciting?" she said.

"Very."

"What do you think?"

I told her that I'd been thinking of suggesting she pioneer somewhere before she exploded from within.

"This", I told her, "may be your big chance. Arise, and go", I encouraged. "Be one of the nine. You can become holy later."

That caused some excitement.

27

I meant it though. I told her to outline her plans, and we would consult upon them later. In the meantime, I'd try to get a job in Utah.

Marguerite was delighted with my generous offer. She said she loved me for it. And demonstrated. When she gave me back my lips, she erupted into a religious outburst. She said she felt sure that because of my selflessness and kindness, that it was I, and not herself, who was that "holy soul" referred to by the Guardian of the Bahá'í Faith.

During this spasm of pioneering ecstasy, Marguerite hallucinated long enough to add, "I feel certain that because of this noble sacrifice on your part, you will become a Bahá'í yourself in Salt Lake City."

"Don't do me any favours", I told her. "And for heaven's sake, don't pray about it. I feel much safer on the outside looking in. Behind the bullet-proof glass of this radio studio. Religiously speaking."

Marguerite's eyes twinkled, "You're sweet", she said.

"Sweet, but not foolhardy."

"How soon can we leave for Salt Lake City?" Marguerite asked me a few days later.

"How soon", I asked, knowing it would thrill both her and the boys, "can the three of you be packed?"

Bill, Jr. with wide, excited, innocent eyes let Marguerite's cat out of her travelling bag.

"We're already packed", he said enthusiastically. "Since yesterday. The bags are all hidden in the closet, raring to go!"

Michael did a noisy "Shuffle Off to Buffalo", slapping his extended right foot up and down, and finishing with his outstretched palm toward Utah, singing: "Goodbye Sacramento, hello, Salt Lake City!"

Slowly I swivelled my head around toward Marguerite. I gave her my most wintry glance. It bounced off her radiant face.

Marguerite giggled, but had the decency to lower her eyelashes.

"The boys", she said, "are impetuous."

"And", I added coldly, "packed. I'm glad you all took time to think it over before our consultation."

"We had complete confidence in your tender heart."

"For tender", I suggested "read 'chicken'."

I watched the three conspirators go through the door of the Radio Station laughing happily, and holding hands in triumph.

Softly I said to myself, "You blind, mad, impetuous, Salt Lake City, pioneering fool!"

I echoed the words which my own father had often used on such trying occasions:

"Dear God, where will it all end?"

DARLING
CANNIBAL

11

The radio drama raced toward its chilling close. The mood music became more ominous and threatening. It signified the end of the final act.

I was greatly relieved when it was all over. It was my last effort on behalf of the Radio Station. My job was finished.

Soon Marguerite and I would be on our way to Salt Lake City heading toward her great pioneering adventure as one of those "nine holy souls". The car was already packed. The two boys, William and Michael, were sleeping on the back seat with our dachshund "Spook".

We had left Spook snoring between the two of them with the tail of a blue rubber mouse in his mouth. All three were tucked in under warm woollen blankets, ready for their all-night journey to Utah. All three of them had been so excited all day, they couldn't keep their eyes open a minute longer.

The theme music swelled to an end concluding the tragic story of the famous Donner Party snowbound so many long years ago while going over the rugged mountain pass in the Sierras between Nevada and California. The very pass Marguerite and I would cross sometime before morning.*

No need to dwell here on the gruesome details of the fate of the Donner Party. They became hopelessly trapped by a violent winter blizzard during icy, below-zero freezing temperatures in the high mountains.

Frozen and starving, trying to survive in some of the most horrendous winter weather ever recorded in the High Sierras, the Donner Party became involved in one of the rare examples of can-

---

* Known in dramatic circles as "the plant" foretelling trouble ahead.

nibalism in North America. Those who survived did so by eating those who did not.

They became famous as the "Tragic Donner Party". The pass over the Sierra Nevada Mountains where they lost their lives is to this day called "Donner Pass". In fact, that was the title of our documentary, now mercifully finished.

Still basking in the memory of our third cup of hot coffee at Uncle Jim's place, advertised in huge red neon lights as the finest coffee in the world, perhaps a slight exaggeration, we piled back into Marguerite's blue Ford. We brought a roasted hot dog out to Spook, tucked everybody back under blankets, and took off.

In no time, the boys, Spook and the rubber mouse resumed their sleeping positions. Two happy-go-lucky newly-weds, two small boys, a dachshund and a blue mouse, none of whom suspected they were headed for a night of terror.

How could we still be newly-weds with a four and a six year-old boy sleeping in the back seat, you ask? Easy. They were my sons by a former marriage. The dachshund and the blue mouse were mine, too. But not for long. Marguerite was rapidly taking them all over as hers.

She was good at that.

Marguerite and I had made a post-wedding vow that Marguerite would learn all about the sports which I broadcast (and she hated) if I would learn to dance, which she loved (and I—never mind).

Marguerite conquered the sports scene very rapidly. She already knew more about the batting averages of the Di Maggio brothers—Dom, Vince and Jolting Joe, not to mention Ted Williams and Stan Musial—than the boys did. I must admit, however, that I had not shown anywhere near the same progress in dancing. I still knew only two dance steps. One was the waltz, which I could "one-two-three" with the best of them. The other wasn't the waltz.

All I know is that the two boys and Marguerite got on fabulously. They seemed to be bound together by carburettors, pistons, RPMs and zingo! driving, as well as by RBIs, stolen bases, and home runs.

And there was I with the waltz.

33

I think what won the boys over to Marguerite even more than her newly-acquired sports knowledge (which must have stuck in her craw*) was the way she handled a motor car. Any motor car. Marguerite began driving automobiles when she was thirteen. Unfortunately, she did have one serious weakness at the wheel. Her weakness is far too grave to be called merely a minor flaw.

Marguerite thought every car she was driving was a Ferrari, and that she was entered in the Indianapolis Five Hundred. Whenever she slid behind the steering column she thought, at that very moment, that she was "on the track!" pitted against the greatest.

"Le Mans, not Indianapolis", Marguerite corrected me, with a twinkle in her eye, as she shot her blue Ford sedan zip! in between two parked oil tankers.

When I hollered, "Cut that out!", the boys applauded and yelled, "Way to go, Mother! We knew you could do it. Give it the old Zingo!"

"Zingo?" I asked.

One morning when just the car and I were parked alone together, waiting for the three of them to come back to our pit-stop with hamburgers and malteds, the accelerator-pedal looked up and whispered to me, cautiously, "Where's old lead-foot?"

All right. So it's Irish whimsy. It is also perfectly true.

Marguerite has a lead foot on the gas pedal when she throws it into high.

---

* Marguerite was, of course, far too lovely to have anything as inelegant as a "craw".

12

We ran into a giant blizzard on the Lincoln Highway as we headed for Salt Lake City. The driving had become extremely hazardous even for a "formula five" driver like Marguerite. We found ourselves sliding along on a Sierra Nevada ice rink.

Marguerite was outwardly conservative and cautious as we ground our way slowly up the mountainside. However, inwardly was another matter. It did not comfort me to hear all three of these pioneering fanatics shout aloud every time we went into a tailspin, or pulled out of a hair raising skid:

"Wagons East! Ho!"

Marguerite's blue V8 Ford was fighting the wind and bucking the drifting snow as we fought our way courageously into the teeth of the gale. She loved it.

The rain had turned to sleet. It was flicking the windshield glass, adding a new storm sound to the monotonous beat of the windshield wipers back and forth. William insisted that the blades were saying: "You can't make it! You can't make it! You can't make it!"

A stern glance from the Navigator, known in happier weather as his father, silenced him, but all of us could see that the sleet had now paved the highway with a solid sheet of ice. We not only could see it, we could feel it as we created an endless series of small "S" curves.

The temperature dropped suddenly. Heavy snow followed. Marguerite found herself the captain of a ship that was sliding along in all directions, not knowing exactly where it was on the highway, except that it was now in the midst of a raging blizzard.

Once we spun around twice in a complete double-circle. Sort of "spin the bottle" with a two-ton Ford. None of us cared for it, but Michael was the only one who yelled out. He shouted at the top of his voice:

"Is there any Remover of difficulties save God?"

"What was that Michael yelled?" I asked Marguerite.

Bill answered. "It was the 'Remover of Difficulties' ", he said. "But he didn't yell it anywhere near loud enough. Not for these circumstances." Bill demonstrated himself much louder as we went into another skid.

"It's a little prayer I taught them", Marguerite explained, cheerily. "For emergencies."

"Why is the husband always the last to know?"

"Hang on!" Marguerite warned. "Here we go again. This one is going to be the worst one of all!"

It was a gross understatement.

We boxed the compass twice, clockwise then, as we hit a dry patch of road, counter-clockwise. We began sliding toward the low steel guard-rail. It was the only thing between us and a three thousand foot drop into the rocky ravine below. To calm myself, I played a word game. I tried to think of other names for ravine: chasm, gorge, gully, cliff, crevasse, abyss, gulch. I didn't like any of them. And it didn't help a lick.

"Look out!" I yelled in despair, "We're going over!"

We didn't.

Each time we were threatened with certain and immediate earthly extinction, Marguerite and the boys would cry out, "Is there any Remover of difficulties save God?" and the car would right itself and start spinning the other way, or do something to lessen the danger.

Sometimes it was Bill, sometimes Michael, sometimes Marguerite. Sometimes it was all three in unison who shouted the prayer out loud. The noise of their piercing voices was nearly as harrowing as the skids.

"What was that phrase again?" I shouted at Marguerite.

"Not now", she cried, spinning the wheel expertly with the slide and gradually bringing us out of another frightening tailspin.

"I need to know", I demanded. "I can use it myself. You were all a little slow that last time."

"I'll teach you later", Marguerite promised.

"At this rate, there may be no later."

I didn't insist. At that exact moment there was a break in the swirling snow. It revealed the highway sign. White printing on a dark green background.

You guessed it.
It read: Donner Pass!
Marguerite no longer loved it.

Avalanche!

13

Marguerite tooled the loaded-down Ford carefully and brilliantly along the icy road. It was now covered over with another layer of freshly fallen snow. You couldn't see where the ice was. It was safest to assume it was everywhere.

We talked continuously. All of us. We were trying to ignore the storm. The boys took comfort in Marguerite's recollection that 'Abdu'l-Bahá Himself had ridden over this mountain pass by train with His party way back in 1912. The written account tells how they had discussed the fate of the famous Donner Party. Marguerite and the boys took more comfort from the story than I did. I was too busy watching the road. Our vigil went on for miles.

The boys were sitting up straight and stiff, and Spook also was sitting up between them. It was an amusing and charming sight. All three of them finally keeled over sideways from fatigue, excitement and exhaustion. They fell sound asleep in a heap.

The blizzard raged on.

Half an hour later, we were over the summit. We started downhill toward Truckee and safety. We sighed with relief and congratulated each other. Just when we thought the worst was over, we were suddenly involved in the most terrifying of all our death-defying skids.

Marguerite had finally decided it was peaceful enough to explain to me about the prayer.

"Wouldn't HELP have been quicker?" I asked.

"Are you complaining about the results?"

"Never! I loved it!"

"It's a short prayer from the Herald of the Bahá'í Faith, the Báb", she explained. "It's called 'The Remover of Difficulties'."

38

Marguerite added significantly, and quite unnecessarily, "It's very useful in times of emergency."

"You're telling me! However, if you have any other Bahá'í material just as powerful, but a lot shorter, let's please use that next time. You were almost too late."

We both laughed.

"I", she said, "have a whole arsenal."

"Look out!"

The car went into another skid. By far the worst. This time, for about one hundred feet down the highway, we turned and floated in a continuous circle, round and round and round. All we needed was calliope music.

We travelled straight down the middle of the road, completely at right angles to both the guard-rail and the mountain. We were a rotary snow-plow sweeping the highway before us.

Express!

Spontaneously I cried out as loud as I could:

"Is there any Remover of whatever she said!"

We were rapidly picking up momentum as we moved down the steep hill.

The Ford, now completely out of control, was racing along the ice like a ski-jumper set to take off. A bend in the road took us directly toward the rocky face of a huge mountain and into the giant snow drift piled up at its foot.

Head on!

At least it was better than the gorge, but as I said later there is little to choose between the cholera and the plague.

We hit the piled-up snow and plunged through the drift toward the rock beyond. We burrowed deeper and deeper into the darkness making our own tunnel.

With a loud whack! we hit a solid wall of stone and came to an abrupt stop.

A mighty roar followed as an avalanche of snow came rumbling down the mountainside spilling over the top of our car.

It totally engulfed us.

The darkness and silence that followed were awesome.

39

14

I put on the dome light and looked around. The boys and Spook had slept through all the excitement. They would be furious. After a long pause, trying to ease the tension, I said to Marguerite:

"The prayer didn't seem to work that time, did it? Maybe because I didn't know all the words."

"What do you mean, it didn't work?" Marguerite objected. "We skidded toward the mountain not toward the precipice, didn't we? At least we're here, not down there."

"You have a very sound point."

Not that I had been knocking the prayer. So many skid winners back-to-back down an icy road cannot be quickly dismissed. Even when you end up buried under an avalanche of snow. At least we were all still alive. It certainly beat all those TV shows you see nowadays where the car goes hurtling down the gorge and keeps bumping into the side of the mountain on the way down until it finally bursts into brilliant flame shooting up a ball of fire as the car smashes on the rocks below.

"I don't know if you'll get the Academy Award for your marvellous driving," I told Marguerite, "but I *am* nominating you for Skid-Mother of the Year. You've earned it."

I think she giggled, but it might have been hysteria.

I reached over and shut off the headlights.

I was worried about Marguerite. We still knew very little about each other. Even less about the size of the avalanche of snow that had engulfed us.

I wasn't sure how Marguerite would react to a crisis like this. She might panic. A snow-slide can be serious in these mountains. Even fatal. Sometimes it can cut off your vital oxygen supply. Both of us were very fond of breathing, so were the boys and Spook.

I wasn't too sure how I was going to take the crisis myself. Especially if it turned out that we really *were* buried alive with no way out. I pushed the car door open against the soft snow. I reached for the long-handled windshield scraper on the floor beside the seat, and began poking upward. I leaned out and made a hole toward the sky.

I could see stars!

I heard strange sounds coming from Marguerite still behind the wheel. I closed the door, and put my hand on her shoulder to tell her that everything was all right. I became alarmed when I felt her shudder. I thought, "This girl is becoming hysterical." Perhaps she was still recalling the terrible last moments of the Donner Party in the documentary she had listened to so recently. The tragedy had happened very near to this very spot.

I slid over toward the wheel and put my arm around Marguerite to comfort her.

"Are you all right?" I asked.

She was more than all right. Marguerite wasn't in a panic at all. She was anything but hysterical. Marguerite wasn't crying, she was laughing.

She looked up at me with a big grin. Smiling mischievously, Marguerite said:

"I won't eat you, if you don't eat me."

I knew right then what my Bahá'í marriage was going to be like.

THE
PLUNGE

15

Marguerite was right about another thing.

I did become a Bahá'í in Salt Lake City.*

The magic moment happened one night after I finished broadcasting the baseball game between the Ogden Reds and the Salt Lake City Bees.

Marguerite picked me up at the ballpark. On the way home, while listening to Glen Gray and the Casa Loma Orchestra, I told her I was thinking of becoming a Bahá'í.

Marguerite wept.

Later, after riding in silence for several miles, I said, "I really mean it."

She wept.

No hand-holding now. Both of Marguerite's hands were on the wheel to keep from driving onto somebody's lawn on the East Bench. Her eyes were on bright, like the headlights. She was watching me out of one eye, cyclopian. Cat at the mouse hole! Excited. Anticipating.

Glen Gray was now playing Malaguena, lots of sax, strings and drum-rhythms.

Marguerite couldn't stand the pressure. She pulled off onto the side of the road and stopped the car. She hugged me, kissed me, and cried. She was too overcome to drive on.

Anyone seeing the two of us hugging, kissing, weeping, and cuddling in the front seat of that car would have thought we were either newly-weds, or about to be newly-weds, separating for a divorce, or simply taking advantage of the full moon of summer. They would never have believed we were talking about religion.

* I have recorded that event in *God Loves Laughter*, George Ronald Publisher, 46 High St, Kidlington, Oxford OX5 2DN, England (1960). There is no need to repeat it here other than these previously unrecorded and significant events.

Marguerite suggested that I shouldn't hurry my decision about becoming a Bahá'í.

"You mean it can wait until I get home?"

She laughed, and said, "Think it over carefully. Don't rush into anything of such lifelong importance."

"You mean longer than the year I've already been studying secretly?"

"Have you really?"

"Can Amoz Alonzo Stagg coach football?"

I noticed that Marguerite had slipped a Declaration Card out of her purse, and was fingering it "at the ready". She showed it to me and said she had been carrying it in her purse ever since the day of our marriage.

"Why such an old beat-up Declaration Card?"

"It was new when I put it there," she said, "but I kept taking it out and saying a prayer or two over it, thumbing it caressingly, and wondering how long it would be before I'd have a chance to use it. If I ever would."

Marguerite dropped the Declaration Card back into her purse. Firmly she snapped the clasp shut and, with a contented smile, said:

"It can wait until tomorrow."

The Ford took off like a shot. With squealing tyres, it zoomed along the East Bench, and threw gravel stones every which-way as it careened toward home and tomorrow.

It took us forever to get home. Marguerite kept pulling off the road and stopping the car. She would hug me and kiss me or cry. Sometimes one at a time, sometimes two at a time, sometimes all three at the same time.

You have to be a Bahá'í wife or husband who has been longing for the day when the family would be united in the Faith to fully appreciate the joy and rapture that filled Marguerite's heart on that occasion.

Over the years, I have learned to value more and more what a truly treasured moment that was for the both of us, that moonlit night high on the East Bench. To this very day almost half a century later, all I have to do is say to Marguerite, "Remember that night on the East Bench back in Salt Lake City with that big fat orange Wasatch Mountain moon shining down on our parked car? When I said to you . . ."

Marguerite's eyes become misty. Her whole body turns into butterscotch pudding. Soon big tears of love start to fall.

Eventually, on that actual long-ago historic night, I had to tell her, "Marguerite, if you don't stop the waterworks, I'll have to go back to the church."

Marguerite showed that she had not been so overwhelmed by the happy news of my wanting to become a Bahá'í that she had lost her sense of humour. Between blowing her nose and dabbing a kleenex at her misty eyes, she said:

"You've been away from the church so long, you couldn't find your way back with a seeing-eye dog."

"No", I admitted. "But I did find my way into the Kingdom, didn't I?"

Marguerite wept.

"The time for small talk", I told her, "is over. Just take that battered old Declaration Card out of your purse, and I'll sign it."

"I'll get a new one at home", she assured me. "For this special occasion."

"No way", I objected. "I want to sign that old friend, that very beat-up card you've been hoarding all this time. That's the card for me. I won't sign any other."

Marguerite took the card out of her purse. Fumbling. I had to finish the job for her myself. Marguerite was too excited. Gently I took it from her.

"I'll sign it right here and now, in front of your very eyes."

Marguerite wept, but she wouldn't let me sign the card just yet.

"It doesn't matter", I told her. "The thing is you've finally landed me, you lucky wife of a brand new Bahá'í husband."

This time, she really wept.

> *"Over my dead body!"*
> *"If necessary."*

16

When Marguerite and I reached home on Beverly Boulevard, we stopped on the porch for one last look at the Wasatch moon that had been lucky enough to have witnessed this night. We hugged and kissed. We were both as excited as two young lovers just beginning their life together. And, of course, we were. It was now a whole new ball game, and I couldn't hit inside fast pitching. I leaned against the door and prepared to sign my Declaration Card by moonlight, figuring that would certainly be a first.

Marguerite stopped me.

As she unlocked the front door, Marguerite said:

"Sleep on it."

"Really?"

"You can sign your card tomorrow."

"Whatever you say. You're the teacher."

"It's already signed in your heart. That's the important thing. The rest is only a formality."

In the morning, breakfast was ready an hour early. The smell of frying bacon gently penetrated my sleep, and hypnotized me into a slow motion awakening.

When I came downstairs into the kitchen, Marguerite, Bill, Mike, and the dachshund, Spook, and the cat who had strayed in during an act of the Metropolitan Opera *Faust* on a Saturday and became known as Mephistopheles, were all gathered around the breakfast table. I felt like Lew Alcindor (Kareem Abdul-Jabbar) of UCLA fame running through the two lines of blue-and-gold cheerleaders at Pauley Pavilion to centre court. Only I knew that this time, I was not the star. The star was plainly visible. All eyes and body angles were pointing toward it.

Out of the corner of my eye, I could see the Declaration Card

47

sitting on the fringe of the table beyond my bacon and eggs.

I ignored the magic sleight-of-hand by which the Card moved from the outer perimeter of the table to dead centre, pushing aside the orange marmalade.

Sometimes I wonder about myself. And worry. Am I cruel and uncaring, sadistic, unfeeling, or am I just full of fun, prompted by the mischievous "little people" heritage I have from the "ficke-looney's fire" swamps of Ireland? I only know that I pretended to ignore the dramatic scene they had set. I looked hurriedly at my watch, then turned toward the back door.

"I'm late", I said. "No breakfast for the wicked today."

I threw my topcoat over my arm and put on my hat. I could hear plainly the low whispered comment: "Wicked is right."

I turned in the doorway with a big smile and said:

"By the way, you don't happen to have one of those Bahá'í Declaration Cards handy, do you?"

Bedlam! Maldeb! Which is bedlam spelled backwards.

Hugs, kisses, tears, barks, meows and general hysteria, including hand-holding and dancing around me. Spook bit me on the ankle because he thought I was the one responsible for all the noise and excitement.

I was, of course.

"Way to go, Dad!" Mike cheered.

"I told you mother could do it", William bragged, punching Mike on the biceps, and getting just as good in return.

William held the chair for me, Michael pushed the plate of bacon and eggs aside, and Marguerite centred the Declaration Card by my right hand. All three of them offered me pens.

"No thank you", I said. "I have my own."

I drew out my gold Parker and showed it to Marguerite.

She wept. What else is new?

"Recognize it?" She nodded through the tears. I told the boys, "It's the pen your mother gave me back in Sacramento. 'You can use it when you sign your Declaration Card', she told me. 'When you find out that it's really you who is one of those "nine holy souls" the beloved Guardian referred to.' 'Over my dead body', I replied." Now, I gave Marguerite a smile and squeezed her arm. "I take that part back."

Before signing, I reached and drew the plate of bacon and eggs back toward me.

"First things first", I said.

"You do," Marguerite warned, "and you'll get your hot coffee on your bald spot."

We all laughed at that.

Every one of us knew that the moment was too sacred and significant for anything else to matter. It was so important to all of us in our lives, that we became flippant merely to keep from shedding the tears of joy we felt.

Except Marguerite, of course. She cried through the entire morning. Every hour on the hour. Silently though. No noise, just sweetly falling large single tears of happiness, like beads to be strung. I never knew until I became deepened in the Faith years later how much that moment really meant to her. I knew when I watched my two sons sign their Declaration Cards, and my niece Fran, and my sister, Frances; they were more than Phi Beta Kappas or PhDs, their doctorates were in love. For all mankind. They had achieved their blessing for both this world and the next.

On that long-ago morning in Salt Lake City, another brick had been placed in the foundation of that great Kingdom of God on earth promised by Christ, and Marguerite had helped in a small way to make it possible. It was part of the "great work" promised in Scripture.

Subconsciously I knew in my heart that I probably would never again experience a moment quite like that moment shared with my wife, my sons, a dachshund, and a calico cat.

I never did.

I picked up the Declaration Card that Marguerite had kept in her purse so long, saving it for this very moment. It looked worse in the daylight than it had on the East Bench last night. I flipped the tired old Card up and down and it flapped loosely like a thin pancake.

"Do you think they'll accept this?"

"I offered you a new one."

"Never!" I repeated. "We were made for each other."

For the umpteenth time I raised my pen and was about to sign. I stopped at the critical moment, and once again everybody held their breath. I was like Peter Falk in Columbo, stopping at the door for one last thrust, before leaving. I smiled mischievously at Marguerite.

"I know you'll want to say a prayer before I take this incredible historic step?"

She was shocked that she had forgotten.

"We really should", she said. "I'm ashamed for forgetting."

Teasingly, I suggested the Fire Tablet or the Tablet of Ahmad. Both quite long, but oh my!*

Marguerite said, "Will someone else say the prayer? Something short, please. I can't bear the suspense."

Bill Jr. said the "Remover of Difficulties", the only prayer he knew by heart, and I signed the Card while he was saying it.

I handed the Card to Marguerite who held it for a moment over her heart.

"Let's not make any mistake about which Bill Sears you're so fond of", I reminded her.

Marguerite kissed me on top of my bald spot which was much better than hot coffee. I arose and embraced her.

"I hope I shall be worthy of such a great gift."

Michael broke the silence and brought us all back to normal.

"Hot diggety dog!" he hollered. "I bet this means the whole family will soon be on its way pioneering somewhere! Dad will be a Bahá'í when he pioneers this time."

"Great!" William echoed. "I'll start packing. It can't be too soon or too far for me."

"Please, boys", Marguerite cautioned them. "Let's be patient. After all, Daddy has to get his spiritual bearings before he goes out to conquer the world."

I had only planned to go to the radio station to conquer my morning programme. Suddenly there flashed through my mind those prophetic words once spoken by my friends the Jew, the Catholic, the Protestant, the atheist and the agnostic:

"That way lies madness!"

Quickly I corrected Marguerite.

"I may have lost my marbles, but not my bearings." To myself I said, as probably many a new Bahá'í has done under similar circumstances as they watch their signature drying on the Declaration Card in indelible ink: "Perhaps I can plead temporary insan-

---

* Wait until you hear about these two prayers. They are part of the deeply moving, volatile, Bahá'í "mountain movers". Remember, these prayers are all part of the free fringe benefits you get when you, too, become a Bahá'í and sign your Declaration Card, you lucky dog!

ity. Or maybe I can steal the Card back tonight while Marguerite is sleeping."

Don't be surprised at my still tentative state. Being "reborn" is much harder on the system than being "born". It takes longer, too.

Every baby born into this material world weeps for what it leaves behind. When he feels that slap of life on his rump, he cries. Gradually, the baby becomes aware of the world around him, the meadows, mountains, stars, the seas, the streams, the fragrances of flowers, flowering trees, the sun, the moon, sweet music, laughter, and voices of dear friends. Suddenly, all he has left behind becomes ashes in his eyes now that he is born into this beautiful new world.

Imagine what it is like when one is born into the Kingdom of God for both this world and the next. Like the baby born from the womb of the mother, the new soul born from the dark womb of this world discovers even more wonderful and glorious things. All the treasures of this world are not "worth the black in the eye of a dead ant" compared to what the world of God can grant.

True, I knew these things only instinctively in those early days, but I knew the step I had taken at that happy breakfast table was the right thing to do. The only thing. It might be a struggle as I, too, subconsciously wept for what I had left behind, but I would never let go. There was no doubt about that.

However, I would have to get my spiritual bearings first. Where had I heard that before?

The whole family came out to the garage to see me off to my job at KUTA. Marguerite was radiant. Her face glistened. She, of course, knew that I had done far more than enter her blue V8 Ford sedan. I had entered the Kingdom of God on earth.

"Without a road map!" I called to her.

Marguerite laughed. She knew exactly what I meant. Throughout our lives, each of us would often reply to an inward unexpressed thought of the other. It was another of the sweet things about our marriage. A great time-saver, too.

However, a frightening thought occurred to me as I sat there looking out the car window at those three shining faces.

"Great Scott! Michael's absolutely right. *This* time when I go pioneering, I'll be a Bahá'í, not an onlooker. Does that mean I'll travel even farther? And faster?"

Don't answer that!

51

17

On the way to work on that wild and wonderful morning, I kept mumbling prayers I had learned from the various religions I knew about. I was still trying to keep one foot on first base even though I knew I had just hit a grand-slam, game-winning home run.

Spontaneously, from my long years of Catholic training, I said, "May the saints preserve us!" And then, just to be on the safe side, because I felt so extraordinarily good, so exhilarated, and so downright beautiful inside, I made up a few prayers of my own and offered them in thanksgiving to Buddha, Krishna, Zoroaster, Muhammad, Christ, the Báb, and to all the-holy souls in the supreme Concourse on High.

I wanted all the friends I could muster for the unchartered seas I knew lay ahead. I closed this religious automobile pray-in orgy with a final outburst:

"In the Name of the Father, the Son, the Holy Ghost, and Bahá-'u'lláh, the Return of Christ. Amen. And glory hallelujah!"

When I finished, I found I had driven six blocks past the Radio Station. I may have found part of my spiritual bearings, but I had totally lost my everyday knowledge of the streets-of-Salt-Lake-City bearings.

When I walked into the control-room, my fellow-announcer said, "What's the matter with you?"

"Why?"

"You look like you swallowed a five hundred watt light bulb. I could light a cigarette off your cheeks."

"I'll tell you all about it during the coffee break."

"If you don't burn out before."

Marguerite called me later that morning. She was still ecstatic. She asked me if I would like to join the family at noon in the park for a picnic lunch.

"You sound on top of the world", I told her.

"I am! All of us. The boys and I have been studying a map of the world from the North Pole to Antarctica in the South."

"Laying out a teaching campaign for polar bears and penguins?" I asked.

She didn't hear me at all, but went right on.

"We went all the way around the world following the equator and marking all the places on the map."

"I might not be able to come to your picnic."

"Please do. It'll be fun. We'll say some special prayers about our future."

"What specific future are we talking about here?"

"That's marvellous", Marguerite exclaimed. "How did you do that? With ESP? How astonishing that out of the blue you would say Pacific. In fact—"

"I *didn't* say Pacific", I interrupted hastily. "I said *specific*."

I was glad I hadn't said she sounded a trifle *frantic* because I've never been fond of the Atlantic. I realized all too quickly that my radiant "glow" had been only a local glow, and that I'd better tone down Miss Skyrocket before she took off for some Swahili-speaking landing-strip.

Marguerite laughed merrily. "I was only teasing. I made those remarks just to get even for 'first things first' this morning at breakfast."

"Okay, I deserved it."

"I'm bringing all your favourite prayers and your favourite sandwiches. We'll really celebrate."

I didn't like the sound of any of it. Especially the world map and the prayer books. Not one bit. I had seen Bahá'í prayers in action too many times with Miss Seven League Boots at the helm. I whispered softly to myself,

"May Day! May Day!"

"What did you say, darling?"

I said, "Pray Day! Pray Day!"

"How sweet. That's exactly what we'll do in the park."

At that moment, I said to myself,

"Fasten your seat-belts!"

And that's exactly what we did. From then on. We fastened our seat-belts on Pan Am, TWA, Air France, BOAC, Swiss Air, KLM,

El Al, Lufthansa, Air Canada, United, Sabena, Alitalia, Qantas, SAA, Western, BEA, Air India, Lan Chile, SAS, Olympic and Air Japan among many others.*

In a short span of years, my left arm now became a veritable pincushion for the "slings and arrows of outrageous fortune" including smallpox, cholera and yellow fever, repeated as often as required in those early days. My arm resembled the body of a freshly plucked duck.

I have already, symbolically, taken you twice around the world, and we haven't as yet even reached our first destination, San Francisco. However, I want you to know that I am developing a series of travel shots of my own to inject into our "little outward bound goose". The series is called:

"Immobilized."

* My son William's only reaction to this implied catalogue of unending airline travel was: "What's wrong with Allegheny Airlines?"

NORTH

WEST

EAST

SOUTH

"Go west, young man!" – Horace Greely
"Go south, young man!" – Marguerite Sears
"Go north, young man!" – Teaching Committee
"Stay in San Francisco!" – The minority voice of
William Sears

18

As you may have already suspected, Salt Lake City was not the end of my pioneering for the Bahá'í Faith. It was only the earliest beginning. After Salt Lake City, we had to deal with the cold harsh realities of a place called San Francisco.

We arrived in the East Bay Area the day before Pearl Harbor, on 6 December 1941.

Naturally, Marguerite had an infinite skill, even a magnetic attraction, for wars, border skirmishes, street brawls, race riots, guerrilla attacks, and every variety of individual and group confrontations. How innocent I was. In the next half a century, Marguerite was to involve me in trips to:

Northern Ireland	Beirut	El Salvador	Uganda
Cyprus	Írán	Nicaragua	Egypt.

And you know what's been going on in those places.

Marguerite was distressed about our leaving Salt Lake City. She didn't feel that the local Community was yet strong enough to stand on its own feet. Consultation is a fundamental Bahá'í principle, and I had disregarded it.

I still hadn't the faintest idea about the majesty and greatness of a Bahá'í Local Spiritual Assembly, any Bahá'í Assembly. I'm hoping that my experience shared here may save you from making the same grave mistake.

It wasn't until some time later that I read those powerful Words from the Bahá'í sacred Writings about these Spiritual Assemblies, an Institution created not by the followers of the Bahá'í Faith, but by the Pen of the Founder Himself, Bahá'u'lláh.

The Writings of His Faith say:

> "These Spiritual Assemblies are aided by the Spirit
> of God . . . [They] are shining lamps and heavenly
> gardens, from which the fragrances of holiness are
> diffused over all regions, and the lights of knowledge
> are shed abroad over all created things. From them
> the spirit of life streameth in every direction. They,
> indeed, are the potent sources of the progress of man,
> at all times and under all conditions."

I was learning, but I was still green and fractious. Otherwise, we
would still have been in Salt Lake City suffering, instead of San
Francisco, living it up. It had not yet even dawned on me that
what we, the Bahá'ís, were doing the world over, was raising up
these Bahá'í Assemblies so they could become part of the *Christ-
promised Kingdom of God on earth.*

Of course you don't believe it either! Nor did I.

Not then. But perhaps, like myself, you will begin to believe it by
the time you have finished this book.

You can certainly see that the reality is a lot bigger than my
personal feelings for San Francisco. You can also better appreciate
Marguerite's point of view with which I had not yet caught up,
that it would have been wiser to have remained at our pioneering
post and not moved on so hastily. This whole San Francisco episode with all its hullabaloo was merely an hors-d'œuvre of the
disasters yet to come.

Whatever happened to me, I had coming. It was the first time
we had ever gone anywhere that wasn't a pioneering goal. I'd been
offered the job as Radio Director of a big San Francisco advertising
agency, and I'd snapped it up. I told Marguerite and the family
about it later. I shouldn't have done that.

Marguerite I could see felt that it was a minor religious calamity
since there were more Bahá'ís in California than in any other State
in the country.

I must say however, that Marguerite took my San Francisco
booboo in stride. She always began the teaching work wherever
the Fates placed her. She was sweeter to me than ever, and said:
"We have to give serious thought to your career also, now that
we're here. Bahá'ís must be the best at whatever they do."

"Don't be sweet to me", I told her. "It makes me nervous."

"Don't be. We'll try to help deepen and strengthen the Local
Assemblies in this area."

57

"I feel as though I've wounded both you and myself."

"Aries people are very vulnerable to wounds", Marguerite explained.

"Vulnerable?"

"To sharp instruments, jagged corners and especially head injuries."

It sounded as though she might be prepared to inflict one.

"You're talking to the old pin-cushion", I admitted.

"Aries injuries", Marguerite pointed out, "are mostly self-inflicted."

"Ha!" I retorted. "Is that a Bahá'í teaching?"

"Not at all. Bahá'ís believe in astronomy, not astrology. To quote Julius Caesar, 'the fault dear Brutus is not in our stars, but in ourselves, that we are underlings.'"

"Right!" I told Marguerite. "And once they turn me loose on San Francisco Radio, I plan to be an overling. A *big* overling. Stick with me, kid, and we'll really go places!"

How hollow that all sounds now.

I have laughed about it in Nagasaki, Montevideo, Luxemburg, Perth, Casablanca and Cape Town.

It was quite the opposite. I stuck with Marguerite, not Marguerite with me. Why, only the Supreme Concourse knows. But, I did. I was right about one thing. We really did go places! Five continents, sixty countries, and everything in between!

But first, we went to San Francisco because of my mistake. Freely admitted as I licked my wounds in the city of my dreams.

Marguerite could see that the more I learned about the Bahá'í Faith, the more I was troubled about my not consulting with her and the boys before moving to the city by the Golden Gate. She encouraged me to forget the past and set my face toward the sun, which is hard to do in San Francisco because of the fog.

"Don't worry", she said. "We'll make up for it. Besides, our stay in San Francisco is probably only temporary. There's an urgent call out for pioneers to the Deep South this year. Perhaps later on we can all go to Jackson, Mississippi."

That appealed to me like mashed potatoes with uncooked lumps.

I was not yet that repentant.

58

"By *later on*, do you mean when I start to grow old, or do you mean next month?"

"That", she said, "is not in my hands."

Somehow I always felt that these things *were* in Marguerite's hands. Especially if she was going to pray about them. That always put me on the alert.

I'm talking about "fickelooney's fire", that "will-o'-the-wisp" stuff mentioned earlier that leads people astray into swamps and quagmires and unpleasant places which they would have much rather avoided.

You've heard the old expression "I feel as though somebody just walked over my grave"? I felt that way quite often when Marguerite looked at me in a certain manner and said:

"We'll see what the future holds. We'll pray about it."

You can't tell me she didn't already know.

Otherwise, why would I be writing this particular chapter of *All Flags Flying!* seated at a table in the National Bahá'í Centre in Umtata, Transkei, Africa, having coffee with my niece and nephew, Art and Fran Del Moro and their daughter Kate, when I thought I was going to be at the Rose Bowl in Pasadena watching the Rams and the Steelers in the Super Bowl game?*

Being as yet "perfectly innocent" (as Michael would say) of my real mission in life as a Bahá'í, I learned to love San Francisco. If I had known then what I know now, that the Sears family was warming up in the bull-pen for some fifteen dramatic pioneering posts yet to come even beyond the Deep South, even North America, I would have turned my back on Marguerite, and swum out to Alcatraz Island and broken into the prison instead of out.

---

* Marguerite detests these "flash-aheads" instead of "flash-backs". She keeps telling me so as she proof-reads the book. I didn't have the heart to tell her that soon I would be adding a few "flashes-right-where-we-are"!

"Emm-eye-ess-ess-eye-ess-ess-eye-pee-pee-eye"

19

I didn't mind the maps of Mississippi that kept appearing mysteriously on the walls of my study with a big red circle around Jackson.

I ignored the once occasional, now frequent, songs on the record player such as "Ol' Man River", "Down Mobile Way", "Mississippi Mud", "Are You from Dixie?", and that great novelty hit "Emm-eye-ess-ess-eye-ess-ess-eye-pee-pee-eye. That spells Mississippi!" If they'd had the record in those days, I'm sure they would have focussed on "I'm Going to Jackson!" Fortunately, they didn't.

Perhaps I should not have broken the long-playing album with "Emm-eye-ess-ess" on it against the corner of the fireplace mantel, but I did feel that throwing the broken pieces at the obviously guilty retreating back of my son William was justified.

My waste basket one morning was filled to overflowing with long-stemmed artificial cotton-blossoms that looked surprisingly like Marguerite's make-up puffs. It was the last needle.

I laid my cards on the table which now had two magazines featuring Magnolia Blossom covers. I rolled one up and used it as a gavel.

I called an immediate Sunday morning family meeting. All four of us were present. One man, one vote. We lived and died by democratic process. Dachshunds didn't vote. Although they barked a lot. According to our rotating chairmanship, Marguerite was due, but I pre-empted.

"This", I declared, "is war."

I told them frankly and bluntly, "I am not yet prepared to pioneer to the other end of the earth."

Michael said, practically, "From here to Jackson, Mississippi, is not as far as from here to where you were born in Duluth, Minnesota, Daddy."

"Thank you for the geography lesson," I said, "but where a man is born and where he dies is not the issue. We are speaking symbolically."

I looked as steely eyed as possible. It wasn't easy with the dachshund sitting in his own chair at the table between the boys, with a small apron around his neck, and on the front the word: "Dixie!"

"The dachshund", I said, "goes! That is an executive order. It begins now. We are here to deal with Jackson, Mississippi, not with dachshunds."

There was stunned silence.

Michael spoke up.

"Shall we put it to a vote?"

"This decision", I said, "is not up for grabs. There will be no discussion. You are about to hear the utter, complete, absolute, unchangeable, over, kaput, finished, non-negotiable, answer about anything concerning the high, shallow or deep South."

Silence.

A quiet reply came from Marguerite, who, with a sweet, tender smile said:

"That seems democratically fair."

Another silence.

There was a soft whisper from William, and a heel click under the table.

"Heil," he said, "Hitler."

"You three", I answered abrasively, "are far more like Josef Goebbels than I am like Hitler, if you'll pardon the expression. You have persecuted me unfairly, unduly, and every-daily."

"Can we talk about it at lunch?" Marguerite suggested.

Marguerite loved to postpone crises from meal to meal. To be fair, however, she always faced up to it by the final midnight snack.

Now you know another reason I'm overweight.

"No, we will *not* discuss this one at lunch", I told her.

"Dinner, then."

"Not at dinner."

"Midnight snack?"

"Never."

Michael said to his mother, "He's still weak on consultation."

"It is not a matter for consultation", I said. "The subject is closed. The case will not be reopened. I am not yet ready for pioneering again."

As it turned out, Michael was right again. I came to look upon Jackson, Mississippi, as not being at the other end of the earth. By the time I recognized that truth, Marguerite and her two clones had already boxed and shipped me to South Africa, Uganda, Zambia, Kenya and Israel.

When last I checked the mileage on myself, it was the equivalent of fifteen times around the world.

I *know* I said ten times in *God Loves Laughter*, but a lot of water has gone by the steamer since then, and many fields and farms have fled beneath the wings of our outbound and inbound planes.

If it were possible to have a "nose cone" committee for Bahá'í travelling teachers, I'm sure Marguerite would be on it, and have me scheduled for one of those *Apollo* Rockets. I'd be listening ominously to the count-down inside my astronaut suit wondering how I got there. And for what planet I was destined. Of course, the commander of that astral, far-off fireside flight would be you know who, assisted by her two pint-sized Aliens, and a fair-legged helmeted hound. Was I hallucinating?

I can hear myself now.

"Hello! Houston?"

No reply.

"Help!"

That's how I happened to pioneer to Santa Rosa instead of to Venus. I dug my heels in and fought furiously for California, beginning with San Francisco. I must admit that I still can't remember clearly how I wound up riding a bus every day from San Francisco to Santa Rosa.

When I could run fast enough in the fog to catch it.

The unprepared "prepared" soul

20

All of us knew that the battle for San Francisco was on!

My opening salvo in the campaign to remain in the city by the Golden Gate sounded quite impressive to me.

"As a sportscaster," I explained to Marguerite hoping she'd fall for it, "I can't possibly go pioneering to Jackson, Mississippi. Not for some time."

"Why can't you?" she asked.

"Because."

"I'm still listening", she said from those Olympian heights.

"A young ball player", I explained further, "never goes straight up to the New York Yankees and the Big Time. He spends a while preparing in the Minor Leagues first."

"So?"

"First he goes to a smaller farm club. Then, when he's ready, they call him up to the Yankees."

"You mean Jackson, Mississippi, is too important a pioneering post for a young rookie Bahá'í teacher like yourself to start on?"

"Right!"

"You mean you want to work your way up?"

"Give that girl a big cigar!"

"You're so right", Marguerite agreed, startling me. "Perhaps you should begin at someplace smaller, closer to home." She thought a moment before exclaiming aloud: "I have the answer. Santa Rosa!"

"Where's that?" I asked. Nervously.

Marguerite pointed north.

"Up there", she said, happily.

"How far?"

"How far what?"

"How far *up there*?"

"It doesn't matter."

"It matters", I told her. "Is Santa Rosa a Ukiah, California 'up there'? Or is it an Anchorage, Alaska 'up there'? There's a crucial difference."

Marguerite laughed. She was delighted at the turn of events. She didn't care where she pioneered as long as she was in the flow of the Plan. If she could fill a vital pioneering goal anywhere, and at the same time make my life more exciting and easier, too, it was perfect.

"Santa Rosa is a goal city," she explained, "that's the important thing. The Teaching Committee has been searching all year for some prepared soul, some hero, to go to Santa Rosa."

"Good luck to them," I said. "I hope they find somebody."

"They have!" Marguerite cried out. "*You.*"

Marguerite warmed to her task enthusiastically. "*You're* that prepared soul."

"I am?"

"And best of all, you volunteered."

"I did?"

"Symbolically you did, by not wanting to go up to the Yankees."

I tried to hoist myself off my own petard.

"I thought you wanted to go to Jackson, Mississippi?"

"I *do*. More than anything else in the world. But right now, your career is important, too. The boys and I want *you* to be happy. A goal city nearby like Santa Rosa makes it possible for all of us to pioneer and for you to commute to the studios at NBC in the San Francisco you've come to love. Isn't that exciting?"

"Halle", I said, "lujah."

"It *is*", Marguerite insisted. "It means the whole family will still be pioneering, and in the spirit of the Teaching Plan. That's marvellous!"

I began to rebel. It wasn't that marvellous.

"Santa Rosa", I said, "is too far away."

"You don't even know how far it is."

"Wherever it is, it's too far."

"No such thing. You can reach Santa Rosa from here with a nine iron."

You couldn't, of course. You had to take a Greyhound bus and two seven irons.

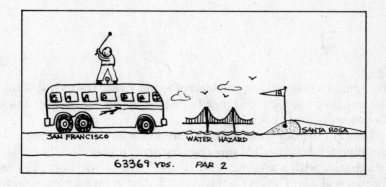

"Now hear this, Marguerite Sears!"

21

We rented a farm on the outskirts of Santa Rosa. It was still within the city limits so we could legally be part of the Santa Rosa Local Community and Assembly.

I caught the Greyhound bus to San Francisco each morning. By the time the bus reached our country area, it was already packed to capacity with war-time commuters. With all the stops, I stood for two and a half hours each way, each day, giving me ample time during which to meditate.

If I was lucky I could snag one of the last free hanging-straps. Otherwise, when the bus lurched, you clung desperately to the clothing of the passenger nearest to you. This could lead to assorted rude, sordid and insulting remarks.

While I didn't have much luck reading the San Francisco *Chronicle* one-handed, standing up and lurching from side to side, and poking my unfolded paper in people's faces, I did enrol three new Bahá'ís during that six month period.

One of them I hadn't even been talking to. He was accidentally trapped between myself and the person whom I was teaching, and he overheard what I said about the Faith. The one I was talking to had all the fire of a swamp, but the one trapped between us became a real live wire, an active Bahá'í.

"It's the first time eaves-dropping ever paid off for me", he said, enthusiastically.*

Naturally none of the Bahá'ís I enrolled lived in our goal city of Santa Rosa. They were all from Petaluma, Sausalito or somewhere else.

But that's show business.

* Incidentally, I was told later that he was pioneering in Latin America. Probably developing his own crowded-bus teaching technique in Spanish. We tend to teach others the way we ourselves came into the Faith.

66

Every time I crossed that glorious Golden Gate Bridge, my personal love-affair with San Francisco deepened. From my office window in the Knox Reeves Agency on the corner of Market and Montgomery, I could watch my friend the fog slide slowly up Market Street each morning and disappear into the Pacific Ocean beyond the top of the Twin Peaks.

In the late afternoon, the wispy grey fingers of the fog would claw their way back over the top of the Twin Peaks, and finally like a crouched leopard ready to attack, it would slowly crawl toward the Embarcadero.

Foot by foot the fog would fasten upon everything that stood in its path as it pulled itself down Market Street, quietly swallowing up one parked car after another, devouring store fronts, traffic lights and tall buildings. Softly and silently, the fog would gulp in people, trucks and streetcars, until it reached the Oakland–San Francisco Ferry building at the foot of Market Street, ingesting them all, leaving only an impenetrable mist over what once was San Francisco.

I loved it!

From out of that mouse-coloured void, still trying to survive, came the sound of the streetcars clanging, police sirens shrieking, and the constant, uninterrupted, insolent blast of the ferry boats as they took off or approached the Embarcadero, fog or no fog.

The entire city below my window was in the stomach of a great grey whale. It happened every afternoon. My office window was a TV screen.

San Francisco was heaven!

I could endure an almost unendurable amount of suffering, including standing on the bus two and a half hours each way in my mist-dampened clothes; stepping out into the frequent rain, hacking away at a nasty hollow chest cough; anything, rather than give up the joys of San Francisco.

Besides, wasn't I filling an important goal right where I was? Not overseas, it's true, but still vital. Who was to say which goal city was more important in the eyes of the Supreme Concourse, I asked myself.

Unfortunately, I also asked Marguerite.

"How about the National Teaching Committee's suggestion?" she replied. "They've put Jackson at the top of a high priority list."

"Don't", I told her, "confuse me with facts."

I knew it was becoming touch-and-go as to who would win our battle for the City by the Bay. Unfortunately for my side, Santa Rosa now had fifteen people resident in the city without the Sears family, and there was still that urgent call for the Deep South and Jackson, Mississippi.

I knew that if I didn't watch my step, Miss Robin's-Egg Blue Eyes and her high-priority Teaching Committee would peel me away from California like a banana skin.

I could feel the family peer pressure building. The dachshund Spook would run around the house in a brown paper bag with holes for his head and feet. On the sides someone had drawn a railroad train with the engine spewing out black smoke which spelled out the words "Choo Choo South!"

At unexpected times, the record player treated me to loud blasts of Al Jolson's rendition of:

> Oh, I wish I were in the land of cotton,
> Old times there are not forgotten,
> Look away! Look away! Look away!
> Dixieland!

I felt I could "look away" no longer. It was show-down time at the Sears hacienda. I decided to have it out with the family that very night, once and for all, as they say in melodramas.

I laid my plans carefully as I rode home on the bus from NBC and the *Dr Kate* soap strip. I had two and a half bus hours to prepare and rehearse my California vs. Mississippi speech. I knew exactly what I would say to them, and how I would say it. I called it *The Case of the Countless Can'ts*.

I put notes inside a manila folder. I marked it boldly in black, underlined in red, with three huge exclamation marks!

NOW HEAR THIS, MARGUERITE SEARS!!!

"I wouldn't be in his shoes for all the money in the world."

22

Immediately after dinner, the great show-down began. Influenced by the war-time Navy talk from the base at Vallejo across the Bay, I cleared my throat and roared out in a commanding voice:

"Assemble! On the double! Everyone!"

They did.

"Now hear this, Marguerite Sears!"

The boys started to turn away. I added, loudly, for their benefit: "And company!"

They came back to immediate attention.

At the sound of my Day-of-Judgement voice, the dachshund Spook slunk off into the woodpile beside the stove with his tail between his legs. I bellowed at him.

"You, too, Choo Choo South!"

Spook burrowed deeper toward safety.

"Perhaps we should have a prayer before we begin", Marguerite suggested.

I replied coldly. "In particular we shall not pray about it. The matter is not negotiable. It is settled. Once and for all. I am not leaving San Francisco. Ever. Especially not for Jackson, Mississippi. Only one thing can now make me change my mind. One thing and only one thing. Are there any questions?"

There were none. I could tell by the quick flash in their eyes and the glances they surreptitiously cast at each other, that they were all waiting to hear the one thing that could make me change my mind, so they'd know where to direct their immediate and future attacks. But I was on to them.

I took out my game-plan from the manila folder. I thumbtacked it up on the bulletin-board, and using my pointer, I read it aloud to them. It stopped them cold. Dead in their tracks. I knew I had won at last. I laid it out a second time, slowly, word for word, so there could be no mistake.

"It will take a miracle, nothing less", I insisted. "A veritable, genuine, full-blown miracle. Colourful and unmistakable. There cannot be the slightest doubt in anyone's mind that it has to be a miracle. Clear?"

"Clear."

"That is the only thing that will ever get me to leave San Francisco for Jackson, Mississippi. Is that understood?"

"Understood."

"And I will accept only a miracle of the first order. Not a second-rate miracle. It must be authentic and unimpeachable. A miracle that any pin-head can recognize immediately."

Silence.

"Capish?"

"Capish."

"The miracle has to hit me like a ton of bricks. Wham! so I will cry out: 'My God! It's a miracle!' Is that clear?"

"Clear."

I looked Marguerite, the ringleader, directly in the eye.

"You have always insisted that the Bahá'í Faith could perform miracles. Right?"

"Right. If one has a pure and detached heart, there's no reason why—"

"No heart could be more detached from Jackson, Mississippi than mine", I told her interrupting coldly. "And no purposes for staying in San Francisco could be purer than mine."

Silence.

"That's it", I concluded, taking my game-plan down from the bulletin-board and putting it back into my manila folder. "Now, let's see your miracle. Put your money where your mouth is."

Every Bahá'í reading this is already laughing. They are saying to themselves, "Poor Bill Sears!" They knew I was throwing stones at the sun to try and put out its light.

Marguerite stepped forward. She hugged me and kissed me on each cheek. She smiled up at me with that sweet, tender, loving, benign smile that always infuriates me and burns my biscuit. Have I said that before?

"We'll do exactly what you say, dear."

I knew I couldn't back off now. She was trying to undermine me with kindness and understanding. I looked directly into her soft sympathetic eyes and drove the nail home. I said:

"Have I made myself perfectly clear on this subject of miracles?"

"Perfectly."

"Did you all hear every word I said?" I asked, taking in William and Michael as well.

"Every word, Daddy."

William turned and whispered behind his hand to his brother Michael, "Boy. I wouldn't be in his shoes for all the money in the Bank of America."

Michael nodded.

"Bahá'u'lláh's gonna *zap* him for sure."

"And", I raised my voice, "I don't want any whispering or smart-alec remarks from you two. Clear?"

"Clear."

Marguerite slid her hand slowly across the coffee table toward her prayer book. I froze her with an arctic blast.

"And we won't pray about it. We'll let nature take its own course."

"Whatever you say, dear."

"And no praying behind my back. Understood?"

"Understood."

More silence.

I looked over at the stove. Spook's tail was all that remained visible.

"You can come out now, hound-dog", I told him. "The storm is over."

Spook refused to budge. I could hear him burrowing even deeper into the woodpile until his tail disappeared from sight too.

I summarized the Council Fire for posterity. I told them,

"It will take a miracle, a clear, unmistakable, full-blown, genuine, live and in colour, miracle to get me out of San Francisco heading for Jackson, Mississippi. You hear me?"

"We hear."

Silently, the three of them joined hands.

"A *miracle*", I repeated.

"A miracle", they echoed in unison.

"A M-I-R-A-C-L-E—"

"We *know* how to spell it", Marguerite objected, her voice edged with rising heat.

I closed my address to the troops:

"Until such a time, Jackson, Mississippi is a subject that is c'est fini, kaput, ausgespielt, finished, ended, closed, terminated. Over and out."

Which is where I went, stomping thunder with my feet, but terrifying no one but myself. The technique has never been effective. Especially not with your own children who can read your "father-sounds" like a familiar book.

I could see their lips moving.

I suspected they were already praying. Or were up to something. So, just to be on the safe side, I stopped in the doorway, turned, and gave a final blast in parting. I yelled a warning to cover every weird, bizarre and shameless shenanigans they might be up to.

"And cut that out! Whatever it is the three of you are doing! Mississippi is as dead as a doornail!"

There was a lethal silence. One of those that is so quiet that it is almost noisy. As I closed the door gently, having chosen not to slam it which is what the dramatic circumstances demanded, I thought I heard William singing softly to himself:

"Emm-eye-ess-ess-eye-ess-ess-eye-pee-pee-eye. That spells Mississippi!"

For someone who had laid down the law and been so obviously triumphant, why did I feel so totally defeated?

THE
MIRACLE

FIREWORKS!

23

I remember all too clearly how it began.

My doctor, an incurable optimist, told me, "Perhaps you have gallstones. That would account for your saffron colour."

I've put in all this light-hearted medical talk since this is supposed to be a somewhat humorous book. The doctor entered into the spirit of things, saying,

"The X-rays will tell us."

"Don't worry", Marguerite comforted me. "We'll all be praying for you."

I shuddered.

"Please don't", I entreated. "Let nature take its course. But no prayers. No fireworks. I'd rather be saffron, if that means yellow."

"It does, dear, and saffron is very expensive."

"Wait until you get the bill for this gall-bladder operation, you'll think saffron is sand."

"I was only trying to comfort you, dear."

"If you want to comfort me, don't pray. No fireworks."

What else?

Already, I had turned as red as a Harvard football jersey from the pill they gave me to quiet me down. My blood pressure could have driven the Santa Fe *Chief* to Palm Springs.

"You were allergic to the pill", Marguerite explained.

"You could have fooled me. I thought my head was a red balloon. That could happen to anybody."

"It'll be different this time."

"Of course. There are still lots of colours left."

When they rolled me into the operating room, my doctor was extremely cheerful and bright.

"You", he said, "are one of the lucky ones."

"Naturally", I told him. "That's why I'm here."

"You're one of the very first civilians to have this new wartime anaesthetic tried on them."

"You mean I'm a guinea pig."

"You're a war hero without ever leaving home. Who knows what medicine may learn here in San Francisco this morning?"

"Hip! Hip!" I said, "Hurray! Shall we send up rockets?"

"You're about to receive the new wonder drug Sodium Pentathol. Before you can count from ten backwards to one, you'll be gone. If you make six I'll be surprised."

"But will I return?"

"Have faith."

"What about my allergies to everything new? Shouldn't we test it first?"

"We shall", he said, gallantly. "Under fire."

His laugh was hollow and so was the pit of my stomach. Especially when he said, "Let's play it by ear." He said, "Count backwards from ten."

I tried.

"Ten, nine, eight, sev—"

I didn't make six.

I woke up later in my hospital-room.

Marguerite was sitting beside the bed smiling at me.

"Welcome home", she said.

"Was the operation a success?" I asked.

"The truth is," Marguerite said, "you were allergic to the Sodium Pentathol, too. You turned black on the operating table."

"Great."

"It took the doctors some time to get you back to your normal colour."

"White?"

"No."

"Red?"

Marguerite shook her head.

"Still yellow?"

She nodded.

"Well," I mumbled, "at least that will improve now that the gallstones are out."

Marguerite coughed. "Well," she said, "the truth is—".

"Don't tell me, let me guess. You prayed."

"The doctor said your gall-bladder was misplaced, and it would be too dangerous to take it out this time. Perhaps later."

"Never."

"So they took out your appendix."

"They took out my *what*?"

"Your appendix."

I was disgusted.

"Maybe I had appendix stones."

I had already lost confidence in my doctor when, through the anaesthetic haze, sometime during the operation, perhaps when he found the misplaced gall-bladder, I thought I heard him say:

"Oh, my God!"*

---

* Marguerite insisted that one of the most intriguing parts of the miracle took place years later by which time a special surgical technique had been developed for removing just such misplaced gall-bladders; and "miraculously enough", she added, poking me in the ribs with her elbow, "you had your worst gall-bladder attack in the very hospital where the surgeon who developed that surgical technique practised. Now be honest", she added, "is that miracle-stuff or not?" Meanwhile, back in San Francisco.

24

We were on our way home from the hospital.

"Unless I'm mistaken," Marguerite said smugly, "you promised to pioneer to Jackson, Mississippi, when the proper time came."

Always beware of people who begin a sentence with "Unless I'm mistaken."

"I must have been hallucinating", I told Marguerite.

"You actually said it, Daddy!" the boys chipped in from the back seat. "We both heard you."

"Did you or did you not say it would take a genuine colourful miracle of the first order to get you to change your pioneering post from Santa Rosa to Jackson, Mississippi?"

Always beware of people who start sentences with "Did you, or did you not?"

Marguerite was right, of course. I *had* said it.

"Okay", I agreed, "and when that colourful miracle *does* take place, we'll go to Jackson. But not a minute before."

"Bill! Bill! Bill!" Marguerite cried, shaking her head from side to side, "Are you blind?"

Always beware of people who start sentences with your name three times in a row: "Bill! Bill! Bill!". Especially with that sad, empty echo sound. Only disaster can follow.

As it did in this case.

Especially be warned if they add a pitiful: "Are you blind?"

Any fool, of course, should have seen it in a flash. I don't understand how I could have missed it. I berated myself, apologized to Marguerite, and began beating my fist against the rain-drenched car window.

"Bill, Bill! Bill!" I asked myself, "how could you be so blind?"

To myself, inside, I added: "You poor, mad, Jackson-bound fool!"

I cried into my basket of hospital fruit.

No use keeping you in suspense. About the colourful miracle, I mean. You've probably already guessed it. Every potential and actual Bahá'í pioneer reading this book saw the truth immediately, in a burst of light.

Marguerite's voice cut through all of my objections, making it clear that from now on she would brook no interruption. She had the floor and she meant to keep it. She was centre stage with all flood and spotlights on. And two boys were in the prompter's box.

"You said that with the coming of the miracle, you would be ready for the Deep South and for everything that teaching the Black and White in Dixie stood for. Right?"

"Right. But only when the colourful miracle—"

"When that happy miraculous day came, you said—"

"Never mind the editorial," I told her, "get to the punch line." Somehow I knew that this time it really would be a punch line.

"Number one: When you came to California from the Midwest you were pale and pasty-faced until you acquired a nice deep California suntan. Am I right?"

"What does that have to do with—"

"Then, poor dear," she continued, ignoring my interruption, "you turned a bright saffron yellow from the gallstones."

"So?"

Marguerite clucked in her teeth sympathetically.

Icily, I said, "I'm still waiting for the part about the miracle."

"Put him out of his misery, Mother", Michael encouraged.

"Right!" William added, "Put him down for the count! Give him the old sockeroo!"

I objected. I asked Marguerite to quiet down her bloodthirsty troops.

"*Where* and when", I insisted, "did God work this marvellous miracle? I don't see it."

"You will", Marguerite said serenely.

"When?"

"I'm saving that part for when we get home. It's the most thrilling part of all."

"I want to hear it now."

"Later", she said. "In the meantime, think about it. See if the answer doesn't come to you yourself, with a terribly guilty rush, and overwhelm you."

Marguerite gave me another of those infuriating molasses-sweet smiles. I know I keep saying that repeatedly, but now I can tell you why.

The truth came to me for the first time right then in that rain-drenched car. Unmistakably. Marguerite's smug, superior smile almost invariably precedes some sudden unexpected disastrous defeat for me. It always comes at one exact precise moment. When? Just before I hear the trap-door spring open, and I fall headlong down into Fu Manchu's cellar.

The old rainbow!

25

I finally woke up from my convalescent nap. I was still surrounded by smiling faces. Marguerite, William, Michael and Spook. The dachshund leaped up onto the bed along the permanent ramp Marguerite had constructed for him* and attacked me with all four feet. He landed on my bandaged scar, so I knew I was home.

I panned my eyes along the three faces: Marguerite, William and Michael. They were bursting with eagerness to finish off the miracle story and give me the old *coup de grâce*.

"This is it?" I asked. "The old sockeroo?"

As if I didn't know.

"This", Marguerite told me, "is it."

I don't know whose face was the brightest with excitement, Marguerite's, Bill's, Mike's or Spook's, who was now chewing on my ear.

Marguerite gave it to me straight and put me out of my misery.

"You were white," she said, "and acquired a California deep brown tan. When the gallstones struck you changed to yellow. The pill they gave you to calm you down turned you red. And the anaesthetic, the Sodium Pentathol, turned you black on the operating table."

"So?" I knew it was lame, but all I could dredge up was, "So?"

"So," she said, "where else in the entire Bahá'í world today do we have a follower of Bahá'u'lláh who in less than one month, has been white, brown, yellow, red and black? All of the colours of the five races of mankind?"

---

* The first thing Marguerite always does, even before we unpack our bags, is fix an incline up from the foot of the bed for the dachshunds. She has done it for all eleven of them. I've given the grisly details in *Tokoloshe*, or: *I Married Eleven Dachshunds* which Marguerite and I are writing together.

"Nowhere", I told her. "It's impossible. It would take a real miracle to accomplish something like—"

"Exactly!"

"It's you, Daddy!" the boys shouted gleefully, clapping their hands. "The old rainbow! You, yourself are the miracle!"

Marguerite went on inexorably.

"If such a five-skin-coloured person is not ready to arise and pioneer for Bahá'u'lláh, and to teach the Oneness of Mankind, in the Deep South, without fear and without restraint, then no human being ever born on this planet will ever be ready to do so."

"Curtain!" I called out, applauding. "End of Act Two."

In the long silence that ensued, I just stared at Marguerite. Amazed.

"And *that* is the colourful miracle?"

"It is."

"Me?"

"You."

"Let me get this straight. All three of you think that I, myself—that *I* am the colourful miracle?"

"Well, aren't you? Isn't that what happened? A colourful, authentic full-blown miracle of the first order?"

"Don't you get it yet, Dad?" Michael asked.

Bill, Jr. chipped in, delighted. "You've been every one of the colours of all five races of mankind: Black, White, Yellow, Red and Brown. And all in one single month!"

"And that's a miracle!" Michael insisted.

Marguerite nodded. "You're unique."

"One of a kind", William added proudly.

"But all of those skin colours were temporary", I protested. "And symbolic."

"And", Marguerite added, "colourful and miraculous. You are now ready to pioneer. As promised."

William, Michael and Marguerite Sears all spoke together, like the Andrew Sisters:

"Isn't it terrific?"

"Have you three rehearsed this?" I asked, suspiciously.

They drowned out my voice. They were now giving me a standing ovation, applauding loudly while Spook barked and ran wildly back and forth, up and down the bed, and twice across my bandaged stomach.

81

Sometime later Marguerite poured my tea and buttered my croissant.

"Isn't it marvellous?" she asked. "Really?" She kissed me again, soundly, and ate my croissant.

It *wasn't* marvellous at all. Not to me. But all three of them knew that my walls had caved in. I had destroyed myself with my own allergic body.

"Admit it", Marguerite coaxed. "It *is* a truly genuine, colourful miracle, isn't it? Yes or no?"

It was. I couldn't deny it, but I hated to give in.

"The jury's still out", I told her.

I sent up a forlorn hopeless trial balloon.

"Whether it's a miracle or not, depends upon the eye of the beholder."

"God is the Beholder this time", Marguerite pointed out significantly. "Are there any questions?"

There were no questions. And certainly no answers.

"Clear?" Marguerite added.

"Clear."

"Understood?"

"Understood." I grinned.

"Capish?"

"Capish."

She really did it quite well.

How could I resist any longer? To paraphrase the words of Abraham Lincoln, you can fool all of the people some of the time, and some of the people all of the time, but you can't fool *The Man Upstairs* any of the time.

I knew I was a goner, "you all", as they say in the Deep South —such as in Jackson, Mississippi.

"I hope you will always stay yellow like that, Dad", William grinned during dinner. "I like you better that way."

"Me, too", Michael seconded. "Only a deeper yellow."

"You can depend on it", I told them. "But from now on, the yellow will be on the inside where you can't see it."

William summed up the entire San Francisco miracle-caper in one sentence:

"Now hear this! Just when Dad thought he had successfully escaped pioneering to Jackson, Mississippi, God reached down and finger-painted my father."

26

We were taking the Southern Pacific scenic route to Jackson, Mississippi. It would carry us through Palm Springs, Yuma, Phoenix, Las Cruces, Texas and on to New Orleans, Louisiana. There we would change to the Illinois Central for Jackson. I always had the forlorn hope that the engine would develop "flat wheels" or that the famous San Andreas fault would swallow up a thousand feet of track in front of us.

As I look back on that historic pioneering journey from my present-day mountaintop of wisdom over a quarter of a century later, I am inclined to indulge in that flip-flop process of "flash-backs" and "flash-aheads" that Marguerite finds so confusing and annoying.

Once again, with masterful strokes, I am going to blend the past, the present, and the future into one; but only briefly, and only on behalf of the State of California, my home town.

Marguerite deprived me of California at a tender, impressionable and relatively youthful age. Not once, but three times, Marguerite forcibly removed me with her prayers from the warm womb of mother California.

I still stand in awe and trembling, pleasured beyond belief, when I look towards the West Coast and speak that magic word.

California!

All rise, please.

I loved San Francisco, but I adore Southern California. Marguerite and I lived the longest part of our western Bahá'í lives in that paradise. Marguerite, of course, refers to Northern California as No Cal, and to Southern or Lower California as Lo Cal. Unfortunately, Marguerite is prejudiced in favour of the Continent of Africa, and can take California or leave it—by car, bus, train, or plane, whichever is the fastest. "And the sooner the better, and let's not come back."

But for me, on the other hand, the State in which I grew my own rainbow will always be my home town.

I know. I know. Some wise guy once said: "You can criticize California, especially Hollywood, and you can ridicule all that 'tinsel' in Tinsel-Town, but if you are really fair-minded and sincere, and you look behind all that 'tinsel' you'll find the real 'tinsel'."

I am able to withstand all these sarcastic Eastern, Midwestern, Southern, Mountain and Florida generated insults because I personally know where the real gold is buried.

The Bahá'í Community of Southern California is a mother lode and the land on which she stands is hallowed. Marguerite spells it with an "o".

I have lived a good share of my Bahá'í life in and around Los Angeles, Palm Springs, Palm Desert, Thousand Oaks, Beverly Hills, Sierra Madre and Simi Valley. I wouldn't change one oleander bush in Los Angeles, Ventura, San Bernardino or Riverside Counties for all the blooming trees in the rest of the planet. Materialistically speaking.*

Why couldn't Marguerite see in those early days that it was impossible for me to pioneer so soon, and to be swept away from all those gorgeous soul-crushing materialistic things my immature soul still craved for so desperately? That, of course, was before it became the popular and the "in thing" to curse and denounce all these material, worldly entrapments such as Fedco, Gemco, Standard Brands, Aaron Brothers, Sears, Broadway, May Company, Robinson's, Bullock's, Pic'n'Save, and all those luxurious malls and plazas that not only turned me on, but set me ablaze. As Professor Higgins would say, "How frightful! How delightful!"

I'm not prejudiced, mind you. I don't care *who* the Southern California Trojans beat at football, or the UCLA Bruins at basketball. The Lakers are lovely, the Kings are classy, and the Dodgers are darling. I'll even go as far as lauding the California Anaheim Angels, the San Diego Padres, the Chargers, and the newly-fledged Los Angeles Raiders.

These were my kind of people.

*The Holy Land, naturally, is exempt from all these earth-bound comparisons by an underling soul. In that case, there is no contest.

85

Naturally, I have now matured and have outgrown all these —Please remove your hat. It's true that when we fly over Los Angeles *en route* from Mexico to Canada, Marguerite and the boys still lash me Ulysses-like to the plane's galley till we're past. Certainly an unneeded precaution now, but *then*—Aaahhh!

When I can't breathe a little of that invigorating Los Angeles smog, or get caught in the fierce bumper-to-bumper San Bernardino Freeway traffic between Los Angeles and West Covina, or quiver along with a jolly little minor San Andreas Fault earth tremor, life is not really worth living.

Jack Benny and Fred Allen used to feud over the comparative virtues of Los Angeles and New York City back in the halcyon days of Radio when there really were Sunkist orange groves all over Southern California instead of high-rises and army bases. The slopes of Mount Baldy were white with pure snow, not grey with pollutants. To cite the words of Fred Allen, "There's nothing wrong with Southern California weather that you can't pump out of your cellar."

Marguerite and I have had mud-slides in our living-room in Sierra Madre. We've outraced forest fires *en route* to several places in those dry brown valleys between Thousand Oaks and San Bernardino. We've watched the large plate glass window in our living-room in Palm Springs bend and quiver back and forth without breaking during an earthquake as we sat, nonchalantly, on top of the San Andreas Fault enjoying breakfast while our newly-arrived niece from Wisconsin cried out: "What was that?"

Where else in all the world could you have the dramatic excitement such as California had in 1983, with the streets caving in from flood-like rains, houses encased in goo sliding into the sea, piers at Santa Monica and Seal Beach being ripped apart by huge tidal waves, mud-slides blocking city streets, and two tornadoes, one after the other, accompanied simultaneously by two minor earthquakes? In fact, a flood, an earthquake and a tornado all in one day! That's disaster-movie material.

Of course you didn't hear about it. You were too busy digging out from under your own multiple blizzards and highway icings.

You can't tell me Southern California is all bad. Otherwise, why would those wise birds, the swallows always keep coming back to Capistrano?

Right?

Those swallows don't come back to Rio, or Tokyo, or Paarl Valley, or Paris, or Rome, or New York, or Miami, or Panama City, or Whitehorse in the Yukon, do they? You bet they don't!

They come back to Capistrano! And that's in Southern California.

Everybody please rise and bow towards the West.

I'm always willing to arise myself, anytime, anywhere, with only a moment's notice, to fly along home with those brilliant swallows, piggy-back, every year, if there was only some way to do it. From wherever I was in the world.

To California!

Cue the closing music!

"That's Christian, isn't it?"

27

The Southern Pacific Passenger train carrying us away from the City by the Golden Gate was winding its inexorable way toward Jackson, Mississippi. The "Choo Choo South" was just approaching Las Cruces, New Mexico. Spook was in the baggage car ahead.

Marguerite, Bill Jr. and I came back from breakfast in the dining-car. Michael hadn't been hungry.

When we approached our seats, Michael was deeply engaged in a conversation with two Catholic Sisters, Nuns. The ones with the attractive large pointed head-dress.

Michael was fascinated.

We sat down a few seats behind them rather than interrupt a genius at work.

Michael, as always, was direct.

"You have very funny looking hats", he said.

They laughed, pleased at his interest.

"They're not hats", they told him. "They're part of our habit, our dress. We're Catholic Sisters."

"Oh", Michael said, interested. "That's *Christian*, isn't it?"

This rocked the religious pair.

"Yes," they said, "it is Christian. Aren't you Christian yourself?"

"Oh, yes", Michael admitted. "I'm Christian, and then some. I'm all sorts of things. East and West. It's terrific! You name it, and I'm it."

The Nuns looked at each other, puzzled.

"We don't understand."

They didn't either.

"What other things are you?" they asked, perplexed.

"Well", Michael said, trying to remember clearly himself. "I'm not only Christian, but I'm also Jewish, Buddhist, Hindu, Muslim, and a lot of other good stuff."

The Nuns giggled.

"You're joking, surely."

"In a pig's eye!" Michael replied, deadly serious. "We believe in everything. That there's only one God for everybody. And that He's not working only for the Christians."

"We believe that, too."

"That's good."

"Are your folks Christian?"

"Some are. Not these with me here on the train now."

"What are they?"

"Those on this train?"

"Yes."

"We're all Bahá'ís, of course."

"Bahá'ís? What's that?"

Michael was shocked. His sympathy showed in his eyes.

"You mean you don't know about the Bahá'í Faith?"

"No, we don't."

"That's mighty funny. You're certainly old enough."

"Not that old", they said, laughing.

"My father claims that anybody who doesn't know about the Bahá'í Faith today, must be living in a cave, or have their heads stuck in the sand like an ostrich. No offence."

None had been taken. Michael's blue eyes, that wavy blond hair, that beguiling (and misleading) look of complete innocence had bowled them over.

I started to get up and put an end to Michael's consultation. Marguerite put a restraining hand on my arm.

"What do the Bahá'ís believe?" one of the Sisters asked.

Michael didn't know where to begin, the subject was so vast. He admitted it quite frankly.

"I don't know exactly, it's so big. But I do know that we love everybody."

"We love everybody, too."

"Yes," Michael said, extending his arms way out, "but we love them universally."

This tickled the two Sisters. They confided in Michael who, obviously, they found enchanting.

"We're on our way to our new teaching post in Las Cruces", one of the Sisters explained, "to work among one of the poor minorities, among the Spanish-speaking people."

89

"So are we", Michael replied, delighted. "I guess we're both pioneers. Only we're going all the way to Jackson, Mississippi, to work among the poor Black people, the *real* minority."

Michael's manner said: "Take that."

One of the Nuns asked:

"For Christ?"

"Him too. Among others."

"That's it", I told Marguerite. "The great Southern Pacific religious confrontation is now at an end."

I cleared my throat loudly. Michael turned around and saw us sitting behind them. He said to the two Nuns:

"I have to go now, my parents are here. But if you want to go into this deeper a little later on—"

Louder cough.

"We do!" they said, laughing. "We certainly do. It's been fascinating."

"It's big, all right", Michael assured them, over his shoulder. "Bigger than anything any of us earth-people have ever dreamed about. My father said that. He's here now. If you'd like him to elaborate any particular points I've brought up, or answer any questions that may be troubling you—"

"Michael!"

I used my Billy-Goat-Gruff voice. Michael knew immediately that the evil Troll was hiding under the bridge.

He leaned back and whispered to the two Sisters:

"Later", he said. "There's some things even bigger than religion."

Michael joined us.

"It was all perfectly innocent!" he said. "They asked me. I couldn't refuse to tell them about the Faith. Could I? They're pioneers, too. I liked them."

I waited until Michael had wound down. Then our entire family went back to the dining-car for more coffee and milk.

And more privacy.

The next morning, the *Daylight Limited* slowed down as we approached Las Cruces. The two Nuns were getting off at this charming New Mexico town. They walked past us, stopped, turned around, and came back to our seat.

"You have a very unusual son", one of them said.

It was obvious they wanted a closer look at his parents.

"Thank you."

"He does seem a little bit confused, religiously", the other added.

We laughed.

"Not really", I told her. "Michael's fine. It's just the world that's confused. It hasn't caught up with him yet."

"I see. It's a *family* thing, then?"

She said it as though it were a raging, contagious disease.

"You might say that", I agreed. "We're all in it together. We're Bahá'ís."

William offered her a postcard of the Bahá'í Temple in Wilmette with the Bahá'í principles listed on the back.

"I always carry a few of these", William said, "for people who are interested."

"Thank you", the taller Nun said, "but no."

"They're free", Bill explained. "The Bahá'ís pay for everything themselves. Nobody who's not a Bahá'í can give a cent towards the teaching work."

I closed down his hard sell, and thanked them for their interest in Michael.

The elder Sister handed the postcard back to Bill, and said, "We're much too busy with religion."

Michael said, "This *is* religion. This is the real thing I was telling you about."

"We'll pray for you", the Sister said. "Five Our Fathers and Five Hail Marys."

"We just finished praying for you", Michael countered. "Nine Remover of Difficulties."

It was a Mexican stand-off in a New Mexico town. The heavenly Concourse must have been quite tickled. I heard Bill, Jr. over by the window whisper to himself, "Nine of a kind beats two fives".

The Sisters clucked in their teeth sympathetically, shook their heads, but couldn't restrain their giggles as they walked down the aisle. They took their luggage down from the rack and prepared to leave the train at Las Cruces. One of them dug the other in the ribs. We could hear her chuckle as she repeated Michael's words.

"We love them universally!"

Spontaneous laughter.

Louder.

The Nuns waved cheerfully to us as they descended the steps.

The great Southern Pacific Railway Religious Confrontation was over.

I told Michael, "I think you still have some spadework to do there."

We were jerked back in our seats as the train puffed and huffed. The wheels squealed and the iron monster began moving slowly toward El Paso and on to Jackson, Mississippi.

Michael summed it up for all of us.

"I'm hungry", he said. "This Fireside teaching is murder."

It *was,* too. His style.

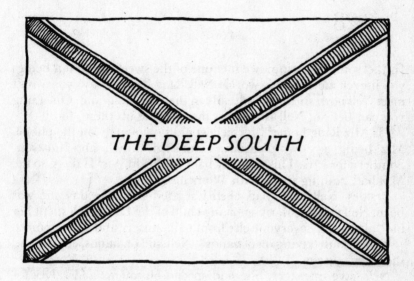

THE DEEP SOUTH

28

In Jackson, Mississippi, we met one of the sweetest human beings you'll ever meet in this world: Nell Ring. Sad to say, you won't meet Nell now, since she's already in the next Kingdom. One thing you can bet on, Nell is making them hustle up there, too.

"Is Miz Ring home?" a voice would say lovingly on the phone. Miz being a slow, pleasant, elongated drawl, and Jackson-Southern for Mrs. This was way back in World War II days, so the Miz had nothing to do with Women's Lib.

Besides, Nell Ring had been liberated from the day she was born. Nell was a real, rip-snorting child of the Lord. Nell spent her life "liberating" everyone else from pain, misery and unhappiness.

Talk about "laying on of hands"! Nell laid on hands, elbows and shoulder muscles.

Nell gave massages. She had special ointments and salves for every human misery. Nell had marvellous healing hands, and a happy-go-lucky outlook on life that cured even more of her patients than her jars, bottles and massages. Nell also had a million dollar grin which made her smile priceless for healing.

Nell Ring was a big woman, both up and down and around. When Nell started to laugh, which was often and infectious, she shook so violently that it took every bit of her light-footed balance to keep the car on the road.

Nell was a darling, delightful human being. She spent most of her time giving free massages, food and hand-outs, including small bills and loose change which she showered on her needy patients. Nell had both Black and White patients. She could never tell the difference.

If you reminded Nell of her dwindling bank balance and the charity-bazaar she was running for a business, and warned her, "Nell, you'll go broke", she'd answer happily, "Honey, I'm so rich in the Lord and so far ahead on blessings, that if I was starving, I'd still feel like an over-fed glutton."

Then off Nell would go into gales of laughter. The real kind that made you feel good deep down inside.

Nell Ring had honeysuckle and magnolia blossoms in her accent. If it was any *more* Southern, you wouldn't have understood a word she said. I love it. I used to prod Nell into telling me how she became a Bahá'í, just to hear that marvellous incredible voice. I'd give her another big hug and tell her how much I loved her accent.

This always surprised Nell.

"Me?" she'd say, wide-eyed. "Look here, honey. I sound just fine. You're the one who talks funny. Down here, I'm home stuff, Yankee Boy. It's you who stands out like a blueberry on a white plate."

Of course, it was true. In Jackson.

On the other hand, you take Emmy Lou Patten and her Southern accent. It was musical, sweet as hominy, and like a bluebird on a tree. Nell on the other hand simply got carried away. If Nell had tried out for the role of a matronly Southern lady in a Broadway play, they would have turned her down cold and said: "Thank you, Mrs Ring, but what we need is someone authentic. You have quite obviously worked hard on your Southern accent. Congratulations, but you've overdone it this time. Sorry."

I couldn't get enough of Nell's way of talking, myself. But then, I was in love with Nell Ring. All of us were, Marguerite, William, Michael and myself. Even Spook, our dachshund. No wonder. She was Miss, Miz and Mrs Mississippi to all of us, even the hound-dog.

"Don't give that critter dog-food from a can", Nell would say. "He eats chitlings and greens and live garden food from the table just like the rest of us folks."

Maybe her accent was a trifle exotic, but Nell, herself, was one hundred percent authentic. In every way. In all the ways that count. Suddenly I found myself listening to how she became a Bahá'í rather than to her Dixie melody.

It was intriguing. Nell Ring was a true seeker. In the search-and-seize manner. All of her life, Nell had been looking for something better. Her words.

Her daughter, Laura Nell, said that for as long as she could remember her mother had been wading her way through almost every religion, and every off-shoot of every religion, known to man. Searching. Always searching.

Her mother would say, "I *know* there's something better out there somewhere, darlin'! Something a lot more exciting and wonderful than what I have now. I've simply got to find it."

"Yes, mother."

Laura Nell had been a kind, loving, patient daughter, at least fairly patient, as the religious casualties mounted up. Finally, she said, "Mother, why don't you give up? Why don't you just settle for being the kind of proper Christian you were raised to be?"

"Because I'm not that kind of Christian any longer, child. I haven't got a proper bone in my body. I'm on the look-out for the *big* one. It's out there hiding from me, and I'm going to find it."

Nell would tap her breast and say fervently, totally convinced, "Something in here tells me, keep searching, Nell Ring. It's out there somewhere just waiting for you. Don't give up."

Laura Nell reminded her, "You say that about every new religion you find, mother."

"I know, darlin', but once I dig a little deeper they don't live up to that first great exciting promise. Besides, I *can't* give up. I'm closing in on the real thing every day. Closer and closer. You just watch my smoke!"

"Mother!"

"I mean it. Don't you fuss, darlin', this is between God and me. He can't get away with His slippery tricks forever."

29

Nell was too busy helping other people with their problems for her to search for God as diligently and as ardently as she would have liked. Even so, Nell had already worked her way through the various branches of Christianity from Anglican to Zionism, then on to Spiritualism, Palmistry, and Rosicrucian and a dozen others. She loved them all. Those are Nell's own words about her search. She never lumped them all together. Each one was precious and unique.

Nell even delved for a while into the Occult. She had something good to say about all of them. She admitted that she had learned something of value from each.

Nell visited religious meetings of all kinds regularly. Avidly she read the new religious publications at every library and book store in town, buying selectively those items that intrigued her.

Nell was omnivorous. Religiously speaking.

Nell would rush home from every meeting with fresh early enthusiasm. She would inflict an excited account of her latest hopeful discovery upon her patient and long-suffering daughter, Laura Nell.

"This may be it", she'd say, eyes sparkling.

Laura Nell would nod sympathetically. "Yes, mother. But you've said that before. A dozen times."

"I know. I know. But you can't find the needle if you don't mess up a few haystacks."

Days, or weeks later, Nell would say, sadly, with a heavy heart, "This isn't it, darlin'. It just didn't prove out. Pity."

Nell didn't begrudge the time she spent investigating.

"Don't think me ungrateful," she'd say, "I'm better off for knowing about all these darlin' religions. They're all true and beautiful in their own way, but they're only a small part of something much bigger somewhere. I just *know* it in my heart. They're like a piece of the Sun of truth. A small ray. It's beautiful, but it's not enough for me. I want the whole blessed thing. All of it! I want to see the entire Sun of truth which takes them all in. That's what I'm after. It's out there somewhere, I know it is. Just waiting to shine down on me, Nell Ring."

That was about as long a speech as Nell ever made.

"Can't you see, mother," Laura Nell objected, "that you're just wasting your time? It's been years."

"I know, child. I just have to be more patient, more persistent. Besides, I can't help myself. Something's driving me on."

"You're not as young as you used to be."

"No, but I'm wiser. Just think of all the things I know that are *not* it. That's progress."

Back Nell would go to the books in the Library. She made a special study of the religious ads in the local newspaper. She would cut out any announcement of visiting evangelists or speakers on various religious subjects. Nell would carefully underline the latest series of promising religious lecturers listed in the College calendar, and make a careful note of the dates.

"Maybe *this* one is it", she'd say, as she dressed for the occasion. "It's so close I can taste it!"

One night when Laura Nell was reading quietly in her armchair, she heard her mother's Chevrolet come careening into the driveway. It steamed up the gravel path lickety-split. Laura Nell could tell by the frenzied sounds of the car that her mother, Nell, had been to another religious meeting. Apparently fruitful.

A friend had invited Nell that afternoon to hear a surprise speaker from out of town, a brilliant lecturer, Nell was told; one who had come to Jackson for a week-long series of lectures on the Bahá'í Faith.

"Not another new religion", Laura Nell said, despairingly. She was worried about her mother.

"I can't take a chance missing it," Nell explained, "even though I'm dead tired tonight, honey. I'm bone-weary and tuckered out. But supposing this is the real thing?"

"It won't be, mother."

"You can't tell", Nell replied, the bulldog in her coming out. "If

I miss this wonderful something out there," Nell vowed, pointing a finger at heaven, "it's going to be His fault, not mine!"

Laura Nell sighed, tenderly. Inside she must have felt: "Here we go again. Will there never be an end to it?" Aloud she said, "You could miss this one time, mother, if you're so weary."

"No I can't, darlin'. I dassen't."

Laura Nell understood and accepted.

"Of course, mother. Have a good time."

Now, just before midnight, her mother was zooming into the yard obviously anxious to get home and report.

The car brakes were jammed on so hard the old Chevy rocked back and forth. Laura Nell heard the car door slam and her mother's quick footsteps hurrying across the loose gravel. The car was still rocking back and forth when the front door flew open.

Nell literally burst into the room.

She strode to the centre of the carpet, raised her right hand high above her head in a tight triumphant fist, and cried out:

"I've *got* it!"

She had!

Nell had found the Bahá'í Faith.

She was thrilled. It had happened like steel-filings flying toward a magnet. Bang! And Nell Ring was home free!

All those years of search had finally paid off. Her eyes were brighter than the headlights of her Chevrolet sedan which, by the way, she had forgotten to turn off in her eagerness to rush inside to share the good news with her daughter.

Laura Nell had seen and heard it all a dozen times. True, her mother had never been quite so dramatic, forceful or confident before. Usually Nell said, "This *may* be it."

Never: "*This is it!*"

Nell stood in the centre of the room in her house in Jackson, Mississippi. She was Balboa looking at the blue Pacific, Eric the Red landing in Nova Scotia, Edison at the burning globe of electricity in Michigan, Sutter at his mill of flowing gold in California, Columbus approaching the Caribbean Islands.

"I've got it, honey!" Nell shouted, with a smile that went up into each ear. "And I'm never going to let it go! Never!"

And she never did.

RICE CHRISTIANS
vs
HOLIDAY BAHÁ'ÍS

30

Our first Christmas in Jackson, Mississippi, was quite unique.

Marguerite and I later referred to it as: "The Twelve Days of Christmas our young son gave to us: *One* large Principal, *Two* Parent–Teacher Meetings, *Three* small disasters, and an *Albatross* in our pine-tree."

Our son, Michael, aged ten, going on sixty, brought the world-wide wonders of Christmas home to all of us that first Yule-tide in Jackson. Michael was in so much trouble that even Santa Claus lost his address.

Michael flew in and out of scrapes with a casual dramatic flourish. It was his style even at such a tender age. You are, I believe, familiar with the words *flair* and *panache*? Michael wasn't, although they were written for him. Mercifully, Michael remained totally unaware that he was the original Sorcerer's Apprentice.

It all began harmlessly.

"I was completely innocent", Michael explained.

Over the years, as a parent, I have become quite inured to that brief phrase of William and Michael's. However true it might be. On rare occasions, very rare, of course, it was true.

Bahá'ís, as you no doubt know, do not celebrate Christmas. Not as the Christians celebrate it. That's only natural.

Bahá'ís do, of course, honour and revere Christ.

Bahá'ís respect the Holy Days associated with Christ's life with the same honour, respect, and love with which they pay tribute to the Holy Days of all the great Religions of the world and the Founders associated with them.

However, just as the Jews do not commemorate Christmas, nor the Christians Rosh Hashana, other than friendly best wishes and affection to all, in like manner the Bahá'ís do not commemorate

Christmas. Nor do the Hindus, the Buddhists, or the Muslims.

One of the most attractive things about the Bahá'í Faith to our son Michael when he first began to reason things out, was this love and reverence which the Bahá'í Faith held for all the great Religions of the world, without exception, without preference, without prejudice.*

"Now, that", Michael said, "is what I call Religion. That's great."

In fact, unbeknown to us, Michael had already developed his own imaginative concept for a great Teaching campaign based upon this universal principle of religious unity. We didn't know what Michael had in mind or why he was quizzing us in such detail and with such intensity. I accused Michael of giving us the *Third Degree* without the bright spotlight or the "rough stuff".

"This is serious, Dad," Michael said, "I have some important questions. And I want some decent answers."

"Fire one!"

"Do we or do we not, accept and believe in the Founders of all the great Religions?"

"Yes, Michael, we do", his mother assured him. "You know that."

"And we, as Bahá'ís, do honour and respect all their Holy Days? Right?"

"Right."

"I mean *all*. Without exception, without preference, without prejudice?"

"End of quotation", I told him.

"I mean it. There's absolutely no doubt about any of this?"

"None whatsoever."

"The Bahá'ís are never going to change their mind about it?"

"Never!"

"That", he said, "is just great!"

"Agreed," I told him, "but why the sudden enthusiasm? What's behind it?"

"This oneness and unity is the thing I like best about the Bahá'í Faith", Michael admitted frankly. "It's always appealed to me. Wait until I spread this good news at school. I told the kids I was loaded with dynamite. They didn't believe me when I told them I

* One of my favourite expressions. You may hear it again. And again.

owned a real honey-pot. They said that such a good thing as I was talking about, was impossible, and that I was filled with low Yankee cunning."

I looked at Marguerite. She shrugged.

"It's all news to me."

"What were you talking to your fellow-students about, Michael?"

"My great new plan."

"What plan? Clue me in. I'm not sure where you're coming from."

However, I suspected and feared where he might be going.

"You'll have more new Bahá'ís than you can handle," Michael assured us, "once I get rolling at school with my new teaching plan. Zowie!" Michael was delighted. "The Local Spiritual Assembly of Jackson will have to stay up nights just enrolling the new Bahá'ís", he promised. "You can tell them so from me. This may be the beginning of that 'entry by troops' foretold by 'Abdu'l-Bahá. And, I'm going to do it all by myself."

"Really!"

I was starting to feel quite nervous. Maybe queasy is more accurate.

"Really!" Michael replied confidently. He was so elated he did his familiar "Shuffle off to buffalo" dance step. "Hot", he said, "diggety dog!"

Michael started for the door. "I can't wait to spread the good news!"

The word "*Freeze!*" hadn't become popular yet, so I had to rely on a rather old and prosaic equivalent of *Freeze!*.

"Hold the phone!" I yelled, but I put a lot of "*Freeze!*" into it.

Michael stopped, turned, and looked surprised.

"What do you mean, exactly, Michael," I asked him, "when you say 'Spread the good news!'?"

Michael's enthusiasm came back with a rush. He was entranced with his new teaching project.

"Well," he said, "if the Bahá'ís accept all the Holy Days of all the great Religions, we'll have a marvellous year at school. It's already pretty good getting the nine Bahá'í Holy Days off, but when you add in all the other holy days of the Christians, the Jews, the Muslims, and the Buddhists, Wow! I'm sitting on a religious gold-mine!"

Michael was enraptured by the magic of his new-found "freedom from school" concept. I cut him off at the pockets before he had time to add in the Hindus and the Zoroastrians.

"It doesn't work that way", I told him.

It was a blow. Michael was disappointed and dejected. Shocked, perhaps, is not too strong. He tried to weather it.

"You mean all I get are the *Bahá'í* Holy Days?"

"You're on 'Easy Street' now", I told him. "Living in a Christian society, you also get all of the Christian Holy Days, too."

"And that's it? No Hindu, no Buddhist, no Muslim?"

"I'm afraid not."

"Finito?"

"Kaput."

"That", Michael said, "is rotten news."

"You still get nine more holidays than the Christian students."

"Yeah, but I was counting on Chanukah, Yom Kippur, Passover—all that stuff. *And* the Buddhists and Muslims. I promised the kids at school that I'd keep springing new holidays on them until they were blue in the face, if they'd become Bahá'ís. You'll spend more time at home than in school, I told them. They were keen about it! I had them eating out of the palm of my hand. I already had them practising how to pronounce Bahá'u'lláh and Riḍván. I figured we could take off the whole twelve days of Riḍván. That was my big bonanza. I had everybody writing the word Bahá'í with all the accent marks. I was teaching them the Bahá'í principles: Science and Religion go hand in hand. All that stuff. I had them eating out of my hand. I figured . . ."

"You figured wrong."

Michael was indignant about the injustices of life. He just couldn't believe that the roof had fallen in on his great project.

"I was big!" he said. "Now I'm nothing."

"You'll weather it."

"What am I going to tell the kids?"

"Tell them the truth."

"I'm going to have to lie", he said.

"You can't do that. Bahá'u'lláh says that truth is the foundation of all virtue. Keep teaching them, but take back the free holidays."

"All of them?"

"All except the ones they are legitimately entitled to have."

"I could get hurt bad doing that. Physically hurt I mean. Did you ever face a mob of angry kids who were just beaten out of several weeks of free holidays?''

His brother Bill was philosophical.

"I told Michael not to jump the gun."

"Gun, nothing. This will be a lynch mob!"

I sighed. Marguerite suggested prayers and an emergency family consultation.

"We'll come up with something", she promised Michael.

"My dead body!"

Bill made a suggestion. "Michael could offer them nine extra holy-day holidays if they became Bahá'ís. It's not the whole world he promised, but it's better than nothing."

"Yeah!" Mike said, snapping up any possible solution. "That's *not* bad! Nine extra holidays. I told them it would be around fifty, but what can I do—" Michael was off and running.

"What you can do," I interrupted sternly, "is to remember that Bahá'ís do not teach their Faith that way. People have to become Bahá'ís because they love the Faith, not because of some reward. What you would be doing is the equivalent of making 'Rice-Christians', a practice Jesus Himself would deplore."

"I believe", Marguerite inserted, "that the new term being developed by Michael, is not *Rice Christians*, but *Holiday Bahá'ís*. However,—"

It didn't help any when both she and Bill began to laugh.

"It's not funny!" Michael shouted.

He gripped his throat and stuck his tongue out like he was being strung up to a Mississippi lamp post.

"When you have to cut me down cold and stiff, and still only a child, you'll be sorry", he said.

Then we all laughed.

Michael went into a very un-Bahá'í-like snit.

"You've ruined my whole Teaching Campaign."

"Tough."

"And endangered your own son's life."

Michael whirled and stalked to the door. He turned, doorknob in hand, and left us with a sobering thought.

"No wonder we have religious wars", Michael said.

"Don't bang the door on your way out."

He did.

31

One afternoon Marguerite and I heard a brisk, fate-laden, knock on our door.

It was Miss Bertina, one of Michael's teachers. She was quite embarrassed and very hesitant. She was also very lovely.

Our hunch is that by now, Miss Bertina has retired, and is a Bahá'í pioneer in some far-off land. In truth, however, we do not know. We're not even sure her name was Miss Bertina. It was so long ago. The episode itself, however, is burned into our consciousness in "letters of gold upon tablets of chrysolite".*

"You have quite an unusual son", Miss Bertina said to start things off.

Marguerite and I had heard it all before.

"Which one? Of our sons?"

It was always better to know at the outset which fuse had blown. Apparently the thought that there might be more than one such son in her school alarmed Miss Bertina.

"*Michael*", she said, quite definitely, as though everyone should certainly know that.

Miss Bertina suggested that Michael should be present so he wouldn't lose confidence in her. It wasn't difficult to find him,

---

* Marguerite insists that this episode should have been written about William instead of Michael, but I write them as I remember the anguish. You've met them both, I leave it up to you. They can fight it out later themselves, but if anything ever fitted Michael like a pair of rubber gloves too small, this is it. My proof-reader notwithstanding.

since Michael was eaves-dropping behind the rubber plant.

I said to Miss Bertina, "I hope Michael didn't upset your class."

"No, not at all. The students loved it. Even applauded. It was the parents Michael upset."

Now we were worried.

Fellow-students are one thing, but parents dwell in the power-zone.

I think Miss Bertina giggled. If so, she adroitly turned it into a cough.

"My bronchitis", she apologized. "It's that time of the year."

In spite of her frequent bronchial spasms, Miss Bertina continued her recital. Her bronchitis seemed to become dangerously aggravated as she approached the climax of her story.

"The Christmas pageant itself had ended," she explained, "and the three prize-winning essays were being read by Betty Clemont, George Schneider, and Freddy Harris on the *Three Wise Men*, *The Shepherd and His Sheep*, and *The Manger in Bethlehem*, in that order."

I looked at Michael. "I thought you said *your* essay had won special honours?"

Michael blushed. He was basically honest, but like his father sometimes his Irish poetic ancestry might colour—

Miss Bertina came immediately to Michael's rescue.

"Michael's essay won special attention," she said, "not special honours. It was interrupted several times when he read it to the class during the preliminary judging last week. There were whistles, foot-stomping, hisses and boos."

Marguerite and I were both alarmed.

"What", I asked, "in heaven's name was Michael's essay about that they hissed and booed him? At Christmas time?"

"Oh, the class wasn't booing Michael. They loved his essay. They were booing the parents. The children voted Michael first place by acclaim. However, because of the nature of his essay and what he called it, Michael had to be disqualified."

"What", Marguerite asked, both suspecting and fearing the worst, "did Michael call his essay?"

When Miss Bertina recovered from another violent attack of brought-on bronchitis, she told us, reading from her notes,

"It was called 'How come we can't have fifty-one weeks of Christmas spirit every year, and one week of punk stuff? Instead of just one short week where everybody's decent to each other until

Christmas is over, after which everybody puts on his robber's mask again, and starts singing: 'Come All Ye Bandits'. How come? I'm not asking that. *Jesus* is asking. Can't you hear His sweet little voice? From His tiny manger?"

"Is that the title of the essay?" I asked, "or is that the essay itself?"

"That", Miss Bertina said, again hampered by her bronchitis, "was only the title." Glancing at her notes again, she said, "The essay itself began: 'Xmas is a phony word. X marks the spot where a crass commercial world has taken the '*Christ*' out of '*Christmas*' and—'"

"I believe", I told her, interrupting, "that the song '*Come All Ye Bandits!*' and '*X marks the spot*' originated with Michael's quite original great-grandfather in Minnesota, and not with Michael at all."

I looked at Michael, smiled, and whispered to him out of the side of my mouth, "If they convict you, I'll come to your hanging."

"Jesus was perfectly innocent!"

32

Miss Bertina didn't spare us.

"When the party was over," she explained, "the Open House began. Questions were asked from the floor by the parents. The fathers and mothers were free to ask the children anything they wished about the pageant, the essays, or about Christmas itself. And the children were free to answer."

"Sounds like fun", Marguerite said.

I nodded. "Dangerous, too."

"The Open House is a Christmas tradition at our school."

"So far, so good", I interjected.

Miss Bertina continued.

"Unfortunately, being a new student, Michael didn't know that only the parents were permitted to ask questions. He was quite innocent when he raised his hand."

Michael burst out, "I *told* you I was innocent. At our Sears' family forum anybody can talk or ask questions at any time, right? So naturally—"

I used the old hand-over-blabbering-mouth ruse.

"And that", I suggested to Miss Bertina, "is when the roof fell in?"

Miss Bertina smiled. "Religiously speaking you might say that."

Marguerite was puzzled. "What question did Michael ask?"

"Oh, not a question. Michael made a short impromptu speech on the general spirit of Christmas."

"Unasked?"

"Totally."

"It was perfectly innocent", Michael insisted, breaking free. "At the Sears' family forum, anybody has the right to speak up. Whenever the spirit prompts them, as long as they're courteous and not long-winded. Even my father says—"

I put my hand over Michael's mouth again, and nodded for Miss Bertina to go on. It was hard for her as her bronchitis was worsening. Still she tried.

"Michael told the parents and the School Board that he couldn't understand why we had spent the entire afternoon talking only about Christ when there were so many other wonderful Messengers of God and Prophets who had appeared in the world. *Manifestations of God*, I believe, is the term Michael used."

"It's the right term", Marguerite admitted, "but certainly the wrong time."

"I can imagine the consternation those comments might have caused", I added sympathetically. "I suppose there was quite an uproar."

Miss Bertina shook her head.

"No uproar at all. Only silence. A *stunned* silence, I might add. Michael took advantage of these quiet moments to name all of the Messengers of God Whom he felt the School Board had been overlooking and neglecting at our Christmas party. 'Just in case', Michael said, 'that some of you are not as familiar with them as you should be.'"

Michael stirred restlessly, and pulled my hand aside.

"You left out Zoroaster and Bahá'u'lláh", he told Miss Bertina. I applied a tighter security-hold.

Miss Bertina nodded. "So I did."

"And *that*", I suggested, "is what occasioned the consternation and uproar?"

Miss Bertina giggled, recovered quickly, and turned it into a cough before going on quite soberly.

"Michael suggested to the assembled parents and teachers that we should hear something about each one of these other great Messengers of God, too, so we wouldn't have to go home during the Christmas season spiritually deprived and with a one-sided limited view of the fine work God was doing out in other parts of the world. It would help us, Michael said, to appreciate the oneness and greatness of all Religions."

"Didn't anyone object?" I asked.

"I believe", Miss Bertina replied, "that they were so stunned to hear such concepts and words coming, as it were, 'out of the mouths of babes' that they were too taken aback to object."

It wasn't at all wise of Marguerite to laugh. You don't encourage Morgan, the Pirate. Marguerite was laughing because Michael had used several almost exact quotes from my public talk at the Heidelberg Hotel. I couldn't tell for sure, but I suspected that Miss Bertina had joined Marguerite, and they were both trying to suppress their laughter.

"They did not remain taken aback for long", Miss Bertina assured me, hurrying on. "The chairman of the meeting was the Pastor of one of the leading local churches. He tried to be very gentle and kind with Michael. He explained that perhaps the reason they were all talking so much about Christ today was because December 25th was Christ's birthday."

"'It's not, you know', Michael interrupted. 'I mean it's not really Christ's birthday. It's a pagan holiday which the Christians adopted. Of course, that's not Christ's fault. You can't blame Jesus for the dumb way those knuckleheads back in those old days ran His wonderful religion. Right?'"

"In the shocked silence that followed, Michael came to the defence of Christ. 'Jesus Himself', Michael pointed out, 'was perfectly innocent!'"

"You're hurting my hand," Michael muttered to me under his breath, "and you're squeezing my arm too hard."

"You'll have your turn at the family forum tonight", I promised him.

"Before a hanging judge!" Michael objected.

"Michael", Miss Bertina said quickly, sensing our conflict, "realized he might have gone too far. He said he would apologize if that were so."

"'You may not be ready for all this love and unity yet', Michael told them. Fortunately, the meeting was closed at that moment with a loud and unmistakable concluding gavel by the chairman."

"I can believe it."

Miss Bertina, sensing that Michael might be in trouble, came quickly to his defence a second time. She was that fine rare kind of teacher who defends her students against misunderstanding in public, and plans to deal with them later in private. Besides, you could tell that she was taken with Michael.

"You can be proud of your son", she assured us. "His apology was quite moving, and he was very courteous. Michael thanked everybody for their kind attention. He wished them all a Merry

Christmas, and said he was sorry he didn't have his father's visual aids with him so that he could demonstrate the complete Oneness of God, His Messengers, and His Religion which he was sure would clear up all the trouble, and remove any misunderstanding he might have caused. Michael called it the story of *The Sun and the Mirrors*. He told the audience that unfortunately his father was using his visual aids himself this weekend at an important Bahá'í meeting at Jackson State University. Michael insisted, however, that if he *did* have his father's visual aids, he could have knocked them right off the edge of their chairs. Those, I believe, were Michael's exact words. These additional, unexpected and unsolicited comments from Michael made the crowd restive and necessitated a second and even louder series of closing gavels."

"Bang! Bang! Bang!" I said pantomiming, and seeing it all only too clearly.

Miss Bertina hastened to explain that she had *not* come to make trouble for Michael, but rather because Michael had intrigued her with the story of the *Sun and the Mirrors*. She was quite serious, she said, about wanting to know more about it, if we were willing to take the time to tell her.

I excused Michael who rubbed his arm where I'd held him so tightly.

"That's religious persecution", he said, grumbling.

"Tell me at the family meeting. You'll be chairman, as I wish to act for the prosecution."

"Great!"

I sent Michael to the library to bring us a copy of Bahá'u'lláh's *Book of Certitude*.

Miss Bertina, Marguerite and I spent the rest of a beautiful afternoon and evening discussing that wonderful theme the *Sun and the Mirrors*. In almost every Bahá'í book I have ever written, I have told this remarkable story. We shared it that day with Miss Bertina, and if you will pardon our bronchitis coughs, Miss Bertina agreed that if Michael *had* been able to use the "visual aids" he might indeed have carried the day, and prevented the repeated closing gavels.

The next three brief chapters are the heart and soul of this entire book, *All Flags Flying!* They will give you in one brief capsule one of the truly intriguing stories concerning all the Religions of the world. They will also tell you why the Bahá'í pioneers are so eager and willing to arise and go anywhere in the world on behalf of their Faith, as the Sears family chose to do.

We hope you will derive as much pleasure from it and be as deeply moved as Miss Bertina.

THE SUN
AND
THE MIRRORS

The Sun and the Mirrors

33

An old Chinese proverb says that one picture is worth a thousand words. Or was it the Editor of the *New York Times*?

Whichever, it is certainly true of our illustration of The Sun and the Mirrors as shown on the opposite page.

Examine it carefully.

The drawing demonstrates clearly why it would be impossible for a Bahá'í *not* to love Christ. It explains without words the overwhelming devotion that surrounds all Bahá'ís when they contemplate the station of Christ, Founder of Christianity, or that of Bahá'u'lláh, Founder of the Bahá'í Faith.

The *Light* of God that shines in the *Mirror* of Christ is identical with the *Light* that shines in the *Mirror* of Bahá'u'lláh, as you can plainly see from the drawing.

This love which Bahá'ís have for Christ is not a casual affection such as one might feel for a distant relative or a dear friend. It is something far deeper.

Every Bahá'í has the same profound and sacred reverence for the Founders of all the great Religions. They are all *Mirrors* and Messengers of the one same truth. Bahá'ís have been taught this truth by the Founder of their own Faith, Bahá'u'lláh. It is not optional, it is obligatory.

Thousands upon thousands of Bahá'ís have already sacrificed their lives in martyrdom to demonstrate the sincerity and truth of their belief in the oneness and unity of God and His Messengers. Bahá'ís believe in *All* of His Messengers, all of the *Mirrors* of His *Light*, no matter what time in history they may have appeared. Bahá'ís believe and defend this truth without exception, without preference, without prejudice.

Bahá'ís consider each one of these Messengers as a perfect *Mirror* of God's *Light*, reflecting upon mankind His Wisdom and His peerless Virtues. Consequently, what is true concerning Christ and Bahá'u'lláh, is equally valid for the Founders of all the great revealed Religions. There are no exemptions from this fundamental truth. The love which every Bahá'í feels for Them all, will never alter or fade. It is a permanent and beautiful part of Bahá'í religious life.

Our drawing of the *Sun* and the *Mirrors* completely does away with any misconceptions about the oneness of the world-healing Religions and their Founders. They are all part of one, progressive, Grand Redemptive Scheme of God for man.

Nowhere in all Sacred Scripture is this unity and oneness more evident than in the Teachings and Message given to the world by both Christ, the *Son*, and Bahá'u'lláh, the *Father*.*

Their Message is not separate and contradictory. It is the same Message from God shared with the world by both Christ and Bahá'u'lláh at different times in history, progressively unfolding this one same truth.

In reality, it is not *Their* Message that shines in the *Mirrors*, it is the Message of God reflected from His *Sun* of truth. This is what gives it power and healing.

Our drawing makes this unmistakably clear to every impartial and unprejudiced observer.

From our drawing it becomes immediately apparent that if a Bahá'í sincerely loves Bahá'u'lláh, then he or she must just as obviously love Christ. It could not be otherwise.

If a Bahá'í does not have this same deep abiding love for Christ, such a Bahá'í cannot possibly love the Founder of his own Faith, Bahá'u'lláh, for the two *Mirrors* are inseparable. The Light within these *Mirrors* is one. Their love is one. Both for each other and for that Source of all their Light, God, the *Sun*.

We repeat. What is true of Christ and Bahá'u'lláh is equally true of the Founders (*Mirrors*) of all the great Religions. A follower of any one of these *Mirrors* who repudiates any of the others in effect

---

* For a more detailed and moving description of the story of Christ, the *Son* and Bahá'u'lláh, the *Father*, see the documented story of Isaiah's thrilling prophecies concerning the *Prince of Peace* and the *Everlasting Father*, same author (to appear).

repudiates Them all; and thus denies the *Light* of God that shines in any *Mirror* of God, including his own.

Therefore, any Bahá'í who lacks this unquestioned, unlimited love for any one of these great spiritual World-Educators and Prophets, is, in reality, not a Bahá'í at all. This oneness of God and His Messengers is a basic fundamental Bahá'í belief, never to be compromised.

In the Words of Bahá'u'lláh, the Founder of the Bahá'í Faith:

> "All the Prophets [Mirrors] of God abide
> in the same tabernacle, soar in the same
> heaven, are seated upon the same throne,
> utter the same speech, and proclaim the
> same Faith."

The Bahá'í Sacred Writings make it unmistakably clear that Bahá'u'lláh did not come only to the Bahá'ís, He came to the world. Moses did not come only to the Jews, He came to humanity. Christ did not come only to the Christians, He came to all peoples.

This is true of the Founders of each and every one of the world's great revealed Religions. Their Messages were all planetary in scope whatever the geographic limitations of their outpouring.

Bahá'u'lláh Himself has written that each one of these Messengers, *Mirrors* of God, is a "champion" of the Cause of God in whatever age He appears. Each One invariably proclaims and upholds the one same ever-advancing Religion of God.

In Bahá'u'lláh's Own Words:

> ". . . His holy and chosen Messengers are, without
> exception, the bearers of His names and the embodi-
> ments of His attributes.
>
> "They Who are the Luminaries of Truth and
> the Mirrors reflecting the light of Divine Unity, in
> whatever age and cycle they are sent down from
> their invisible habitations of ancient glory unto this
> world to educate the souls of men and endue with
> grace all created things, are invariably endowed
> with an all-compelling power and invested with
> invincible sovereignty . . . These sanctified Mirrors,
> these Day-Springs of ancient glory are one and all
> the exponents on earth of Him Who is the central
> Orb of the universe, . . ."

The Bahá'í Writings also point out:

> "Any variations in the splendour which each of
> these Manifestations of the Light of God [These
> Holy and Luminous Mirrors] has shed upon the
> world should be ascribed not to any inherent superi-
> ority involved in the essential character of any
> one of them, but rather to the progressive capacity,
> the ever-increasing spiritual receptiveness, which
> mankind, in its progress towards maturity, has in-
> variably manifested."

In the poetic Words of Bahá'u'lláh: God, through His Messengers, those Mirrors of His Light, uncovers "the Face of Wisdom" in
direct proportion to the "capacity" and "ability" of mankind to
"sustain the burden" of God's world-healing, world-redeeming,
ever-progressing, one religious truth.

Every great Religion, since the beginning of time has played its
own distinctive, independent, absolutely essential God-given role
in this great drama.

Including yours.

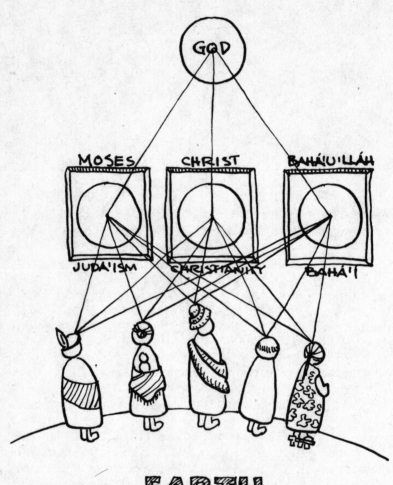

"Seed, bud, flower and fruit"

34

Our second drawing as shown on the opposite page confirms everything said in the previous chapter concerning the eternal oneness of God, His Religion, His Messengers and His people, mankind.

We have selected the *Mirrors* of Moses, Christ and Bahá'u'lláh to further demonstrate this truth. These three have been chosen merely for the sake of simplicity, brevity and convenience, in telling the story.

Our drawing should in reality include all of the *Mirrors* and Messengers of God, the Founders of all the great Religions, but because of space, it would be an impossibility. However, as long as we understand clearly that every word written about these three *Mirrors* is equally true and valid for all, it will not matter.

In order to establish this essential truth, let us examine the exciting, wholesome and world-healing story of the *Sun* and the *Mirrors* in its simplest terms.

God is like the sun. His Messengers, the Founders of the great Religions, are like the *rays* of the sun.

They are the pure *Mirrors* of His, God's, Light and Truth. These Messengers (*Mirrors*) reflect the Light of the Sun (God). It shines within Them. Every *Mirror* reflects the one same light of truth upon the world. They have done so from the beginning of time. They will do so until the end of time. Progressively. Each One appearing at a different time in history. Each One following the other, successively.

They are all equal, all true, all valid, all beautiful, as we have seen in our drawing. The truth is unmistakable. We must accept all of these Messengers (*Mirrors*). ALL!

Without question. Excluding none.

The sun brings all physical light to the world. Without that sunlight, regularly, in progressive appearances each day, humanity, all human life on the planet earth, would gradually perish.

God, in like manner, is the spiritual Sun. He brings the spiritual Light to the soil of the hearts of humankind.

Without that Light, that guidance, that spiritual Teaching shed progressively upon an ever-developing humanity, all human creation would cease to progress spiritually. It would never advance higher than the stage of the animal kingdom.

This, of course, is unthinkable and unacceptable. Such a concept is not, and never has been, a part of the Plan of God for man.

God is infinite, unknowable, indescribable. He is beyond the definition and comprehension of man. Even to use the pronoun "He" is misleading. Man knows God *only* through His Messengers, through His (God's) Sunlight which shines in each of these pure *Mirrors* of His Light.

The physical sun does not come down to earth, it sends its rays. God, the spiritual *Sun*, does not come down to earth. Such a concept is not only sacrilegious, but inconceivable.

God sends His *Mirrors*, His Messengers, Who bring the Rays of His spiritual Light, His knowledge and His Teachings to mankind. These Messengers, *Mirrors*, reflect the virtues and attributes of God so that man may, through this outpouring of the Holy Spirit, develop into a finer human being, a better person, one that is made in the image and likeness of God.

These *Mirrors*, these great World Educators, come to earth, One after the Other, successively, progressively, to accomplish this "Great Work".

The Bahá'í Faith does not seek to obscure the divine origin of the other religions that have preceded it. It does not attempt to dwarf the admitted magnitude of their colossal achievements. The Bahá'í Faith countenances no attempt that seeks to distort the features or to stultify the truths which all these great Religions instil in their followers. The Teachings of the Bahá'í Faith do not deviate a hair's breadth from the verities which these past Religions enshrine, nor does the Message of the Faith of Bahá'u'lláh detract one jot or one tittle from the influence which these past Religions exert, or the loyalty they inspire.

Far from aiming at the overthrow of the spiritual foundation of the world's religious systems, the avowed, the unalterable purpose of the Bahá'í Faith is to widen their basis, to restate their fundamentals, to reconcile their aims, to reinvigorate their life, to demonstrate their oneness, to restore the pristine purity of their teachings, to co-ordinate their functions and to assist in the realization of their highest aspirations.

It is not the Founders of these great Religions, but their followers that divide, separate, and make exclusive their own Religion and its Messenger. They consider their Faith and its Founder, His *Mirror* and His *Light*, to be the last and final outpouring of God's truth for the world. Hence, the tragic consequences. The results of such actions require no comment here. We need only look at the world around us.

It is what mankind has done to religion that has obscured its beauty, its truth and its Light. It is this product of his own perverseness that man does not admire and which he refuses to acknowledge; the religion which he, man himself, has created from his own lack of spiritual values. It is for this reason that God has renewed in each Age His wholesome, healing outpouring of true Religion.

In the Words of Bahá'u'lláh, God's *Mirror* and Messenger for this Day in which we live, we hear the Message of Power, Truth and Beauty once again.

> "Religion is the greatest of all means for the establishment of order in the world and for the peaceful contentment of all that dwell therein. The weakening of the pillars of religion hath strengthened the hands of the ignorant and made them bold and arrogant. Verily I say, whatsoever hath lowered the lofty station of religion hath increased the waywardness of the wicked, and the result cannot be but anarchy."

It is, of course, the Religion of God as seen in this story of the *Sun and the Mirrors*, that one progressive ever-developing Religion of God, that Bahá'u'lláh is referring to; and not to the feeble lifeless body without a spirit which passes for religion in this day, a religion which man by his godlessness has debilitated and for which he now expresses such contempt and dissatisfaction. The beauty, the joy, the wonder of his own glorious Religion is thus lost to him, unless he awakens to the renewal of that same Sun of Truth revealed in God's *Mirror* for today.

Bahá'u'lláh writes:

> "Religion is a radiant light and an impregnable
> stronghold for the protection and welfare of the
> peoples of the world, for the fear of God impel-
> leth man to hold fast to that which is good, and
> shun all evil. Should the lamp of religion be ob-
> scured, chaos and confusion will ensue, and the
> lights of fairness, of justice, of tranquillity and
> peace cease to shine."

That is a pretty fair description of our world as we see it today. The "fear of God" referred to here, is above all a fear of our own shortcomings, our own critical lack of those godlike virtues, the acquiring of which makes us in the image and likeness of God, and is the purpose of our life upon the planet.

Could there be a greater fear than mankind's own awareness of its failure to achieve that balance between the material and the spiritual which makes a man a true human being? That he and humanity are drawing farther and farther away each day? The realization that as a part of that humanity, he and the world around him, have permitted their animal nature to dominate their lives, resulting in an unbridled, cancerous materialism which has led to the chaos, confusion, injustice and un-godlike nature of mankind's increasingly unloving, uncaring lives?

Bahá'u'lláh pays tribute to those dearly-loved people of every Religion, whatever the Name and the *Mirror*, who have been faithful to their trust. As for the others, unless they change, they are regressing backwards toward their animal nature rather than progressing forward toward their human, spiritual nature. They are losing the game of life.

Naturally, we fear that tragedy and the consequences of our own actions which have prevented us from developing a "seeing eye" and a "hearing ear" which might draw us nearer to God and the *Mirror* of His Light; a God who has tried so mercifully, and continues to do all He can through His Messenger and *Mirror*, to help each one of us to become numbered with the *Elect* and the *Chosen*; so that each one of us may fulfil our destiny on this spinning ball of dust, our temporary home and testing-ground.

The Writings of the Bahá'í Faith, in a desire to prevent this separation from God which ends in such sorrow and suffering, say clearly that to contend that "all Revelation is ended, that the portals of Divine mercy are closed, that from the daysprings of eternal holiness no sun shall rise again, that the ocean of everlasting bounty is forever stilled, and that out of the Tabernacle of ancient glory the Messengers of God have ceased to be made manifest" would indeed be "nothing less than sheer blasphemy".

These great Religions have only one goal: To enrich and purify your living and draw you ever nearer to God and to your own true human worth. These great Religions are all one, equal, progressive, and beautiful. They do not contend with each other, they embrace, defend, and support each other. The fault lies with the followers, not the Founders.

Our drawing of the *Sun* and the *Mirrors* makes this truth self-evident.

In the teaching of Moses we see the Bud of the one tree of Religion. In the teaching of Christ we see the Flower, in that of Bahá'u'lláh, the Fruit. The flower does not destroy the bud, nor does the fruit destroy the flower. Not one of them destroys. Each one of them fulfils. The bud-scales must disappear in order that the flower may bloom. The petals must fall that the fruit may grow and ripen.

Were the bud-scales and the petals wrong then? Or useless, that they had to be discarded? No, both in their time were right and necessary. Without them there could have been no fruit. They are all, every one without exception, an absolutely essential part of one great process.

So it is with the various prophetic teachings. Their externals change from age to age, but each Religion and *Mirror* is the fulfilment of its predecessor. These religions are not separate nor incongruous. They are one. They are different stages in the life-history of one Religion. A Religion which has, in turn, been revealed as seed, as bud and as flower; and now enters on the stage of fruition.

This tree of Religion includes each and every one of the great revealed Religions: seed, plant, tree, branches, leaves, flowers and fruit. All, without exception. Your own included.

The story of the *Sun and the Mirrors* from whatever direction we may view it, remains that simple, that clear, and that beautiful.

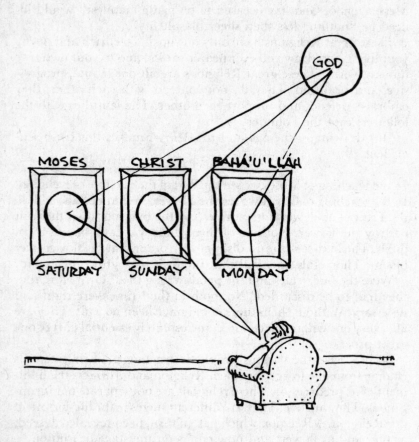

35

We have come to the final chapter in the story of the *Sun and the Mirrors*.

To explore it in further detail, and cite all the passages from the Bahá'í Writings about it, would require a volume much larger than this entire book, *All Flags Flying!*, so let us bring it to a close.

Our last drawing on this subject is shown on the page opposite. The sketch depicts an experiment which we hope you yourself will perform out in your own backyard, "live and in colour" as they say.

Ready?

Good! Let us begin.

This time take three mirrors, exactly alike. Go out into the real sunlight.

Now, hold up the three mirrors to the sun. Let the sunlight reflect in each mirror at the same time, so that you see three suns shining, one in each mirror. The real sun, of course, still remains by itself in the sky above.

Right?

I heard that grumbling. You said, how can I expect you to hold up three mirrors by yourself, and still stand back and look into them?

You're right.

I suggest you go back inside and telephone three good-natured friends and enlist their help.

It will do them a world of good, too.

Now, we're ready.

Let each friend hold up one mirror as shown in our drawing

opposite the first page of this chapter. Look at the three mirrors again.

Before you start your experiment, on the top of the frame of the first mirror write the name, Moses. On the top of the frame of the second write, Christ. And on the third mirror write, Bahá'u'lláh.

On the frame under the mirror of Moses write Saturday. Under that of Christ write Sunday. Under the mirror of Bahá'u'lláh write Monday. Exactly as shown in our illustration.

Now, at last, we *are* ready for our experiment.

Repeat: Let each friend hold up one mirror as shown in our drawing opposite the first page of this chapter. You are now looking into the three mirrors. You can see three bright suns. One shining in each mirror. Four suns, of course, if you count the real sun still shining in the blue sky above, and now reflected clearly in all three of the mirrors your friends are holding.

Oh, sorry about that!

I forgot the sunglasses. You'd better go back inside and get them.

Be patient.

Humour me on this. I promise you it will be worth while. Did I say that before?

Ah, that's better. The sunglasses are very attractive, by the way.

Now comes the interesting part. Stand back a few paces from your friends who are holding the three mirrors. Look once again at the mirrors: Moses, Christ and Bahá'u'lláh. There is an identical sun shining in each one of them, isn't there? Each mirror shows a perfect reflection of the real Sun still shining in the heaven above.

Right?

Now, for the moment of truth.

As you stand there, looking at those three *Mirrors* your friends are holding, with the live sunlight shining in each one of them, the *Mirror of Moses*, the *Mirror of Christ*, and the *Mirror of Bahá'u'lláh*, you tell me, which *Mirror* do you think conveys the real truth of the Sun?

Which *Mirror* is best?

Which has more sunlight?

Which is more beautiful?

Which *Mirror*, with its reflected sunlight, do you appreciate, respect and love, most?

Which *Mirror* do you prefer?
Which *Mirror* is the one and only *Mirror* for you?
Christ, Moses, or Bahá'u'lláh?
Ask your three friends about it. See what they say.

Of course!
What else could anyone say?
All three *Mirrors* are identical. All three!
The same Light of the same Sun shines in each one of them.
You love them all equally.
How could you do otherwise?

That's the way it is with Religions and their Founders. They are all *Mirrors* and Messengers of the one same Truth in this *Grand Redemptive Scheme of God for man.*
It is called "Progressive Revelation".
Religious truth has been uncovered to the eyes of men gradually, progressively, uninterruptedly, until it has reached us now in this long-anticipated, eagerly-awaited Day which was promised to us in all the Holy Books of the past. It is the Day of fulfilment, the Day of maturity, the Day of the coming of age of the human race. It is the Day of the *One Fold and One Shepherd,* the Day of Bahá'u'lláh, the Lord of the Vineyard, the Promise of All Ages, the Supreme Redeemer of men.
Of course, it's exciting and challenging.
As we look at these three identical Suns shining in the Mirrors, we realize that any One of Them could have fulfilled those promises. It is the time in history that governs the outpouring of Light, not the Name on the *Mirror.*
This does not mean, or imply, that with the appearance of Bahá'u'lláh, the *Spirit of truth,* that the story of the *Sun and the Mirrors* has ended. Far from it.
When mankind has understood, accepted, and put into effect the Teachings which Bahá'u'lláh, God's Messenger for today, has brought to the world for the spiritualization and unification of all nations, peoples and religions into one peaceful, progressive, harmonized society, there will, in the ages to come, be other Messengers, Divine Educators, *Mirrors* Who will appear and deal with the problems which are puzzling and affecting human society in that later time in history so that the spiritual progress made will not be lost, but always improved upon until we reach that "golden

age" foretold. An age that is not merely a dream but a reality.

These *Mirrors,* these Messengers of God Who will come in the future, like all the *Mirrors* gone before them, will shine with that same pure Light of God in their *Mirror.* They will reflect God's Purpose for mankind in that particular later age in which *They* appear.

The Religion of God is a "living and growing thing", not something temporary, lifeless and unchanging. It is not an outward appendage to be applied to our lives on special Sabbath days such as Thursday, Friday, Saturday and Sunday.

Religion is the heart and core of our very lives, both our individual lives, and the life of our society.

The spirit of Religion is to the life of human society what natural law is to the life of the mineral, vegetable and animal worlds.

The Religion of God is eternal. It will never cease. It will continue to comfort and guide each successive age in human history. It is the *Rainbow of God,* the symbol of His Covenant, which Scripture promises, will always join heaven and earth. God will never abandon mankind. He will, as foretold to Noah, always send His Rainbow, the Sign of His eternal Covenant, that links earth and heaven; and which is seen following the storms that plague mankind.

No, don't remove the sunglasses yet. There is yet one more experiment.

Gaze once again upon those three wonderful mirrors. Each is shining with exactly the same radiant sunlight and beauty there in your own backyard. Those three mirrors your friends are holding make yet another basic and fundamental religious truth crystal clear to all of us.

If we had the time, we would have asked you to send for more friends, and we would have used more mirrors, one for each of the Founders of every one of the great revealed Religions.

I trust I need not repeat again what we have already said and shown you about these three *Mirrors.* Every word is true not only about these three, but about every one of the Others, without exception, without preference, without prejudice.*

All. *A-L-L!* All have exactly the same power, the same love, and about the greatness of All, we must have the same conviction.

* Sorry about the repetition, but nothing else says it quite as well.

What these three *Mirrors* of Moses, Christ and Bahá'u'lláh make self-evident as you look at them now, is the principle that there is no exclusive salvation for the Hindu, the Jew, the Zoroastrian, the Buddhist, the Christian, the Muslim, or for the followers of the Herald and Founder of the Bahá'í Faith, the Báb and Bahá'u'lláh. There is no exclusive salvation for the people of any one Religion.

God is not in competition with Himself. No Religion, nor the Founder of any Religion, is greater, more holy, or closer to God, than any other, whether preceding or following.

If you look at the three Names: Moses, Christ and Bahá'u'lláh, they are different, one from another. But, if you look at the sunlight shining in each *Mirror*, they are one and the same. Their reflection of the *Sun* in the heavens, is identical, both with each other and with the *Sun*, God, the Source of all their Light.

If you look at the names of the days of the week which you have written on the bottom of the frames of these three mirrors: Saturday, Sunday, Monday, they are different. But, if you look at the Sunlight of God that shines in each *Mirror* on the Day of His appearance, they are the same.

You see that all of God's "Days" are one and the same. They are all identical, one with another, and all with God. They are perfectly interchangeable. Their Light is one Light, the Light of God. They have appeared at different times in history, but the Light is the same Light. Always. And always will be. Now and forever.

Okay, you can remove your sunglasses and go back inside with your friends for a well-deserved tea-break.

Our story of the *Sun and the Mirrors* has come to an end.

All that we have written here in these three brief chapters, has been nothing more than the overture, the opening chords, of this planetary melody of love. Some day you will read the entire story, in Bahá'u'lláh's Own Words.

This has been merely the first movement in our eternal symphony on that unforgettable theme of the *Sun and the Mirrors*.

Now where was I in *All Flags Flying!*?

Oh, yes. The time when Marguerite, Michael and I sailed to Cape Town, South Africa.

FULL
STEAM
AHEAD!

36

On our first night out, Marguerite and I went into the tiny movie theatre on board the *African Sun* to watch the day's newsreel. We had seen them bring it aboard just before we sailed.

It was quite sensational. Some amateur photographer had been standing at the rail of a New York bound passenger liner beyond the Pillars of Hercules when a volcanic island suddenly rose up like magic from the sea. It was a gigantic chocolate ice-cream cone, sending the foaming waters of the Atlantic cascading down the side. Fortunately, the photographer was holding a loaded movie camera pointed right at the scene, and was able to film the entire dramatic event.

Marguerite and I watched with delight as that new-born island came boiling up out of the Atlantic. I leaned over and whispered to her.

"Don't let the beloved Guardian find out about this island or he'll make it a goal of the Ten Year Plan."

It was a whimsical amusing comment on my part since Shoghi Effendi, the Guardian of the Bahá'í Faith, had taught the entire Bahá'í world about geography. He hadn't overlooked a single corner in any part of the planet. He introduced us to countries we'd never heard about before, with names we still couldn't pronounce properly. Hence my pleasantry.

Marguerite, however, appeared to take my comment seriously.

"It could be an important future goal", she agreed.

Quickly, I added, "I don't want to go there."

"Pity", Marguerite sighed.

She was already jotting down figures in her green notebook on longitude and latitude, and was obviously contemplating the easiest way to get there.

"Just in case", Marguerite confided.

Marguerite couldn't restrain her giggle, so I knew I'd been had.

I didn't want her to think I'd taken the bait, so I said, jokingly, "Besides, it's probably near the Lost Continent of Atlantis or maybe even Mu."

"Mu is somewhere in the Pacific", Marguerite said, her eyes lighting up at the thought.

I knew immediately that any further comment on my part about such a dangerous subject might prove to be a grave, even foolhardy mistake. I could visualize myself, Bill and Mike all taking scuba-diving lessons in preparation for our next underwater, or should I say "under-sea", pioneering post.

Don't laugh, trying for Atlantis or the Lost Continent of Mu is not as far fetched or exaggerated as it sounds. Not if you're married to Marguerite. She was exceedingly fond of dreaming up the most remote and outrageous places to reach on the planet. Or off. The difficult "goals" were the ones she admired the most.

The more remote, untouched, previously unvisited, and completely virgin the area might be, the better she liked it.

No challenge was too great for Miss "Around the World in Eighty Prayers".

"I'm thinking of a pioneering post somewhere in the world that begins with the letter A."

37

Marguerite couldn't sleep so she tapped on the bottom of my top-side bunk with a ball-point pen. Naturally, the noise awakened me. It was intended to.

Immediately I recognized that Marguerite was tapping out a musical rhythm. This is another of her favourite pastimes when she can't sleep. It usually happens late at night just as I'm dozing off. When we are in the same bed, Marguerite will reach over and drum the rhythm of a particular song on my right shoulder because I sleep on my left side when not rudely interrupted. If I do not guess what the song is, but continue pretending that I am still asleep, the piano player can get quite rough!

I am told that most married couples play musical shoulders. I, personally, hate to be jarred out of a bitterly won sleep to be tortured by Tin Pan Alley "oldies".

I usually try to make out the name of the song Marguerite is sending as quickly as possible as it is the best way to get back to sleep.

"Are you awake?" Marguerite.

"Now I am." Me.

"What was the song?"

"*The Beale Street Blues*?"

"No."

"*I'll be down to get you in a taxi, honey*?"

"Not even close."

"Was it *The Night They Shot Old Maggie Dead*?"

"There is no such song."

"There should be."

"Don't be nasty. I was merely trying to get your attention."

"You've got it."

"It was *Blues in the Night*."

"You're telling me!"

Marguerite immediately switched to another of her favourite games. Most of them have to do with quizzes on the Bahá'í Faith, and obscure historical data associated with its history. I don't function too brilliantly when jolted out of dreamland, so Marguerite may call upon her endless repertoire of other simpler games. If she can't think of one, she makes up a new one.

"I had this wonderful new idea tonight", she said. "I had three, actually, but this is the one I decided to try out on you."

"Lucky me."

"It's completely new. And fits right in with pioneering."

Marguerite loves games, and her enthusiasm for them is infectious. They help spice up her study classes and Firesides.

I think these games are one of the reasons Marguerite gets along so well with children, and has such hilarious summer school classes with them. Of course, Marguerite would be the first to admit that she can't compare with her good friend, Helen Gardner. Helen can dream up some real doozies, right on the spot, even while you are standing there watching her. Helen astounded the Bahá'í friends attending THE GATHERINGS at Batterwood with her multiple stunts, games, quizzes, and surprise packages year after year. Without once repeating herself.

But mind you, Marguerite is no slouch. She can make up new games a mile a minute, too. Especially when the sun goes down, and I am sound asleep.

If Marguerite had saved up all the various games and ideas she invented until the coming of computers, she could easily have put Atari and Colecovision right out of business. Pac-Man is a piker alongside several of Marguerite's weird midnight concoctions.

On that long-ago night on the *African Sun,* Marguerite sprang another brand-new one on me.

"Are you ready?" she asked.

I faked being sound asleep with a loud snore that fooled no one. "Zzzzzzzz!"

"Good!" Marguerite said, reaching into the upper berth and squeezing my biceps. "I like it when you're wide awake. Now listen."

The name of the game was "PIONEERING POST: WHERE AM I?" What else?

"I", Marguerite said, "am thinking of a pioneering post somewhere in the world that begins with the letter A. Where is it?"

"Zzzzzzzz!"

"I said the letter *A*, not *Zzzzzz*."

"Africa?"

"No, silly. We're on our way to Africa now."

"Argentina?"

"No."

"Ali Baba and the forty thieves?"

"Be serious."

"Afghanistan?"

"No."

"Agamemnon's Cave?"

"No."

"Aleutian Islands?"

"No."

"Allee Allee Outs in free!"

"You're not trying."

"Alaska?"

"No."

"I give up." I turned over to go to sleep.

"Don't give up." She poked me a few times. "If you guess where it is, we'll go there. All of us."

"Ah!" I said. "At last you've captured my complete rapt attention."

I began to snore again.

"Stop that. It begins with the letter A."

"The Abhá Kingdom?"

Disgusted with me, Marguerite put out the light and went to sleep herself. *That* trip I was prepared to make with her.

Oddly enough, now that Marguerite was sound asleep, I was wide awake. Why is it that that kind of people always marry our kind?

A few hours later I awakened. I was alone in the cabin. I went up on deck. Marguerite and Mike were both at the rail enjoying a spectacular display of unique fireworks. Not in the sky, in the water below.

"I was just going down to get you", Marguerite said. "No one should miss this sight."

We stood at the rail together watching a fascinating drama in the sea below us. The storm was over and the stars were out. We had entered the phosphorescent waters and they were filled with flying fish.

Every time a fish leapt into the air, he would trail a fiery green comet of phosphorescence in his wake. The sea was alive with these flashing green comets under a canopy of brilliant stars and a friendly moon.

It was one of the most moving displays I had ever seen. We watched for a long time. All of us thought of it as a good omen. Marguerite was particularly pleased.

"It must mean we'll have a very active life."

I agreed.

"It reminds me of the first year of our Bahá'í life together."

"Go to your room."

I started to leave, but Marguerite pulled me back. I drew her closer, put my arms around her, and looked deep into her eyes. I said:

"I'm thinking of a place in this ship, quite nearby, where we can find a magic dreamland. It begins with the letter B."

"Baloney", Marguerite replied. "I'm staying out here with the flying fish."

"Baloney is not the right answer. Try again. You'll love it."

"Bunk!" she snapped.

"That's it! Although it was Berth I had in mind."

Marguerite laughed and squeezed my hand.

"Isn't it all wonderful? Far better than we expected?"

We were both caught up in the magic of the moment.

"Can this really be happening to us?" Marguerite asked, her eyes rivalling the two largest stars.

I kept asking myself that same thing all during that entire fantastic African journey from Brooklyn to Cape Town. As I turned back to our cabin, I could still see Marguerite and Michael silhouetted against the moon which had come out round and full.

If only I had told my seventeen year old son that night, as the three of us floated on toward Walvis Bay and Cape Town, that some day he would pioneer himself in the land we would first touch upon; that he would design a school and a police station in an adjoining country; and that years later, within but a few miles' journey from where our ship was soon to dock, he, Michael, Ruth, his dear wife to be, and myself, his father, would come to the capital city of that very land, South-West Africa, to represent in that order, the World Centre of the Bahá'í Faith, the Continental Board of Counsellors, and the Mother Assembly of the newly born National Spiritual Assembly of South-West Africa/Namibia, a new Pillar of the Faith of Bahá'u'lláh.

If I had said that night on board the *African Sun* that he, Michael, would write and produce programmes, both live and on film, for some of the biggest and most illustrious companies in South Africa, he would have said (jokingly, of course): "Dad, you'd better give me a drag on that before you put it down."

Yet, it has all come true. That and far more.

These are the things that dreams are made of. They were too incredible, too impossible for any of us to have envisioned. I didn't have even the least hint or intuition of such majestic coming events as I stood watching my two loved ones at the rail captivated by the flying fish and the phosphorescent waters of the South Atlantic.

As the prow of the small freighter split the waves of the South Atlantic, it threw brilliant turquoise phosphorescent foam all along the side of the ship. I followed it with my eyes all the way to the stern and out into the radiant shining wake until it was absorbed into the dark navy blue Atlantic.

I stood there silently for some time looking back toward the homeland we had left behind. There was a slight tug on my heart, but I weathered it. I was lost in the endless wonder of the entire experience.

Before going below, I called out to Marguerite.

"America is gone", I told her. "Both North and South. You can no longer see any trace of her shoreline. That's all behind us."

Marguerite turned and called back to me.

"Never mind what's behind us", she said. "What's in front of us. That's the thing."

I pointed to the south-west.

"Africa", I answered.

Marguerite smiled, put her arm around Michael's shoulder, and said:

"Our new homeland."

HOME IS WHERE
YOU FIND IT

38

The next thing we knew, we were in Africa. Up to here!

In succession, we visually conquered Walvis Bay, Cape Town, Johannesburg, Salisbury, Entebbe, Kampala, Jinja, Nairobi, Mombasa and Dar es Salaam.

I stood on the equator and stomped my foot.

"I can't see you, you wonderful, magical, symbolical, imaginary Equatorial Line," I said, "but I know you're down there somewhere, and I love you!"

Marguerite, Michael and I took a small-gauge train from Kampala, Uganda over the Eldoret Pass to Nairobi in Kenya. We shopped and "bargained" out the open train windows with the Africans who besieged the train at every stop, peddling every kind of fruit and vegetables. We envied the experienced travellers who knew what they were buying and eating. We were far too choosy and I'm sure missed out on some of the most tasty things.

We purchased pineapples, pawpaw, mangoes and ndizi, a small very sweet and tasty banana, paying for them with our still unfamiliar East African shillings, "shillingis".

A short time later, still in a numb state of general ecstasy and sheer delight with everything, we found ourselves in an automobile on our way from Nairobi to Mombasa on the coast. We were driving with Sue and Aziz Yazdi, pioneers to Kenya.

Our dream had come true at last. We were about to participate in our first travel-teaching work among the Africans. And what a way to travel! We were going by road right through the National Game Park with animals on both sides of us. Sometimes close enough not only to identify, but to saddle and ride.

I shouldn't have said that because in the shortest time imaginable, I was to saddle and try to ride the wildest beast in the East.

All three of us kept crying out the names of the first wild African animals we recognized.

"Giraffe!"

"Lion!"

"Buck!"

"Zebra!"

"Michael, don't fall out the window!"

I was sure that the animals were looking us over, too; and talking among themselves about us, saying: "Hey! Look at that! The Sears family finally made it to Africa. Let's saunter over for a closer look. I understand that these Americans are really weird."

"That's sheer Irish whimsy", Marguerite said, enjoying my thoughts.

"Don't be so sure", I told her. "Did you know that when St Patrick drove the snakes out of Ireland, he drove out all reptiles?"

"So?"

"So, a lot of them came to Africa."

"That's nonsense!"

"Only because you can't talk to the animals the way I can. That famous Irish animal family the O'Diles came to Africa and became famous through their great ancestor Crock O'Dile. The O'Gator family went to Florida, and their great, great, grandfather, Al, started the Al O'Gator dynasty."

"Over and out!" Marguerite and Michael cried in unison.

Sue and Aziz were fascinated.

"I'm going to do a TV series on that", I told Marguerite.

In fact, I did write the story for children some time later.

When Aziz and Sue told us something about the Bahá'í Community on the shores of the Indian Ocean, I couldn't restrain myself.

"Did you hear that, Mike? Marguerite? The Indian Ocean! We're really going to see it!"

Right at that very moment, an elephant became the centre of all our attention. He had passed across the highway, but had pushed over a big tree right in our path.

Marguerite was driving on the way down. It should have been a breeze for her. Of course, it wasn't the San Diego Freeway or Interstate 10, and it *was* a strange car belonging to Aziz Yazdi.

Mike and I hadn't helped Marguerite's concentration by shouting aloud every few minutes: "Look out! You just drove over the
equator!" My raucous, outrageous laughs of sheer joy didn't add
to her serenity.

I think what fooled Marguerite completely was having the elephant push over that big tree smack across the road. You get very
little of that between Oceanside and Laguna Beach in California.

We didn't see the tree until we whipped around a sharp corner
and there it was. Seeing that huge tree for the first time so suddenly, only a few yards away, pumped us all up. Marguerite called
upon her Indianapolis Speedway reflexes, and took to the ditch to
protect her passengers.

Her passengers were all safe, but it did some rather nasty things
to the right wheel and axle of Aziz Yazdi's car. Aziz couldn't have
been nicer to Marguerite. She had stranded our entire party half-
way between the summit and the sea, but Aziz was angelic. Well,
semi-angelic. He did mutter something in Arabic.

We were lucky though. There was a lovely tea-house and restaurant nearby.

It was Mtito Andei, which is Swahili for: "It's time a tree pushed
over an elephant." Mtito Andei was the half-way point between
Nairobi and Mombasa. We were offered a fine British "high tea"
by the Innkeeper.

We were sitting out on the flagstone terrace having our tea and
scones, and admiring the beautiful African cloud formations in the
sky. Once seen, one never forgets the East African skies with those
incredible gathering thunder-head clouds and the magnificent
trees like huge umbrellas on the horizon.

"Maybe because they are umbrella trees", Marguerite suggested.

"Don't", I told her, "confuse me with facts."

I had just lowered my cup, when the cloud formation in the sky
before our eyes broke wide open. There, in front of us, like a picture
within a huge frame of nimbus clouds, stood the snow-capped peak
of Kilimanjaro!

I had heard for years about the "snows of Kilimanjaro" (now
called Uhuru Peak). I had even read Steinbeck's book, but I had
never dreamed that a Philadelphia sportscaster, and a fledgling
Bahá'í pioneer to Africa, would ever behold that incredible sight
with his own eyes, in person.

"Look!" I cried out to Marguerite. She did and was equally impressed. The waiter didn't even bother to look up. He saw it every day. The British gentleman on my left who owned a farm in the area lighted up another Rothman, yawned, and without turning his head said, "Oh, that."

Marguerite and I held hands. In some ways neither of us had ever grown up. Such sights filled a deep empty longing inside us. It was a moment of pure joy. Bordering on ecstasy. I needled the rancher.

"You don't mean 'Oh, that'", I told him. "You mean: 'OH, THAT!'"

We continued our journey at midnight, looking forward to our big weekend meetings in Mombasa. We boarded the narrow-gauge East African Railway passenger service between Nairobi and Mombasa.

The train was full. There was no space for the joining Mtito Andei passengers. However, out of the kindness of his heart, the Conductor permitted us to use the empty dining-car.

Dining-car chairs are fine for a brief lunch or dinner, but for an overnight journey between Nairobi and Mombasa, they have a tendency to shut off your circulation. For comfort on long journeys they fall just short of the gas chamber at San Quentin.

We took turns trying to sleep on top of the small dining-car tables. This is not only tricky, it is impossible.

There is quite a bit of parry and thrust to a fast-moving small-gauge train. It can suddenly and unexpectedly propel you backwards, zoom! right off the top of one of those slippery formica tables. Or with a violent brake, at an urgent unscheduled stop, it can chuck you in the opposite direction, forward, zip! You slide abruptly head first off the table in a heap, or crumpled over the adjoining table, half off, half on.

Either way, you eventually end up on the hard tile floor which is a long drop and extremely painful to your person, even worse to your dignity.

Ribald jeers and insults from the spectators who witness your humiliation, people who are normally your tender, loving Bahá'í friends and family, do not help.

Of course, it was all in fun, as long as we didn't run out of Band-Aids and Dettol.

And remember, it wasn't the *Broadway Limited* between New York and Chicago, or the Santa Fe *Chief en route* to Phoenix, or the Southern Pacific *Lark* between Los Angeles and San Francisco.

This was Africa.

We were between Nairobi and Mombasa with wild animals looking in from each side. What were a few wounds? This was more exciting than riding broncos at the Rodeo in Calgary. Nothing really mattered, nor could anything dampen our enthusiasm. Marguerite and I spent the whole night laughing.

I believe that Marguerite was the only one to shout out any encouragement to me as I got back up on top of that dining-car table. Hair of the dog.

"Ride 'em cowboy!" she yelled.

Cowboy, of course, couldn't.

"I thought it was terrorists."

39

The meetings in Mombasa were spectacular. Both Marguerite and I agreed on that. We have recorded the delightful experience of our Fireside in the Kit-Kat Cafe in Mombasa in our article "Black Sunlight" in *The Bahá'í World*, volume twelve, page 925.

Those were precious, never-to-be-forgotten days and hours.

We were taught many wonderful things about Africa, and interesting new ways to approach the teaching work in our new homeland. Our guides were Aziz and Sue Yazdi.*

Both Sue and Aziz are now in the Holy Land, that "land of unfading splendour". Aziz serves as one of the members of the Continental Board of Counsellors, and is also a member of the International Teaching Centre on the side of Mount Carmel. That Body has been described in the Bahá'í Writings as one of those "world-shaking, world-embracing, world-directing" Institutions of the mighty Order of Bahá'u'lláh referred to in "The Sun and the Mirrors".

Mombasa was aflame with colour. Flowers, blossoming fruit trees, coconut palms, flamboyant oleander trees in red, white and pink, jealously competed with multicoloured bougainvillaea vines. Unbelievably huge and twisted baobab trees, and Marguerite's favourite, the mango, were all a part of the setting for our Bahá'í meetings as we taught out in the open under the overspreading shade trees.

It was so breath-takingly lovely and unique to us, that we both were worried that as soon as our meetings were over, some stagehand would appear and holler: "Strike the set!"

We gathered beneath several different varieties of shade trees,

* Other wonderful Bahá'ís, such as Hasan and Isobel Sabri, were also of immeasurable help to us, and showered us with kindness.

protection against the blazing equatorial sun and the wilting humidity. It was the first time I ever perspired under my fingernails. The passenger ferries and the Makupa and Kipevu causeways between island and mainland were a delight. The cooling breezes from the Port of Kilindini saved our lives.

It wasn't all meetings and hard work, there was some time for fun and games. The most entertaining episode of all was the afternoon Aziz taught Marguerite to "bargain" Middle East style. The protagonist was a cunning skilful Arab trader born in Mombasa. Aziz instructed Marguerite in all the finer points, as well as the fierce spirit needed to capture an "unworthy pineapple" for a shilling. About fourteen cents.

As we walked together down the street eating the pineapple following their triumphant victory, Marguerite and Aziz shook hands and held their locked fists aloft to seal the success of their common effort, and the smashing success of her newly acquired technique of oriental haranguing. Both were deeply pleased.

I refused to advance Marguerite the shilling she had borrowed from Aziz to buy the pineapple. I had insisted throughout that they pay the man the original two shillings asking price.

"It's a bargain", I said.

Both Marguerite and Aziz voted to leave me home next time. I did, however, offer to reward each of them generously with a new American dollar bill for their entertaining floor show. They refused, scathingly. The amount, they said, was totally inadequate to compensate them for their genius.

I wanted to describe the entire "bargaining" encounter in this book, but it sounds so much better in Arabic. No written description by a very minor and unsung peripatetic Irish poet could ever capture the eloquence and elegance of a genuine spontaneous "bargaining" encounter, a verbal duel in an Arab souk or marketplace, between two evenly-matched contestants. Especially if one is watching the natural genius of Aziz Yazdi challenging that of an Arab trader named Abou ben Hassan. I always referred to him after the great pineapple encounter as "Abou ben had 'em and lost 'em."

Several hours later, our Bahá'í mission triumphantly completed, we were all relaxing on board the return train to Nairobi. We had a private compartment this time, no dining-car tables to saddle and ride.

Aziz and Sue were taking turns reading to us. They were translating from Persian into English some of the fascinating stories from the diary of Dr Yunes Khan Afrukhteh. The book is called "Memoirs of Nine Years". The Guardian of the Bahá'í Faith, Shoghi Effendi, is reported to have said that next to the renowned *Dawn-Breakers* by Nabíl, the historian, this book is one of the most authoritative accounts of the days of the Master, 'Abdu'l-Bahá, in the Holy Land, the World Centre of the Bahá'í Faith.

Some of the stories were very tender and brought tears to our eyes. Some were happy, some sad, and some extremely hilarious. Our peals of laughter rang through the Nairobi-bound *Mombasa Express*. The stories occasionally elicited shrill cries of delight as we sped through the night.

Every now and then the conductor of the train would peer into our compartment to see if everything was all right, and that no one was being mistreated or tortured. When he discovered it was cries of laughter, you could tell he wished that he himself were part of that fun and happiness. Apologetically, he would withdraw, shaking his head. We could imagine his saying:

"At first, I thought it was terrorists."

Marguerite was going home to Nairobi a better African teacher, and also a far better "bargainer". Fortunately for our budget, Marguerite could now give up the original method which she devised to conclude all vital purchases in the African markets. Especially arts and crafts shops.

Marguerite would hold out all of her local currency in both hands. She would implore the honest, local tradesman to take the proper amount. Marguerite implemented her trust in his natural integrity by trying to look vulnerable, frail, and above all extremely innocent. I kept telling her that no woman shopper who wants a bargain, ever looks the least bit innocent, let alone extremely.

"Don't do that", I kept telling her, pointing out that the more innocent Marguerite looked, the more money the crafty merchant took from her open hands.

"I've seen it", I told her. Marguerite didn't believe it. She's a better Bahá'í than I am, but much poorer and without funds when travelling.

I tried to demonstrate the truth of my theory to her the day I entered into negotiations with a cab-driver to pay for our fare back to the New Stanley Hotel in Nairobi. I held out the money, à la Marguerite, in both hands, and told the taxi driver to take the proper amount. He was only too willing and eager. He joyfully plucked American dollars out of my hand, one after another, like peeling bananas from a stalk.

"One uh for you, and one uh for me", he explained, smiling happily. "Two uh for you, and two uh for me. Three uh—"

I caught on fast, having dealt with cab-drivers in Rome, Athens and Paris. I grasped his money wrist and scooped back all of the bills, except the proper amount.

I told him:

"None uh for you, and all uh for me. Me Tarzan, you crook."

A barge on the Nile

40

I was day-dreaming again. I was in the upper bunk of the sleeper on the train back to Nairobi from Mombasa. The luminous dial of my watch said two a.m. I dropped my left arm over the side, stretching down toward Marguerite. She reached up as I reached down. We held hands.

We were both too stimulated to sleep. It had been a wonderful trip.

On the top of all that joy, we were in Africa, on an African train, passing through an African Game Park, listening to an African language being spoken by people who passed back and forth in the corridor outside our compartment.

Neither one of us believed a word of what was happening to us. I laughed.

Marguerite said, "What is it?"

"Ecstasy", I admitted, frankly.

"Me, too."

If anyone had told me back in those earlier days when I first met Marguerite at WOMT, Manitowoc, Wisconsin, that I would ever get to such a far-off place as Chicago, I would have expected sirens, and a white-jacketed medico to toss me into the ambulance, and whip me off to Wauwatosa.*

But look at me now. Africa!

How could I possibly have believed on our first sea voyage together that Marguerite would launch me on an endless series of world-wide journeys? I, Bill Sears, head honcho of staying at home; who had trouble getting to the football stadium and back, who would soon be flying from Adelaide to Amsterdam, from Casablanca to the Royal Palace in Western Samoa. Little did I

* Bellevue to you New Yorkers

dream that this day of joy in which I was revelling, this brief train journey from Nairobi to Mombasa and back, would turn out to be a peanuts prelude.

I do suspect, however, that Marguerite knew.

Gradually, my world-wide travels would all become quite run-of-the-mill, just plain average Bahá'í planetary commuting.

I would give talks on the Bahá'í Faith in the Shell at Waikiki, Honolulu; in the United Nations building along the East River in New York City; at Hollywood High School in California where so many "starlets" had been discovered (not me); in the Frankfurt Zoo in Germany; and in the open air African bush country seated beneath giant over-spreading mango, mavuli and baobab trees in Uganda, Kenya, Tanzania, Zululand and Lesotho, to name but a few; I would teach the Faith even inside the Royal Albert Hall in London, England and outside a beautiful Buddhist Shrine in Kyoto, Japan.

Marguerite and I even returned to the port of Kilindini at Mombasa for our second sea journey to Tanga and on to Beira in Mozambique. We took the narrow-gauge train to Salisbury, Southern Rhodesia (now Harare, Zimbabwe) stopping for lunch *en route* at Umtali (now Mutare). Everybody left the train, walked four blocks to the hotel to lunch, then returned to the train when it tooted for departure.

We sent a telegram to Kenneth and Roberta Christian in Salisbury: "Put the coffee on. You know who." They did, too. The coffee wasn't bad.

Once launched into Bahá'í flight by Marguerite, I visited receptive souls in Tilling, Canberra, Port Louis, San Jose, Liberia, Seshego, Ermelo, Addis Ababa, Sugarbush and Rustenburg.

Until I was a Bahá'í, I didn't know the meaning of that old joke, "You can't get there from here." But you can't. Not in a hurry, anyway. Especially from such unrelated places as Lagos, Vallejo, Port au Prince, Dallas, Durban, Adrianople, Jakarta, Indio, Tokyo, Tehran, Walla Walla, Maputo, Mexicali, Annotto Bay or New Delhi.

It's called travel teaching. I visited them all.*

From Anchorage, Alaska in the land of the midnight sun where

* Note to proof-reader: Sorry about this "flash-ahead", Marguerite, but it "sings".

I had my hair cut for ten dollars (*circa* 1961) during a raging blizzard, to Khartoum in the Sudan where I had the same haircut (and not much of it, at that) for forty-seven cents.

The sky at Khartoum was filled with beautiful stars. They seemed only a few feet out of reach as my Cairo-bound Constellation set down. As the passengers walked towards the terminal, I thought, "If only I had a butterfly net, I could scoop me a netful of these incredible desert stars and mail them home to Marguerite."

What happened in Khartoum was this: Before we had finished our soup course, a sudden blinding sandstorm grounded all planes. Since I am "S" on the alphabet, all the hotel rooms were taken. I was miffed but smiled through my tears since I knew the experience was character-building. My vexation turned to bliss when I was invited to sleep on a barge in the Nile River.

I loved it!

I dreamed of Ramses, Cheops, Luxor and Cleopatra's nose. I remember dozing off *en route* to Cairo mumbling, "cue the asp!"

The only reason I didn't see Marguerite more often during those hectic months and years, is that West Berlin, Reunion Island, Zululand, Buenos Aires, Beirut, Naples and Pearl Harbor are such a long way off from Johannesburg. I kept telephoning her, but always missed her. She was off in the villages teaching the Africans.

I sometimes sent Marguerite dates from Indio, California; pecans from Georgia; oranges from the Indian River Valley in Florida; and humorous tape recordings from Birmingham, Brussels, Boston, Canton (United States, not China) and sometimes a letter. Unless I was too busy in Nicosia in Cyprus; Tegucigalpa in Honduras; the Okanagan Valley in British Columbia; Kisumu in Kenya; or Brisbane in Australia; and other lesser intermediate stops.

Marguerite, when she proof-read this part of the book, objected violently. Not to anything I said about her, but as she expressed it, "to your eternal, unexpected, whimsical Irish flash-backs and flash-aheads. Tell it chronologically", she insisted.

"That's totally impossible with half a century to chronicle. I have to jump around to get it all in."

"No one will know where you are, or at what time in your life you were there, wherever it is."

"I will know", I assured her.

"Where? On the train to Nairobi, or in Donegal?"

"On the train to Nairobi, of course."

We kissed as we passed through Mtito Andei. That helped.

The truth is, that slightly balding ex-sportscaster you are watching day-dream in the upper berth on board the Nairobi Express, would someday live in, or visit, every one of those wonderful places listed above, and many others even more fascinating.

In fact, after I became a Bahá'í, I found I had friends everywhere in the world. I had more real friends than any famous or popular movie, television or rock concert star. I had become a member of the world's biggest, most beautiful, and most loving family, the Bahá'í Faith.

The world may be "starved for love" as the psychiatrists keep telling us, but the people who are trying to cure it, are working the wrong side of the street. There's no need for all that inner suffering, agony, sorrow and loneliness if you know the right formula.

It's spelled: "BAHÁ'Í" (Followers of Light or Glory: followers of Bahá'u'lláh, the Supreme Redeemer of men).

The formula works. The Bahá'ís Marguerite and I visited in so many different lands during so many different seasons; people of every racial and religious background who had been complete strangers to us when we first knocked upon the door of their home, their hut, their igloo, their cave, their apartment, or their mansion. Sometimes even their palace. Once they had opened the door to us, heard our Bahá'í greeting, and looked into our eyes:

Ping! Steel filings to a magnet.*

We laughed, embraced, and became instant lifelong friends in that first revealing moment.

These Bahá'ís made us feel that they had been waiting all of their lives for the moment when we arrived at their front door. They were not waiting for someone else. They were waiting for *us*!

To your increasing delight you too will find that this is the case, when, as a new Bahá'í, you journey to every corner of the planet wherever other Bahá'ís reside. You will also discover to your joy and happiness that it holds true for you as well. There are people out there (Red, Yellow, Black, Brown, White, Oriental, Occidental) who really care about you. Even though they haven't seen you yet. They are waiting everywhere. Just for you. Or so you will

---

* I must make a rubber stamp of that expression for myself, and an "I was perfectly innocent!" stamp for Michael.

surely feel when you visit them and meet them for the first time face to face.

They are called Bahá'ís. The word is simple. Bahá(í)— of Bahá'u'lláh; as in Christ(ian)— of Christ. Bahá is one of the Titles of Bahá'u'lláh. It means "Glory"; just as "Christ" is a Title that means "Anointed". See? It is no longer strange. And neither are these people, these Bahá'ís, no matter what part of the world you find them on your visit.

The Bahá'í Writings say about such encounters, and other wonderful experiences like them, which the Bahá'í Faith brings to everyone who embraces it:

> "Let the doubter arise and himself
> verify the truth of such assertions."

No more loneliness. Ever again. For any Bahá'í or friend of the Bahá'ís. Anywhere in the world where there are Bahá'ís.

All hearts are one.

Imagine.

How lucky we are!

It took me some time to appreciate all of this, and of course I had the good fortune to be married to a Bahá'í who introduced me to this heaven on earth. I had to be grateful.

For the first few years with Marguerite, I suffered severely from spiritual "motion sickness". Dramamine didn't help. Neither did Mam-mine.* Marguerite just kept me moving, and did the same herself. She was training me, as the mama goose trains the goslings until she kicks them out of the nest. Marguerite was forever having me get cholera, yellow fever and smallpox injections to be "at the ready" for some sudden, unexpected, urgently needed trip.

However, by the time I had visited Durban, Port Elizabeth and Bloemfontein, and passed through Salisbury, Dar es Salaam, Zanzibar, Nairobi, Kampala, and on to Leopoldville (now Kinshasa), Accra, Monrovia, Dakar, Casablanca, Rabat, Tangier and Cairo, I had already stopped saying, "Where are we?"

Amatu'l-Bahá, Rúḥíyyih Khánum, one of the most illustrious of Bahá'í teachers, when she was Mary Maxwell, once said that Marguerite, prior to becoming a Bahá'í, "Wouldn't say boo! to a weasel."

* Sorry about that.

That was before Miss Seven-League Boots became a Bahá'í, of course, married an innocent bystander, and learned to say *fortissimo voce:*

"All systems go!"

The *Mombasa Express* was pulling in to Nairobi when I returned from my day-dreaming.

I asked Marguerite something that had been troubling me.

"Why is it that I always seem to end up in the upper berth? I thought there was complete equality between men and women in the Bahá'í Faith."

"There is", Marguerite replied, smiling her innocent eyes. "But we have to be fair. You did lose when you couldn't answer the Bahá'í quiz question. Remember?"

"What was that question again?"

"What Bahá'í book would you give to a seeker who was a construction engineer?"

"And what was the answer I missed?"

"*Foundations of World Unity.*"

Marguerite turned away quickly but I could tell she was laughing. I wasn't. She had prepared the quiz. She always prepared them. It was another favourite game of hers. For deepening. Mostly serious, but every now and then, when she wanted to "make points", she invented a "sleeper" question such as above.

"Can I make up the quiz questions next time?" I asked Marguerite.

"Of course."

"Good!"

I scooped Marguerite up in my arms and tossed her up into the upper bunk. I said. "That's where you will be spending your time after the next quiz, so get used to it, sister!"

We both went off into gales of laughter until the porter came to collect our bags.

I was gradually becoming accustomed to Marguerite's viewpoint, and to what she referred to, alternately, as "our great adventure" or the "great work".

Even so, many times, in the early days of those African adventures, I would say to Marguerite: "Tell me again those enrapturing things you told me on the Old Sawmill River Road in Pennsylvania about the joys of pioneering and travel-teaching in far-off lands, and how I would come to love it so madly. Could you run that past me once again? I need it."

"You *will* come to love it", Marguerite promised me. "And madly."

To myself, I whispered:

"Waka Pantinani Bhuphata Makano Planifafa!"

The above sentence is in one of the African tribal languages which freely translated into English, means: "If I had known then what I know now, I would never have backed her blue Ford V8 out of that snow-drift on Donner Pass!"

Remember?

The night when Marguerite had smiled so winningly and so innocently at me, and said:

"I won't eat you if you don't eat me."

I should have eaten her.

"Match that if you can!"

41

The African journeys, as well as those to other parts of the world, undertaken by the Sears family, Marguerite, William, Michael and myself, either separately or ensemble, might appear fairly impressive at first glance. It is true that over the years, these travels included pioneering and teaching in North America, South America, Europe, Asia, Africa, Australasia and the islands of the Atlantic, Pacific and Indian Oceans, as well as the Caribbean and Mediterranean Seas.

Before you say, "Bravo!" let me explain that all of these travels lumped together would never begin to rival the wondrous accomplishments of that heroic teaching example for all Bahá'ís, Martha Root.

Martha Root was the "star-servant" of Bahá'u'lláh. She was designated by 'Abdu'l-Bahá as a "herald of the Kingdom" of God, and a "harbinger of the Covenant" of Bahá'u'lláh, the Promised One of All Ages.

Martha Root's "historic journeys" lasted for "twenty years" of constant travel. They took her "several times around the globe".

The quotation marks are brief excerpts from the many tributes which have been paid to this gallant heroine in the Writings of the Bahá'í Faith.

Martha was still labouring in the "active service of the Cause she loved so greatly" when she laid down her life far from home, on the distant island of Oahu, Hawaii. I took a photograph of Marguerite at Martha's grave in Honolulu. While I was focusing my camera, a beautiful Hawaiian rainbow appeared, that symbol of the Covenant. Through the camera lens, it seemed to come down to touch that much-loved and visited spot.

Shoghi Effendi, Guardian of the Bahá'í Faith, described Martha Root as the "archetype" of Bahá'í travelling teacher and the "foremost Hand" of the Faith raised up by Bahá'u'lláh since the passing of 'Abdu'l-Bahá.

Martha Root taught the Faith in such a convincing manner that she brought Royalty within its fold. She captured the interest of Presidents, Prime Ministers and Leaders of modern thought. One of them, Eduard Beneš, former President of Czechoslovakia, inspired by Martha's visit, was moved to describe the Bahá'í Faith as "one of the great moral and social forces in all the world today." President Beneš went further, saying that the Bahá'í Faith was "one of the great instruments for the final victory of the spirit and of humanity."

Martha Root's example of dedicated, "manifold services" and her life of uninterrupted travel on behalf of the Founder of her Faith, Bahá'u'lláh, have won for her the title of "Leading Ambassadress of His Faith and Pride of Bahá'í teachers, whether men or women, in both the East and the West".

The beloved Guardian said, a pilgrim's note, that some Bahá'ís are heroes, some are martyrs, and some are saints; but Martha Root, the Star-Servant of His Faith, had by her signal international services crowned the American Bahá'í Community with imperishable glory. Martha was all three: A heroine, a martyr *and* a saint.

The Bahá'í world has yet another shining example of teaching and travelling to spur us on in this day. Another pattern we can all follow:

The heroic travels of Hand of the Cause of God, Amatu'l-Bahá, Rúḥíyyih Khánum, become more worldwide with each passing year. There is scarcely a part of our planet that has not already been inspired by her presence.

Amatu'l-Bahá, Rúḥíyyih Khánum, has not only visited the underprivileged areas of the world, so dear to her heart, but has also journeyed to its capital cities as well. She has established an unprecedented record in meeting Kings, Presidents, Prime Ministers, Heads of State, Governors, Mayors, and leading figures in all fields in all the continents along her path of travel. She has met the Press everywhere, and has made her mark on Radio and Television as well.

Like Martha Root before her, Amatu'l-Bahá, Rúḥíyyih Khánum is becoming an example for Bahá'í travelling teachers to arise and follow. With each year that passes, her "star" is on the ascendant in that galaxy of Bahá'í heroines. She has far outdistanced the rest of us and she didn't have half a century to do it in, as we did.

To me, Amatu'l-Bahá, Rúḥíyyih <u>Kh</u>ánum will always be the Queen of the world.

She doesn't approve of my saying these things, but they are true, however inadequately expressed by my pen. I confess I did not ask her permission to write this tribute because I suspected the answer would be a resounding and unequivocal "No!"

I have also refrained, with superb restraint, from going even further with my words of well-deserved praise, but I'm thinking them. I refer especially to her literary masterpiece, *The Priceless Pearl*. There could be no richer reward for any Bahá'í than to read this magnificent tribute to Shoghi Effendi, the Sign of God on earth, and Guardian of the Bahá'í Faith.

Marguerite and I read her book aloud to each other on one of our teaching trips across the United States. Those were truly memorable days!

Marguerite, in more than one part of the world, has acted as temporary curator for the fascinating animal acquisitions which over-zealous Bahá'í friends keep giving to Amatu'l-Bahá, Rúḥíyyih <u>Kh</u>ánum, along the way. Usually just as she is boarding the departing plane.

Thus there is more between Marguerite and Amatu'l-Bahá, Rúḥíyyih <u>Kh</u>ánum than just a deep love for their religion.

I shall stop here, as I do not wish to jeopardize my invitations to tea at the Master's House when Amatu'l-Bahá, Rúḥíyyih <u>Kh</u>ánum is in the Holy Land, and I am lucky enough to be there at the same time.

She forgives me for almost bordering on the impertinent at times because she is fond of both Marguerite and myself. I am counting heavily on that. It is hard for her *not* to forgive me, since she knows that both Marguerite and I love her with all our hearts. As do her fellow-Bahá'ís in more than three hundred separate countries, territories and islands of the seven seas, and in more than one hundred thousand places all over the planet.

We hope you meet her some day.

We all would do anything in our power to help her. In any way we could. At the drop of a hat.

Match *that* if you can!

42

Without a doubt the most happy and exciting years of our Bahá'í pioneering lives were spent in Africa. We had the joy of living in Nairobi, Kenya, and also in Ndola, Northern Rhodesia (now Zambia) where Marguerite ran a small restaurant and made the greatest soft ice-cream south of the Sahara. Old Baskin-Robbins Bill cut into the profits alarmingly.

We were living in Chingola with Knight of Bahá'u'lláh Doris Ballard who typed so many of my early manuscripts. We had a productive, but much shorter, stay with another very dear and close friend, Hasan Sabrí, in his home on the outskirts of Dar es Salaam in Tanganyika (now Tanzania).

Our longest stay however, and the heart of all our early pioneering work in Africa, was on the farm we owned off Muldersdrift Road, twenty-five kilometres outside Johannesburg, the City of Gold, on the great Transvaal Reef.

The Sears' farm at Honeydew, and the experiences of those who visited us, generated a number of stories some of which later became legends among our Bahá'í friends. All were true, but somewhat understated, or so it seemed to the real eyewitnesses. Don't look at me! I'm talking about the "animal lady" of *God Loves Laughter*. My own life has always been quite simple, an ordinary routine of laughable disasters, and sudden cries of "Help!" in the wake of the outgoing ship, M.R.S.

We were presented with a large peacock with a magnificent tail by two dear friends, John and Val Allen, Bahá'í pioneers in Swaziland. It was a "house-warming" present which they thought would dress up our farm and give it a little class. The peacock was also intended to encourage some egg-laying action from the five hundred day-old chicks Marguerite had purchased with an eye to the future.

The very next day, Marguerite saw our peacock high up in the pine-tree branches outside the kitchen window. Since we had clipped its wings, Marguerite couldn't understand how the peacock had escaped from the chicken-run and flown to such a height. She called for help to capture it. Everybody on the farm responded. If we had organized our teaching trips to Lesotho with half as much verve and imagination, we would have spiritually captured Maseru in the first month.

Even so, with all our frantic energetic efforts, it took most of the day to rescue the peacock. Work came to a screeching halt until the final moments of the great tree-to-tree capture. Honours to the entire posse. When we put the peacock back in the chicken-run where it belonged, we discovered that we now had *two* peacocks.

We had hoped they would turn out to be Adam and Eve, but they turned out to be Cain and Abel.

"Don't you mean *unable*?" William said. I won't repeat what I said, or for that matter what Andrew Mofokeng said.

Marguerite advertised in all the local papers. "FOUND, ONE PEACOCK." The second week she said: "HAS ANYBODY LOST A BIG BEAUTIFUL PEACOCK?"

We figured either somebody had, and didn't want it back or had an elfin sense of humour because the next week there was a reply ad that said "NOBODY".

Marguerite finally put up a large notice in the local trading store. No one claimed the him-or-her (as the case might be) peacock. I was informed that male peacocks always have brilliant colours and a fancy tail while the female peacocks are quite plain. I really didn't care. Sorry about that, girls.

If you have ever heard a peacock cry out in the night, especially during mating season, you probably know why no one claimed it. Peacocks look like Jaclyn Smith but sound like Lionel Stander. Since the peacock had flown into the topmost branches of several of our highest pine-trees until capture, we called him Sir Hillary in honour of the latest news from Mount Everest. We now owned both Sir Hillary and Friend.

The point of this story is not the peacocks, but the day-old chicks. They grew and grew, but still had not produced one single egg. Marguerite finally stormed into the hen-house one morning and laid down her ultimatum!

"Starting tomorrow," she warned, "if there are still only chickens in this hen-house and no eggs, we begin eating chickens. Roast chicken, fried chicken, fricasseed chicken and chicken soup. Do I make myself clear?" She tacked up her wanted-poster: "WANTED: EGGS!"

"This", she said, "means you!"

Marguerite slammed the door and stomped out. The two peacocks squawked and fluttered around the corner, not wishing to be lumped in with the threatened fowls, and not caring for the scowling countenance they saw on the boss-lady.

Apparently Marguerite had made herself devastatingly clear. We had four eggs the next day, and by the end of the month, dozens. So many eggs, we began to give them away to our friends, those who would still take them. They would say, "Please come to dinner, but don't bring any eggs. Or asparagus." They mentioned the asparagus because we had 4 500 crowns. Asparagus is slow in starting but once in gear, it goes on alarmingly, prolifically, and pops up daily, forever. Sometimes you fear an asparagus "take-over". Worse, the asparagus has to be cut, every day!

In that wonderful African soil, we could plant lettuce, carrots, cabbage, green beans and assorted other vegetables and have them grow all year long. No season. We also had peach trees from here to there. Two hundred and fifty trees of early peaches, two hundred and fifty normal,* and two hundred and fifty late peaches. I still have a colour photograph of Marguerite on a ladder pruning a peach tree, while Fred Schechter is standing below the ladder reading directions to her from a newly acquired library book entitled: *Anyone Can Prune a Peach Tree*. They switched places from time to time like a "do-si-do" barn dance. I have photographs of both ritual peach dances.

In time, we had a wonderful crop of peaches, middle, early and late. I especially loved the early peaches, large, white, sweet, juicy and delicious. Later, we had a wonderful crop of Bahá'ís, too, but

* I am reluctant to use the word "normal" in connection with anything to do with this farm. You'll find out.

that was the year we forgot to spray the peach trees. Pioneers are always trying to balance their priorities, and usually lose out to teaching, winding up with wilted lettuce and undug potatoes.

We had boysenberries, strawberries, raspberries and gooseberries. We also had orange, tangerine, lemon, grapefruit, apple, apricot, pear, plum, nectarine, fig and cherry trees.

And stomach cramps.

43

One of the most precious crops ever developed on our "West Winds" farm, and one of the sweetest to the taste, was Florence Marumo. Florence worked like a miner, sang like an angel, and cooked like the chef at Maxim's. Florence was a dear, kindly and thoughtful human being who also turned out to be an excellent translator and teacher, as well as a housekeeper *par excellence*.

She still is. This story took place a quarter of a century ago, but last year when we returned to Johannesburg, and lived on the corner of Sabie and Niger Roads among the jacaranda trees, Florence was working as head honcho and housekeeper supreme to a citizen of Dunkeld. Florence wanted to retire but her employer sent a long limousine to her home to entreat her to return. He couldn't get along without her. Neither could we. Like Coke, she was it!

Marguerite taught Florence many things, and vice versa. However, one of the most productive and beautiful things Marguerite ever taught Florence was how to bake cakes. Between them, for three years running, Marguerite and Florence baked and had eaten by visiting Bahá'ís, five hundred and ninety-five cakes per year. More than one a day. That surely established an all Transvaal Gold Reef record: 1 685 cakes! All filled with the tasty flavour of love. The cakes came in as many varieties as there were wildflowers on the farm: Devil's Food, Angel Food, Pineapple Upsidedown, Marble, Gingerbread, Sponge, Spice, Raisin, Chocolate Chip and Coconut. Every cake had its own special frosting that "made the angels sorry they died."

My son William, who was no slouch himself as a pastry chef, and who had been cooking since he was seven years old, also taught Florence a thing or two when it came to baking. During the Bahá'í

Nineteen Day Fast from sunrise to sunset in March, Bill would start baking and preparing at dawn:

> Brownies
> Muffins
> Molasses, oatmeal and date-filled cookies
> Lemon meringue pie
> Chili con carne
> Cinnamon rolls
> Apple turnovers
> Banana fritters
> And his favourite flavours of home-made ice-cream.

Bill, of course, knew that the farm would be filled with hungry people after the sun went down. They were drawn to the farm like a compass needle to the magnetic north! Perhaps ants to a picnic is more apropos. Those of us who were fasting with Bill would, on occasion, enter the kitchen and punch him on the arm muscle for filling the air with such tempting, tantalizing aromas all day long. I believe I was the one who started the fad of wearing a light plastic clothes-pin on my nose during those Bill-baking daylight hours.* It failed completely to discourage Bill. He baked on.

In addition to the above assorted goodies Bill, Marguerite and Florence supplied us with four varieties of berry pies, biscuits, bread and Danish pastry, Yankee style. These were over and above the pot roasts, baked hams, beef fillets (Three shillings for an entire tenderloin! Let us take a moment of silent prayer for the poor souls buying meat today!), lamb roasts and mutton.

The smells that filled our farmhouse on baking day were enough to bring everyone on the run as the sun hit that western horizon. Not only from the farm, but from the neighbourhood. Our friends everywhere from Orlando to Rosebank, from Sophiatown to Germiston knew exactly when baking-day came each week. The cars and bicycles started appearing like rush hour on Commissioner Street just as the sun went down. Of course, what made it an event was the fact that it invariably coincided with one of Marguerite's Deepening classes, Study classes, or Fireside meetings. So you can

* It was Bob Quigley, American pioneer, who, when he spent his first week on the farm, said: "When I was a Roman Catholic, I used to dream of dying and going to Heaven. Since becoming a Bahá'í and pioneering here in South Africa, I now want to die and go to the Sears' farm."

see that the baking and cooking were not excessive when you realize that Marguerite conducted a permanent "open house" at the
Sears' farm. Everybody was welcome and knew it. Morning, noon
and night. It has always been that way with Marguerite and her
home as long as I can remember, which goes back almost to the
Cro-Magnon Man. She not only had open house, she had open
doors and open windows to air out the lingering aroma of frying
bacon and mince pie.

Many of our friends were not Bahá'ís, of course. Not yet. They
still hadn't tasted Florence's cooking or Marguerite's desserts.

Michael used to warn us that we were making "Raspberry Pie
Bahá'ís". I suggested to him that he was a sorehead, and still rank-
ling because we had undermined his "Holiday Bahá'ís" teaching
scheme back in Jackson, Mississippi. Michael took it in good spirit
by spearing the last of my coconut macaroons and vanishing behind the red oleanders.

Anyone who is at all familiar with the Bahá'í Faith knows that
there is no compulsion or pressure of any kind exerted upon anyone to become a Bahá'í. They have to do it all on their own because
they love Bahá'u'lláh and His Faith. Nothing else will do. We
merely tell the people about the wonder and excitement of Bahá'u'lláh's coming, and the astonishing number of prophecies He
has fulfilled from the Bible and other Holy Books. We are delighted
to share Bahá'u'lláh's Teachings of love and unity with everyone
because we feel they are urgently needed, and so perfectly suited to
the problems facing mankind today. Marguerite and Florence's
superb cuisine is merely an accidental fringe benefit.

Whether anyone is interested in the Bahá'í Faith or not, is entirely up to them. No strings attached. Bahá'u'lláh said we should
attract the heart, and not enforce the mind. Offer the cup. If the
seekers drink, fine. If not, leave them to themselves, but still main-
tain your friendship. The important thing, was for us to create an
atmosphere of fellowship, friendship and love for all the peoples we
meet whether they are interested in the Faith or not. Our homes
should welcome them into a warm, happy family atmosphere. All
Bahá'ís know and understand the importance of the home and
children and their need to have a place of safety, security and
serenity.

We only hoped that many visiting friends who felt this spirit and atmosphere of hospitality on the farm, would want to seek further and perhaps eventually join us and become a part of it. There was an abundance of never-failing love offered with "no strings attached" for anyone who came. Where else can you find that in the world these days? And can depend upon it? The "free gift", as it says in Scripture.

Michael nodded in agreement. He had returned surreptitiously, his big blue eyes smiling, as he wiped the last of my coconut macaroon crumbs from his lips.

"And", he said, pointing out the religious implications of coming to the Sears' farm, "Florence Marumo's leg of lamb with the mint sauce, doesn't hurt."

That's when I hit him with the one coconut macaroon he'd missed.

> *"Turn down the lamps, set the alarm, put out the ridgebacks and the cats, and hit the bull- frogs. Gently."*

44

I forgot to tell you about the baritone bullfrogs who lived in our lily-pond. They croaked so loudly all night long that it would on occasion lead to one of our sleepless-night emergency family consultations. We had to discover how we could best get rid of the bullfrogs—no violence. Once and for all. These baritone bullfrogs were not Perry Como, they were Ezio Pinza. Our family being by nature creature-loving people, the first decision was to haul the bullfrogs out to the Hartebeespoort Dam and dump them into that happy hunting-ground. The second idea was to put them in Bob Quigley's swimming-pool.*

My son Bill came to the rescue of his family and the bullfrogs. Bill learned from our neighbour on the adjoining farm that you can put an end to a bullfrog's croaking at night without having to croak the bullfrog. All of us liked that.

Here's how it works. When you are ready to go to sleep, you approach the lily-pond, shine a flashlight in the bullfrogs' eyes, temporarily blinding them, then you gently tap the bullfrogs one after the other, on the top of the head and go back to sleep. Both you and the bullfrogs.

It's a chore, and must be done each night like putting out the cat. If you're lucky the bullfrogs will remain quiet for hours. Sometimes all night. I reminded Bill that with as many bullfrogs as we had, he would look like Lionel Hampton at the vibes before the job was finished.

Try it yourself if you're ever in bullfrog territory. It really works.

Bill overdid it the first night, he started out to the lily-pond with a five-iron. I told him it was the wrong club for a water hazard. I suggested a seven-iron, or maybe a sand-wedge. It's hard to tap gently even with a putter. It was Marguerite who said "Stop the

* This was the first of ten similar ideas Michael offered. All rejected.

nonsense." She settled it by offering us her yardstick. It was perfect. The bullfrogs greatly appreciated the change.

Seriously, it *does* work. But, remember, gently.

We had no electricity on the farm and used Coleman lamps with
gas mantles. For the first month, I would reach out for the wall
switch whenever I came into a dark room. I grew to appreciate
and prefer the soft rosy hue of the lamps. They looked so welcom-
ing through the windows when I drove through the pine-trees and
into the yard after a Fireside in town.

I still chuckle whenever I recall Marguerite calling out to Bill Jr.
when he was on general night duty:

"Turn down the lamps, set the alarm, put out the dog and the
cats, and hit the bullfrogs. Gently."

I wish you had come to visit us on the farm in those days. It was
pure, unalloyed pleasure. Everyone who came, and had the time
to stay was sooner or later beguiled by the surroundings and the
comforting feeling that they were "home". Not to mention the
fringe benefits of Marguerite's exciting Bahá'í classes and Florence's cooking.

If the visitors came for their entire holiday, they were in grave
danger of going home very nice persons. That's how the Bahá'í
Faith works. When you add the spirit of the Faith to all that scenic
beauty and catered food, the farm could become a bewitching
Lorelei of love. The two-part harmony of Andrew Mofokeng and
Florence Marumo on "Sala hantle, Ntate" didn't hurt.*

It was in that warm cheerful atmosphere that our first National
Spiritual Assembly was born on our farm, so you know it was a
place very special to us all. It belonged to Bahá'ís everywhere and
to posterity.

My son Bill suggested that we bottle the spirit and ship it to the
less fortunate parts of the world. All of us on the farm would say
fool things like that from time to time, but only because we were
caught up in happiness; and we were trying to think of some way to

---

* "Sala hantle, Ntate"—"Stay well, Father". Seeing the increasing crowds
that came to the farm, I offered to write new lyrics for Andrew and Florence. But
it's hard to rhyme "Stay well, father, mother, son, daughter, uncle, aunt, cousin,
great grandson and all you dear friends." Especially in Sesotho.

convey the wonder, joy and ecstasy of it all. We knew it was beyond us but we never stopped trying.

We shared the bounty of the farm with many of our long-time Bahá'í friends from many countries, as well as with many of our new local friends. The visitors came week after week, month after month, year after year. Their names are legion.

One of the dearest visitors to our farm, and one of the heroines of that great World Crusade, was Bahíyyih Ford Winckler. She is now one of the Counsellors for the entire Continent of Africa. Bahíyyih was blessed above all of us. She had seen 'Abdu'l-Bahá, the Beloved Master. She had met Him in the Holy Land when she was a child. Bahíyyih had heard Him tell stories in His own voice. Watched His face. Was bathed in His smiles. How she could hold our attention with her stories of 'Abdu'l-Bahá!

Bahíyyih would charm us with her tales about the Master, stories which she had heard from the lips of so many of the great early heroes and heroines of our Faith. Bahíyyih came from an illustrious Bahá'í family.

On a far more mundane plane, I can still hear Bahíyyih's excited voice on the telephone when the news of the arrival of imported canned goods from America reached Johannesburg. Bahíyyih's cue for the great explosion was her pet name for all of us:

"Weasels!"

Bedlam.

Bahíyyih served on the very first Local Spiritual Assembly in South Africa.* She was hostess at the Bahá'í Centre, always gracious, charming and a delight to be with. She attracted the friends like a magnet to that "Sacred Fold". Bahíyyih was a tower of strength for all of us in those hectic early days during which we served together with such radiant pleasure.

Bahíyyih was the very first of all the pioneers to South Africa during the World Crusade to hear the good news of her destination from the beloved Guardian's own lips. When Bahíyyih was on pilgrimage, the beloved Guardian told her that she should go to South Africa, to Johannesburg; and, as Bahíyyih so charmingly recounts it, "He, the beloved Guardian, almost identified the very street he wished us to reach."

* Since the 1930s

Bahíyyih was able to fulfil every hope of that historic pilgrimage. She still labours for the Faith she loves in that same richly-blessed part of the world.

One thing we did not have on the farm, was a knowledge of snakes. We knew there were no green or black mambas in our exact area, but we could have used a briefing on puff-adders and cobras, both the striking and spitting varieties. Those snakes were plentiful. Especially on a farm.

I was alone one Friday afternoon recovering from tick fever when I came face to face with my first large African snake.

It was a cobra.

Did you ever see a snake slither slowly toward you, stop, rise up knee high, open up a huge cobra hood, and begin swaying back and forth? Staring at you? You, a city-boy from Philadelphia?

Neither did I.

Until then.

It was my first cobra. I was as green as the hills of Killarney. I felt that someone should start playing control music on a flute and lure the snake back into his basket.

And it wasn't just *one* snake I faced. There were three of them. All cobras. I had to face them all. At one time. Side by side. Head on.

And *that* was not even the worst part of my day.

WITH SENTIMENT
MP
C# DIM

"*Mama don't want no cobra snakes in here!*"

45

We had two remarkable Ridgeback dogs on our farm. One was named Big Finnegan and the other Scotland Yard. No farm ever had better security guards.

The two Ridgebacks, father and son, worked as a team. We inherited them when we bought the farm. It was I who changed their names. I'd always wanted a dog named Scotland Yard, so in time of trouble I could holler: "Call the Yard!"

The two dogs slept on the porch outside our bedroom. At the least sound of trouble or intruders, they would begin their patrol, going around the entire inside fence of the farm in opposite directions, passing each other, and returning to the porch if all was well. If it was not, they chewed on, frightened off, or held in custody for the authorities, whomever they met, such as night prowlers. The size of the dogs, the deep ominous growls and savage barks, all showing long teeth, were usually warning enough to terrify and scatter all marauders.

Marguerite felt sorry for the "poor dear protectors of the innocent" because they had to sleep outside on the cold stone porch floor.

"Shame!" she said.

Obstinately, in the face of a three to one vote against, the dachshund, Cyrano, abstaining, Marguerite brought Big Finnegan and Scotland Yard inside our bedroom at night. She permitted them to sleep under our beds. I drew Big Finnegan. And I mean *Big* Finnegan. When he turned over, I did.

This happy arrangement came to an abrupt halt the night we really did have prowlers. The two Ridgebacks heard them and the warning ridge on their backs went up. Scotland Yard scuttled out from under Marguerite's bed and went head first through the lower panel of the screen door leaving a wide round tunnel not quite large enough for his son, Big Finnegan, to follow. He widened it.

Big Finnegan didn't scuttle. He just raised up under my bed and threw me flying through the air. I landed near the screen door. By then, Big Finnegan was long gone. Like Ray Guy of the Los Angeles Raiders, Big Finnegan got both height and distance on his kick. It was beautiful. His "hang time" on me must have been a full two seconds.

Marguerite and I have long debated how high I flew and how far I was flung. Marguerite usually won because it is very difficult for the victim to demonstrate a proper measurement when he has one arm in a sling.

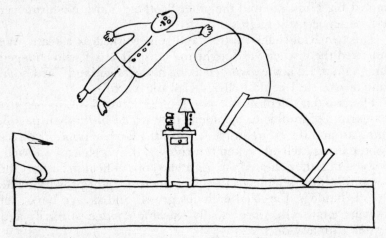

You probably guessed the end result. Scotland Yard and Big Finnegan slept outside from then on. The new lower panel of the screen door came out of Marguerite's household money.

I was in a jinx period as you can see. The cobras and puff-adders were only a small part of it. First, I came down with "Rocky Mountain Spotted Fever". No, I couldn't catch it when I was in the Rocky Mountains which I had crossed at least twenty times. I had to come to South Africa to come down with it. It was really plain old tick-fever, but my doctor who was a colourful character said, "It's what you Yanks call Rocky Mountain Spotted Fever."

It wasn't what this Yank called it.

I was working at the time on a book called *Release the Sun*.

It was an introduction to the early history of the Bahá'í Faith with an epilogue that showed in detail the relationship of the Bahá'í Faith to Christianity, including the most fascinating prophecies from both the *Old* and the *New Testament* fulfilled by Bahá'u'lláh's coming.

I mention it here because, with the kind and sacrificial help of the National Spiritual Assembly of India, we were able to publish the book and sell or give away some 50 000 copies; 16c for paperback and 28c for hard cover. (Eat your hearts and budgets out, present-day Publishing Trusts.)

I had five typists living with us, or visiting us: Marguerite, William, Doris Ballard, Andrew Mofokeng and Fred Schechter. I used everybody's library card and had thirty-six library reference books surrounding me on my single-size bed. The sound of all those typewriters going at one time, made it sound as though the farm was under attack by terrorist machine-gun fire.

Marguerite would pass through the bedroom with pieces of cotton-wool in her ears, look at me, and say:

"Don't think!"

"Why not?"

"We're all tired of typing. We're all going into town to a movie and a little R and R."

"Rest and Recreation?"

"No", she said, "Retreat and Run."

"From me?"

"You said it, I didn't."

To lighten the atmosphere, I said, "I thought R and R meant Return Rapidly."

I saw I was talking to an empty room.

I was feeling as low as a snake's belly in a wagon track before I found out it was just my swollen liver that was depressing me. I use the snake simile deliberately because that was the day I was introduced to my first three-headed cobra.

I mean it. Three heads. Each one closer to me than you are right now.

Suddenly the farm was strangely silent. All machines had stopped typing. My entire family and crew had gone into town as threatened.

I leaned back on my pillows, basking in the tranquil silence.

It was shattered when Franz, one of our African workers, knocked loudly on my bedroom door.

"Come in", I called.

He did. His eyes were huge circles of concern.

"Noga!" he cried. "Noga e kgolo!"

Snake. A big snake. Franz puffed out his cheeks trying to imitate a cobra opening his hood. He did it well enough to send a chill up my fevered back.

"Kgolo?" I asked.

He nodded, vigorously.

"How kgolo?"

Kgolo means big. *How* big depends on the intonation, the emphasis and the volume. Franz quickly demonstrated.

"Kgoooooolo!"

You could have put a small melon in his mouth.

I knew that all work on the farm would stop until the snake had been killed. Since I was the only one left on the farm except for the workers, I struggled out of bed, went to the locked closet, picked up the gun, and followed Franz out to the lair of the cobra.*

The gun was a .22 rifle purchased by my son William, who was very fair minded. He felt that since the cobra was sporting enough to stop, rise up in front of you, and open up his hood, thus greatly increasing the target area, it seemed only sporting for us to buy a rifle instead of a shotgun. People with that kind of reasoning, with luck, can live to be quite young.

By the time I reached the snake's hiding-place behind the oleander bushes, I discovered that my fever had risen during the night and now affected my eyesight. Everything was in double vision.

Franz tossed a stone at the snake. Slowly it turned, and slithered ominously toward us. It stopped in front of me, rose up, and spread its hood.

To myself, I whispered Franz's words: "Kgoooooolo!"

It was indeed.

I thought to myself, as I raised the .22, how peaceful and lovely it was at this time of the year back in Pennsylvania. I wondered what Anna Marie Honnold and all the dear friends were doing on such a nice sunny day in Swarthmore. Or the friends in Downington. Or any place but right there with the cobras.

Eventually, of course, I had to look down the sight of the rifle. Instead of one cobra, or even two cobras in double vision, there

---

* Bahá'ís do not carry weapons. This gun was kept in a locked closet only for the protection of the workers against poisonous snakes.

were now three cobra-heads in triple vision. How much was impaired vision and how much was fear, I cannot say. I can only say that all three cobras were much closer to me than I cared for.

All of this, of course, took place in a flash. I remembered my father telling me about the skills his friends had developed while fighting drunken Irish brawls in the better saloons of County Cork. The in-fighting wisdom he had learned from these encounters, he bragged, was tremendous.

"If you're so tipsy your opponent is facing you with three heads instead of one, and he's swaying dangerously in front of you, there's only one thing to do", my father said. He spit into his palm, drew back his fist, and showed me exactly what to do. "Hit the middle face, my bucko! Pow!"

I followed my father's advice, and shot the middle cobra. May the saints preserve us. I killed all three!

Hurray for the Irish!

I stumbled back towards my bed, swaying from side to side more dangerously than the cobra. I was barefooted and stepped on a broken bottle, gashing open the sole of my right foot. I staggered through the house leaving a bright trail of my lovely crimson blood.

I reached the bed too exhausted to look for the first aid kit, so I did the next best thing. I stuck my foot inside the white pillowcase. Drained of all energy, I collapsed on the bed. I reached my arm up behind me to open the window for a little fresh air. As I rested my hand on the window sill, I was bitten on the thumb by a passing spider.

It was venomous and hurt considerably. In no time, my thumb felt as thick as my wrist.

At that exact hilarious moment, Marguerite returned with her army of shoppers. They were all loaded down with large brown paper sacks containing delicious things: samoosas, raisin bread, apple turnovers, chocolate éclairs, peanuts and egg rolls—or so they said. Marguerite peered from behind her huge Thrupp's shopping bag and smiled cheerily.

"How are you doing?"

I tried to minimize it.

"I am", I told her, "in a losing streak."

Marguerite clucking sympathetically throughout, disinfected

and bandaged my wounded foot, and treated my spider bite.

She scoffed, "You're wrong. That thumb is not nearly as big as your wrist."

"Almost."

"It *is* nasty, but it's hardly any bigger than your nose."

"You have to leave a little room for poetry", I explained, sounding exactly like my grandfather who, on occasion, when the circumstances demanded it, would embroider a trifle in order to give a more accurate and useful picture through symbology, so that everybody could understand the situation better.

"Horsefeathers!" Marguerite replied.

It was then she caught sight of the blood-stained pillowcase into which I had shoved my wounded foot. I tried to distract her from the crimson laundry, I leaned back on my pillow and said, smiling:

"Is there anything you want while I'm down?"

"Yes," she said, "I want to be single again."

I thought it showed a very poor spirit.

46

You can't be this far along in the book without knowing that basically, underneath all her shenanigans, Marguerite loved people and had a special unique way of making new friends. And inviting them home. It had been that way in Salt Lake City, San Francisco, New York, Philadelphia, Palm Springs, Thousand Oaks—Don't worry, I'm not going to review all of our home cities. Although the same thing did happen at each one of them.

Suffice it to say that the visitors to our farm on Muldersdrift Road often came depressed and empty, but left contented and full. They usually carried away with them a big brown paper sack full of fruit, vegetables and baked goods. No one ever dreamed of "doggie bags" like those.

One day, Mother Bountiful gave away the last of my private stock of Billy-baked coconut macaroons. I had a standing order with Bill. The macaroons were much in demand, and if anyone got wind of my private cache—gone! But, that's what pioneering with Marguerite was like—you wound up being loving, generous and quite hungry. And very crafty about your personal possessions. Not only macaroons, but shirts, shoes and trousers.

It was not unique for me to look out the window and see my favourite multicoloured Hawaiian shirt sailing down the road, bananas, palm trees and surfers, without me in it.

"Operation Befriend", Zulu style, courtesy of Marguerite's free, Friday to Monday, flea-market.

Perhaps there is no better way to picture the beauty and wonder of that West Winds Farm than to describe for you a typical day in the script-writing life of a Radio humorist in South Africa, William Sears.

I was over the tick fever, the broken ribs, the coronary and the

Asian 'flu so I felt quite splendid, quite at the top of my form. I carried my card table and chair out onto our front lawn and tuned my portable radio to an FM classical station. I arranged my non-electric typewriter, shoved a carbon sandwich in the machine, and typed: "The Bill Sears Show". Then I went to sleep.

That was often the end of my afternoon's work.

I was surrounded by such serenity and beauty that I often caved in and napped for a few hours. In front of me were both red and white oleander trees, behind me a flame-coloured flamboyant tree, an eight-foot high poinsettia bush against a snow-white wall, bougainvillaea vines in three colours, a golden shower vine creeping along the patio roof and falling in a burnished gold waterfall effect over the side of the house. Along the border of the lawn, and in the nearby fields, I could see amaryllis, cosmos, iris, barberton daisies, and wild flowers growing in profusion.

The colour and backdrop to my work would vary with the time of the year. The two seasons I shall always remember and cherish the most in that sublime paradise of paradises happened first, during the height of the jacaranda season; and second, when Marguerite was standing in the middle of one hundred and ten rose bushes. Imagine my joy during those weeks when the two seasons overlapped.

Marguerite's roses were all blossoming in every hue and shape. She was pruning them to her heart's content. The huge hat she had purchased in Venice, "bargaining" for it from the end of our gondola, was shading and framing her happy face.

Marguerite loved roses, all roses: climbing tree, and plain bush. They blossomed profusely for her. I would sometimes stand, looking through the top half of the Dutch door, watching Marguerite among the buds and full blossoms, pruning shears in hand, rapture on her face. Next to enrolling a new Bahá'í, pruning the roses and giving huge multicoloured bouquets to our visitors was the best.

Naturally, I was happy. I had promised Marguerite way back in the summer we were married, when she didn't have even one rose-bush, that I would someday see to it that she would be surrounded, completely encircled, by her own blossoming roses. New husbands often make wild, irresponsible statements like that. For years, I presented her mostly with thorns and thistles. Now she was almost hidden behind a colourful tapestry of roses: red, white, magenta, orange, scarlet and pink.

My own choice of roses was moss roses until Marguerite taught me that my moss roses were petunias. Each year I would say, at planting time, pointing with a great sweeping gesture, "I want to see petunias as far as the eye can see!"

Marguerite obliged me for years. Until that fateful spring she bought me countless crates of potted petunias with several flowers in each pot. Marguerite told me to put them in the ground myself "as far as the eye could see". I did. And since that time, I have been more than content to receive a beautiful single plant or bouquet as a gift of love from the National Spiritual Assembly of South and West Africa upon my return home from Europe or America.

On those sunny afternoons on the Muldersdrift Road when I worked on my radio scripts on the lawn, Marguerite would always remember me with one of her rose blossoms. She would place one of her deep bronze roses, my favourite, on the top of my typewriter where she knew I'd find it when I woke up.

There I was sleeping, entranced, in the middle of my very own front yard. The lawn had already been cut by someone else. I was alert and ready to begin typing Monday's radio script as soon as I awakened. The entire yard was surrounded by blossoming jacaranda trees.

The two ridgeback dogs, Scotland Yard and Big Finnegan, were lying on each side of my table like book-ends. The two dachshunds, Cyrano and Heidi-Ho, were in the shade beneath my table. Each one had a long nose resting over the toe of a different one of my shoes. I dared not move, nor did I care to. I slumbered on, but one of the five Saturday afternoon lotus-eaters.

It is not surprising that one of our fellow-pioneers, Robert Quigley, would say, "Don't let them find out in America what it's like over here, or the prospective pioneers will empty out all forty-eight states, and ruin everything."

When I woke up, I looked at my script several times. The only words on the page were still: "The Bill Sears Show". Gathering all my strength, I leaned forward and underlined it:

"The <u>Bill</u> <u>Sears</u> <u>Show</u>"

It exhausted me.

It really marked the end of my afternoon of script writing. I leaned back and lost myself in the rapture and reverie of the sounds of birds, the bees, and Wolfgang Amadeus Mozart.

All understatements.

The heliotrope blue jacaranda blossoms were half on the trees, half on the ground. The trees still looked as though they were in full bloom. The other half of the blossoms were spreading themselves over our yard and weaving a magnificent Chinese carpet of that same magic blue. The carpet came almost up to the edge of my table. Like gently falling snow-flakes, every now and then a beautiful blue blossom would drop upon me or my table.

With blue skies above and blue blossoms below, I seemed to be floating in azure space. A soft breeze warmed my cheeks accompanied by the wispy scent of roses from Marguerite's garden. I was enraptured and transported to another world. When the breeze died down, the rose fragrance faded, but others equally enchanting took its place.

A courageous hoopoe bird landed on my carpet not far from the table. He ignored all four dogs, and drove his beak into the soft Kelly-green lawn in search of one of our fat, well-fed angleworms. The hoopoe's American Indian Chief head-dress rose up alarmingly along the back of his neck and head whenever one of the dogs growled. It slowly subsided when the dog moaned softly and went back to sleep. It was Big Finnegan. He, too, was dreaming like the rest of us. The hoopoe bird need not have worried. I looked down at Scotland Yard. His eyes were closed.

The only sound besides the gentle contented murmur of my own breathing, and the varied pitch of the soft assorted snores coming from the four sleeping dogs, was the cooing of the mourning doves who, like all the rest of us, were madly in love with the trees, the flowers, and the lazy South African summer afternoon.

My portable radio was now softly playing *The Dying Swan*.

My own peace and serenity, coupled with the lack of vigorous action I was displaying as a former gung-ho pioneer, can best be depicted by my faithful friend, the ridgeback Scotland Yard. I looked down upon his gently sleeping figure. His pink tongue was peeking out between his teeth. His eyes were closed, his jaw flat on the green grass. A blue jacaranda blossom floated down and landed on the end of his nose without disturbing him or waking him.

Marguerite broke the spell of my reverie. She called out through the open half of the Dutch door.

"How's the script coming along?"

Reluctantly I returned from that enchanted land of bliss. I came back to this material world, over-priced at a farthing.

"Fine!" I told her, pointing to the stack of untouched paper on the table. "You won't believe it, but I have already finished typing 'The Bill Sears Show'."

Was it a lie? Really?

Both Marguerite and I knew exactly how active I had been. The blue jacaranda blossom was still on the end of Scotland Yard's nose, and others had fallen promiscuously all across my card table, my typewriter, and my shoulders, giving me away completely.

"It's my blue period", I told Marguerite.

"Marvellous," she said, her tone letting me know she was "on to me". "You and Gainsborough can read the script to me later."

"Fine!"

To Michael, who was standing in the doorway beside her, Marguerite said lovingly, with a pleasing sigh, pointing at me, Scotland Yard, Big Finnegan, Heidi-Ho, Cyrano, the hoopoe bird and the blanket of jacaranda blossoms:

"One of our more active South African Bahá'í groups."

47

Marguerite's words were prophetic. We became a very active group.

It was already past eleven o'clock, the time foretold by Marguerite for a delightful tea with pound cake and chocolate chip cookies. We called it "elevenses" and so did most of Southern Africa.

The sun had become so hot that our "active Bahá'í group" decided to move to the shade of the patio and really settle down to work. I brought the FM radio with me and fortuitously tuned in on Tchaikovsky's *Pathétique* to follow *Swan Lake*.

My reference material was already on the patio. I kept it in the special little three-sided red brick shelter Bill had built for me to protect my scripts and books from sudden rain, and so I wouldn't always be chasing back into the house for them.

As I began typing, I kept hearing a "hiss! hiss!". I didn't think the script was that bad and looked around to find the critic. I could see no one, but the sound continued. I was about to reach for some carbon paper when a shadow crossed my peripheral vision. I looked at the book shelter, and inside, on top of my reference books, was a cheeky baby ringhals, a South African spitting cobra. He was eyeing me and swaying back and forth.

Talk about the *Raiders of the Lost Ark*, *Indiana Jones and the Temple of Doom*, or even *Adam and Eve*, this junior edition of death had his hood spread as wide as he could make it. I had been told that these "spitting cobras" are accurate up to a quite surprising distance, and go for the eyes. They can nail you with the accuracy of Gabby Hayes hitting a brass spittoon in the Red Dog Saloon in Dodge City. Bill told me that. Michael agreed, but replaced Gabby Hayes with Chester from *Gun Smoke*.

My first inclination was to laugh at the puny size of the little cobra.

My second inclination was to spit right back in his eye because he was sitting upon the very reference book I needed. However, I could do neither of these fearless things. By that time I was already inside the house, slamming closed the bottom half of the Dutch door behind me.

Bill said later that my "help!" had startled the mourning doves out of the tamarisk trees down where he had been hoeing between two rows of carrots. Marguerite, Michael, Florence and Andrew all agreed that I had made some fierce crowd-assembling noises, and they had assembled.

The baby cobra was still there in my private cupola bravely defending his "territorial imperative". We couldn't find the key to the gun closet, so I suggested driving the little snake out with a long stick.

"Not me", I suggested to Bill. "You."

"How *long* a stick?" he asked, wisely.

Marguerite finally found the key, but Bill refused to shoot such a small snake, especially one trapped helplessly the way he was inside a brick box.

"This snake", Bill said, "is not kgolo at all. It's dinky."

"But", I reminded him, "deadly."

Michael agreed with William.

"The baby snake", he said, "is perfectly innocent. He was just going about his normal snake's business."

"Hissing and spitting?" I asked, "And blinding people?"

Michael was in the minority on a vote of four to two, but Bill was on Mike's side, and wouldn't budge on his refusal to shoot the cobra.

"It's like shooting fish in a rain barrel", Bill objected. "He's so tiny that if he were a fish, we'd have to throw him back into the water." Bill grinned at me. "*You*, not me."

We decided to drive the snake out with a few pebbles. Bill and I tossed the small stones at the baby cobra, deliberately missing until we forced him to slither off into the garden.

We didn't chase him.

We both decided to let the little fellow return home to his parents. Bill was particularly pleased.

"As a teenager myself," he pointed out, "I'm always happy to see a juvenile delinquent given another chance."

That was the end of a typical idyllic day in the life of a radio-script-writing humorist. You can easily see why I have developed such a rare and fine sense of humour.

I went back to my typewriter and underlined the first page of the script for a second time: <u>The</u> <u>Bill</u> <u>Sears</u> <u>Show</u>.

There was no hurry. I tuned the FM Station to Alfredo Campoli and his fiddle. They were half way through Rondo Capriccioso, Opus 28, by Saint-Saëns, coming up to the part I liked best.

I leaned back to enjoy myself when Marguerite called:

"Tea's ready!"

"With pound cake?"

"Of course."

"And chocolate chip cookies?"

"Plus cherry tarts."

"Why didn't you say so?" I said. "First things first."

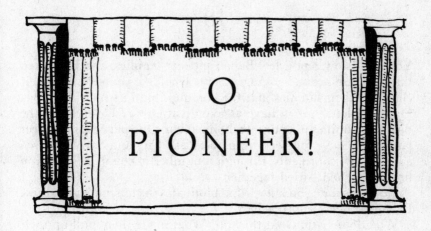

O
PIONEER!

The Catbird's Seat

48

You have now met a few Bahá'í pioneer families, and have seen that they are normal average people who, like yourself, love their children, their families and the communities in which they live. Quite obviously, they have as many varieties of life-styles as the different families in your own home town. One particular pioneer family you have followed from Salt Lake City and San Francisco across a few continents, through a number of countries until you finally reached Africa together.

Now, it is time you knew what motivates the inner life of all these Bahá'í pioneers and teachers.

Why do they do what they do? What made them pull up their roots and leave their former homes where they lived in relative comfort, peace and security? What prompted them to travel to a far-off land where they didn't know a soul, and had no idea what the future might hold for them?

What makes them so eager to pioneer in the first place? Why are they so enthusiastic? So willing? So fervent?

The following chapters of "O Pioneer!" are designed to answer all these questions and to make your new neighbour and his or her motives clear and understandable.

The most important meaning of the word pioneer in the dictionary is "one who prepares the way for others".

The Bahá'í pioneers are doing exactly that. In addition to being a good neighbour and a good friend, they are "preparing the way" so that every person on earth, in every part of the planet, can have his or her chance to enter into that highly praised and precious Kingdom of God on earth promised by Christ in His Lord's Prayer.

The Writings of the Bahá'í Faith say clearly that those Words of

Christ are not *only* a prayer, but also a prophecy. Bahá'u'lláh has appeared in the world to make every one of those Words of Christ come true.

The names of such great explorers as Marco Polo, Ferdinand Magellan, Balboa, Columbus, Jacques Cartier, Father Hennepin, Lewis and Clark and countless others, as wonderful as the stories of their lives may be, are dust compared to the names of these simple heroic Bahá'í men, women, and children, these modern-day spiritual pioneers, we have been telling you about.

For nearly a century and a half, right down to this very hour and day, these heroes and heroines have been laying the foundation for a far greater Kingdom than any ever discovered or dreamed about by those great world-explorers of the past.

Bahá'í pioneers are penetrating into far more remote regions. They are travelling throughout a much more vast area of the world. They have left their homelands in far greater numbers than the famous historical explorers, adventurers and conquerors of old.

These Bahá'í pioneers, these new neighbours of yours, are laying the foundation for a greater Kingdom than any kingdom ever conceived by the mind of man. It is so great, so vast, and so wonderful that it boggles the mind even to contemplate it. It is not a man-made kingdom, but a Kingdom foretold by the sacred Word of God in the Scriptures of the past. It has come at last!

Most exciting of all, this Kingdom is already being built in every part of the planet. It is no longer a hoped-for dream. It is a reality. It is being raised up before your very eyes, as promised in those holy Books of past ages.

Who wouldn't want to be a part of it?

It is a Kingdom of vital importance to the welfare of all mankind. Now and in the future. This Kingdom will eventually cover the entire surface of the planet from pole to pole.

This planetary Kingdom is not being established or maintained by force, but by love. It is being raised up by the voluntary wishes of the hearts of those who hear about it and are eager to arise and help build it. Perhaps even you, yourself, may become one of these world-healing heroes and heroines of God.

Can you think of any explorer or discoverer of the past, no matter how famous or renowned, who could even come close to achieving such a world-transforming goal, or who could have hoped to raise up such an imperishable Kingdom? On a planetary scale?

It is the wondrous Christ-promised Kingdom of God on earth we are talking about. A *spiritual* Kingdom. The Kingdom that makes every other part of life function properly. It is a Kingdom that will reflect on earth the qualities and virtues of the Kingdom of God in heaven.

Christ said so Himself:

> "Thy Kingdom come, Thy will be done
> on earth as it is in heaven."

The Writings of the Bahá'í Faith say plainly that these marvellous words of Christ are not *only* a prayer, but also a prophecy. Bahá'u'lláh has appeared in the world, and has sent out into every corner of the planet His spiritual Army, those pioneers and teachers, in order to make every one of these Words of Christ come true.

It is not some vague, ambiguous, longed-for-but-never-really-expected Kingdom. It is a real Kingdom. Better still, it is already being established in microcosm and is rapidly sweeping the face of the earth toward that macrocosm of love and unity envisioned by all the great Religions, the complete fulfilment of which will come in that far-off slowly approaching Golden Age of the human race.

I know that the eyes of men and women alive today never really believed they would live to see this Kingdom. Above all, they never expected that it would actually begin to take place in their own city or neighbourhood in their own day. Now. Today. Right where they are living at this moment.

Look out your window.*

But that is exactly what is happening. The very earliest beginnings of this universally foretold Kingdom of God are already taking place in your own part of the world. Don't be puzzled or distressed by hearing such incredible news. Be thrilled! It is really happening. To you.

If any one thing is clear in Scripture, it is that. In fact, Scripture even foretells the hesitant and doubtful attitude you yourself may be undergoing right now; now that you have heard about this Kingdom.

* Small joke. Sorry about that. All the rest of it is true.

The peoples of the world in general will be doubtful and negative about this remarkable story when they hear the news. That, too, is Scripture. So you see, the sceptical way you may feel right now is not a bad thing. It's a good thing. You *should* feel that way. The story couldn't be true if you didn't feel that way. Perhaps you will be one of those lucky ones it awakens. Most people, including many of your own friends, won't believe it is happening when they hear about it. Even when they are given proof that it is taking place. Right before their very eyes!

Scripture.

Aren't you lucky to be sitting in "the catbird's seat"? So you can know the truth about it? And don't have to depend upon your friends or family, but can decide for yourself?

This section, "O Pioneer!", next to "The Sun and the Mirrors", is the most significant and important part of this book *All Flags Flying!*

It brings to life and to light the still relatively unknown truth about this Scriptural "great work" that is being carried out today by these pioneers and teachers of the Bahá'í Faith. They have been doing this same "great work" for almost a century and a half.

You are in on the ground floor (how amusing, and how tragic, after nearly one hundred and fifty years!) as our story illumines, in a fresh and clear manner, the close and intimate ties that bind together CHRISTIANITY and the BAHÁ'Í FAITH. Even more meaningful, the tender love and oneness that exist between Christ, the *Son*, and Bahá'u'lláh, the *Father*. This love unites them for all eternity, as together They bring to this sad and disillusioned world the actual beginning of that long-awaited Kingdom of God on earth.*

Hallelujah.

---

* See Chapter 54, "Move over Marco Polo!" in this section "O Pioneer!"

"As the waters cover the sea"

49

This is the shortest chapter of "O Pioneer!", but one of the most significant. It offers confirmation from Scripture which should be comforting to a sincere seeker at this point. You can read the full story in voluminous detail in the book *Thief in the Night*.*

You will see why these Bahá'í pioneers feel so strongly that they are indeed carrying out the "great work" foretold in Scripture, even in the midst of today's sceptical unbelieving world—exactly as foretold.

For example:

ISAIAH

"Therefore, behold, I will proceed to do a marvellous work among this people, even a marvellous
work and a wonder: for the wisdom of their wise
men shall perish, and the understanding of their
prudent men shall be hid."   Isaiah 29:14

That "great work" will happen, Isaiah promises "in that day" when at last the "deaf" will hear and the "blind" will see and the pure of heart will be delivered.

HABAKKUK

"Behold . . . and regard, and wonder marvellously: for I will work a work in your days,
which ye will not believe, though it be told you."
                                    Habakkuk 1:5

Habakkuk goes on to promise that this "great work" and "wonder" will take place at "the time of the end" in the day when "the

*See *Thief in the Night*, George Ronald (1961), pp. 107–77.

knowledge of the glory of the Lord" shall cover the earth "as the waters cover the sea."

Every Bahá'í pioneer knows that the *glory of the Lord* is one of the meanings of Bahá'u'lláh's Name when it is translated into English. Of course, it sets the hearts of the pioneers on fire. Although it is but one of a thousand things about Bahá'u'lláh's life that do.

St Paul

> "Behold, ye despisers, and wonder, and per-
> ish: for I work a work in your days, a work
> which ye shall in no wise believe, though a
> man declare it unto you."   Acts 13:41

St Paul in the preceding verse warns: "Beware therefore, lest that come upon you, which is spoken of in the prophets".

Is that "man" or woman at this very hour "declaring" that wondrous "work" and truth to the people of your city or town?

Yes, all of this is happening right now as you read these words. The wondrous story is being told to mankind once again by God's *Mirror*, Messenger, for today, in your own home town. The "great work" is being unveiled before your eyes by Bahá'u'lláh's pioneers and teachers so that you, too, may have your chance.

The building of this living Kingdom is already on the way! The early stages of this Christ-promised *Kingdom of God on earth* have become a reality in more than one hundred thousand centres in all parts of the world.*

Above all, you should be thrilled, not withdrawn, because the name Bahá'í may seem strange to some of you at first when those Bahá'í pioneers arrive. The name Christ was just as strange to the Greeks and Romans.

That "new name" for God's religion in these "last days" was foretold in both Revelation (3:12) in the New Testament, and in Isaiah (62:2) in the Old Testament. Instead of dampening your ardour, that "new name" Bahá'í (Glory) should set you on fire with an eagerness to hear more, for the name was chosen by God in His Scriptures.

---

* So rapidly is the *Kingdom* spreading through the valiant efforts of the gallant Bahá'í pioneers and teachers that any statistics given about its growth today are obselete tomorrow.

No one has mentioned the name of Bahá'u'lláh, the Glory of God, or "the glory of the Lord" more often than Isaiah. Bahá'u'lláh Himself has said:

> "I am the One whom the tongue of
> Isaiah hath extolled, . . ."

The "Great Work"

50

This is the longest chapter of "O Pioneer!", but I promise you there will not be another.

As I reach the twilight of my years, I feel strongly that the time has passed when I can merely "entertain" and amuse those for whom I write. I dearly long to do just that exclusively, but I feel that the time has come for me to attempt the impossible: To blend together entertainment and Religion. I hope to do it, as the Irish say, with "three laughs and a tear".

This is the "tear".

You will understand why when you have read it. Though in a more serious vein, it is entirely germane to our story of the Bahá'í pioneers and teachers. In fact, it *is* their story: lock, stock and barrel.

Having heard those words from Scripture quoting Isaiah, Habakkuk and St Paul, there remains one vital question to answer. Has the Bahá'í Faith "told" the world about this "great work"? The "work" about which mankind should "wonder marvellously"?

I mean *really* told them?

These Bahá'í pioneers and teachers have covered the surface of the earth carrying the good news of the coming of Bahá'u'lláh, the Messenger, *Mirror*, of God for today with His Message of love and unity, His Plan for the rescue and revival of this sad, bewildered and disillusioned world.

Let us first consider how widespread that "work" has been as we look into the life of the Herald of the Bahá'í Faith, Whose Name means the "Door" or the "Gate".

THE BÁB

His dramatic and thrilling story has been told elsewhere. Here we briefly touch upon some of those events associated with His Ministry that trumpeted His fame to the world.

The Báb directed Messages to the Kings and Rulers of His Day. In His own country, Persia, He wrote a Message of guidance to every religious leader in each city, explaining why they had failed to be aware of the greatness of the hour.

From the outset, the events associated with the Báb were of an international character. The failed attempt to martyr Him with a volley of seven hundred and fifty muskets has been described by a Western author as "a veritable miracle".

What a wonderful, wide-screen, colour film this story would make with all its drama, pathos and heroism. Ten thousand eye-witnesses packed into that Public Square in Tabríz, or sat along the adjoining roof-tops, the better to see this wondrous Figure Who had so magnetized the countryside.

It was yet another Christian scholar and government official who described this remarkable event as "unique in the annals of humanity".

A famous British writer spoke of the Báb, calling His story that of a "true God-man".

The Báb was depicted in France as "The finest product of his country".

A British clergyman, a distinguished divine, described this Faith as the "most important religious movement since the foundation of Christianity".

A far-famed Oxford scholar portrayed the Báb as that "Jesus of the age . . . a prophet, and more than a prophet".

Another account of those dramatic days declares: "Many persons from all parts of the world set out for Persia and began to investigate wholeheartedly the matter."

According to a contemporary chronicler, the Czar of Russia had, even before the Báb's martyrdom, "instructed the Russian Consul in Tabríz to fully inquire into, and report the circumstances of so startling a Movement."*

The renown of the Báb, it has been reported, captured the attention of Western Europe where a profound interest "was kindled, and spread with great rapidity to literary, artistic, diplomatic and intellectual circles."

The French Publicist mentioned earlier, writes: "All Europe was stirred to pity and indignation . . . Among the littérateurs of

---

* This commission could not be carried out in view of the Báb's execution.

my generation, in the Paris of 1890, the martyrdom of the Báb was still as fresh a topic as had been the first news of His death. We wrote poems about Him."

The famous French actress, Sarah Bernhardt, entreated the popular playwright, Catulle Mendès for a play on the theme of this historic tragedy so she might star in it.

A Russian poetess, a member of the Philosophic, Oriental and Bibliological societies of St Petersburg, published in 1903 a drama entitled *The Báb*, which a year later was played in one of the principal theatres of St Petersburg.

The drama was subsequently given publicity in London, was translated into French in Paris, and into German by the well-known German poet Fiedler. The play was presented soon after the Russian Revolution in the Folk Theatre in Leningrad.

On and on go the touching stories of the effect of the life of this youthful Prophet of Shíráz, the Báb, upon society. It has been said that this portrayal of the Báb "succeeded in arousing the genuine sympathy and interest of the renowned Tolstoy, whose eulogy of the poem was later published in the Russian press."

Tolstoy was later to write of the Báb's Successor, Bahá'u'lláh, that through His Teachings, the world was now presented "with the highest and purest form of religious teaching."

No messenger of God ever made such an immediate appeal to the human race over such a wide-scale part of the planet in such an incredibly short time as the Báb.

It is fascinating to see that the great preponderance of all the above tributes, and international publicity, given to the Báb, came from Christians who were members of Catholic, Protestant, and Greek Orthodox congregations. It was an Armenian Christian soldier, Sam Khán, who refused to execute the Báb and marched his Christian regiment out of the Public Square in Tabríz.

How odd that any Christian, or member of any Christian denomination would ever say: "Why haven't I heard of this Faith before? If it is so important?"

Unless, of course, they were numbered among those who would not "believe" the great "work" and "wonder" even when it was being "told" to them; and were "sleeping" as Christ had warned they might be.

Quite obviously it is not possible for us to go into detail on this wondrous story, and cite the tidal wave of world-wide publicity that was given to Bahá'u'lláh, the Founder of the Bahá'í Faith, and to His Successor and Son, 'Abdu'l-Bahá, Who twice visited Europe, and for eight months travelled from coast to coast in the United States and Canada proclaiming the "great work" and the truth of His Father's Mission to the world.*

From now to the end of this chapter, we shall merely cite a few of the highlights that demonstrate beyond any doubt that indeed the "great work" has been told again in our day, to all mankind, in abounding profusion.

BAHÁ'U'LLÁH

Bahá'u'lláh wrote over one hundred volumes. He directed His appeal to the supreme leaders of men. Not once, but twice. He wrote special Messages to the Kings, the Rulers of mankind, the Heads of State, and to those leaders in whose hands was held the complete fate and destiny of their peoples. Bahá'u'lláh wrote to Kings and Emperors in both the East and the West.

He addressed Messages to Ministers of State, to Legislators in every land, to Ecclesiastics of divers denominations, and to the leaders of intellectual and political thought.

Bahá'u'lláh, the Supreme Redeemer of men for this age, remembered every level of human society in His Writings. He addressed Messages to literary circles, mystical circles, tradesmen, scholars, and to the masses of mankind.†

Never since the beginning of time has any religion been so openly proclaimed across the face of the entire earth.

Christ had promised that the day would come when He would

* For a detailed account of how widespread and unprecedented the news of the spread of the Bahá'í Faith was, see: *As the Waters Cover the Sea,* same author (to appear). It tells among other things how the State of California would be worthy to raise the "first flag" of Universal Peace, long before the Charter was written and the United Nations flag given birth in San Francisco. And how New York, called the "City of the Covenant" of Bahá'u'lláh, would later become the International Headquarters for this same United Nations. These are among the least of the wonders to be shared, as these pioneers and teachers raise up the earliest beginnings of the Christ-promised Kingdom of God on earth in every part of this world of ours.

† See *The Proclamation of Bahá'u'lláh,* Bahá'í World Centre (Haifa, 1967), which includes the actual words of Bahá'u'lláh in the most important of those Messages to the Leaders of men, as well as to the peoples of the world.

no longer speak in parables, but would show them openly of the *Father*. Jesus foretold that these things which had been "spoken . . . in closets" would now be "proclaimed upon the house-tops".

Bahá'u'lláh fulfilled that prophecy of Christ.

Bahá'u'lláh also fulfilled prophecy after prophecy as He Himself proclaimed the "great work". Under the most difficult of circumstances, attended by extreme suffering, Bahá'u'lláh was exiled like Abraham; He was stoned like Moses; He was scourged like Christ. He, Bahá'u'lláh, was twice stoned, three times imprisoned, four times exiled, and persecuted "from city to city" as envisioned by Christ, until He came at last to the Holy Land, the site foretold for Him since the beginning of time. He reached at last that "snow-white Spot", the "nest of all the Prophets" where now is located the World Centre of His Faith; and from where His world-redeeming Faith, the *Christ-promised Kingdom of God on earth*, is being raised up in every corner of the planet.

'ABDU'L-BAHÁ

His Son, 'Abdu'l-Bahá, travelled to North America in 1912. He proclaimed His Father's Faith in schools, universities, churches, synagogues, and among the poor and underprivileged as well as among the rich and famous, and the leaders of men: Presidents, Senators, Legislators, Mayors, Scientists and Scholars.

Written records of these events have been preserved for posterity, and have filled several volumes.*

'Abdu'l-Bahá, during His journeys to the West, warned the world of the inevitable coming of the First World War. Following the failure of mankind to establish a lasting peace, 'Abdu'l-Bahá foretold the coming of the second more terrible war. He foretold the horrible persecution of the Jews that would take place on European soil. He warned mankind against the awesome force that existed in the earth, a "force" mentioned even earlier by His Father, Bahá'u'lláh. It was, 'Abdu'l-Bahá warned, a force that could poison the atmosphere and cause the burning and destruction of the cities of the earth. The strongest of these warnings was delivered in Paris to an Ambassador of Japan, Viscount Arawaka,

---

* See *God Passes By*, *'Abdu'l-Bahá*, *The Flame*, *Two Hundred and Thirty-Nine Days*, *Memories of 'Abdu'l-Bahá*, plus many others. Any Bahá'í pioneer or teacher would be delighted to share them with you.

in whose country the first atomic bomb was to be exploded in that more terrible war yet to come.

'Abdu'l-Bahá said:

> "Scientific discoveries have increased material
> civilization. There is in existence a stupendous force,
> as yet, happily, undiscovered by man. Let us
> supplicate God, the Beloved, that this force be not
> discovered by science until spiritual civilization
> shall dominate the human mind. In the hands of
> men of lower material nature, this power would
> be able to destroy the whole earth."

'Abdu'l-Bahá, as His Father, Bahá'u'lláh, before Him, entreated the leaders of men to be aware of the day in which they were living. He reminded them that the One promised to them in all the past Scriptures had appeared at last—the "Spirit of Truth" that would lead them to all truth. They should turn to Him, Bahá'u'lláh, for guidance.

The "wondrous work" was being proclaimed to all mankind, for all to hear. In both Europe and North America, 'Abdu'l-Bahá met people from both the highest and the lowest walks of life.

No one was neglected. An account of those days reports:

> "Every day, all day long, a constant stream, an
> interminable procession! Ministers and missionaries,
> oriental scholars and occult students, practical men
> of affairs and mystics, Anglicans, Catholics, and Non-
> conformists, Theosophists and Hindus, Christian
> Scientists and doctors of medicine, Muslims, Buddh-
> ists, and Zoroastrians. There also called: politicians,
> Salvation Army soldiers, and other workers for human
> good, women suffragists, journalists, writers, poets and
> healers, dressmakers and great ladies, artists and arti-
> sans, poor workless people and prosperous merchants,
> members of the dramatic and musical world, these all
> came, and none were too lowly, nor too great, to
> receive . . . sympathetic consideration . . ."

Since those days, the Bahá'í Faith has been proclaimed by the press, radio and television. There are now well over one hundred thousand Bahá'í Centres in all parts of the world, all telling the wondrous story and carrying on the "great work". There are thousands and thousands of Bahá'í Local Spiritual Assemblies representing the cities, towns, villages and reserves of the world in more than three hundred countries, territories and islands of the seven seas doing the same "great work".

In Israel, the Holy Land, there has already been established an International Body, the Universal House of Justice, dedicated to the peace, prosperity and happiness of all the peoples of the planet. *All!* Without exception.

An International Teaching Centre has been raised up there, and it is linked in every continent to a special body of Bahá'í Counsellors, so that no one on earth shall not hear and not be moved by the "Glad Tidings" of Bahá'u'lláh.

The Bahá'í Faith has launched and completed two Seven Year Plans of teaching, followed by a Ten Year Plan, a Nine Year Plan, a Five Year Plan and Bahá'í pioneers and teachers are now engaged in a third Seven Year Plan which will soon come to an end, and be followed by yet other Plans.

During the course of these various Teaching Plans designed to achieve the spiritual conquest of the planet on behalf of the Kingdom of God, there have been more than twenty-five Intercontinental, International, Oceanic, and Continental Bahá'í Conferences held in all parts of the world.

A downpour of National and Regional Conferences followed in their wake. Far too many to mention. International, National and Regional Youth Conferences added greatly to the total. In each case, these gala events were surrounded by coverage in the various media: press, radio, television, magazines.

Five World Conventions have been held in the Holy Land, at the World Centre of the Bahá'í Faith, for the purpose of electing the Supreme Administrative and Ruling Body of the Bahá'í Faith. Hundreds and hundreds of elected Delegates from almost every corner of the earth, and from the five races of mankind, participated.

Each World Convention received international publicity, plus a far greater flood of attention in each of the participating countries and Regions. Both before and after these World Conventions. Those Bahá'ís who attended either the World Conventions, or the many other International, Continental, and Oceanic gatherings, visited city after city both going and coming so they might spread the glad tidings of the appearance of Bahá'u'lláh and His Message of love and unity.

As I examine these pages, I feel ashamed that I have so unskilfully unrolled the scroll of this world-transforming story. Everything I mention leaves ten greater stories untold. Perhaps the unsung song might be the very one that would appeal most to you. I planned to end this chapter on this page, but I feel compelled to add one additional item. It is so beautiful, moving, one might even say, world-shaking.

How could I close without mentioning the United Nations? The Bahá'í Faith has an International Bahá'í Community with offices at the United Nations Headquarters in New York. It has consultative status as one of the non-governmental organizations associated with UNESCO. Among all the organizations around the world, none has been more supportive and helpful than the Bahá'í Faith with the various United Nations promotions: United Nations Day, Human Rights Day, Universal Children's Day. On their own, the Bahá'ís have launched World Religion Day, Race Unity Day, and World Peace Day with others joining in.

And even all this is still the least of the wonders.

Bahá'u'lláh Himself, addressing the leaders of men, declared:

> "The Great Being, wishing to reveal the prerequisites of the peace and tranquillity of the world and the advancement of its peoples, hath written: The time must come when the imperative necessity for the holding of a vast, an all-embracing assemblage of men will be universally realized. The rulers and kings of the earth must needs attend it, and, participating in its deliberations, must consider such ways and means as will lay the foundations of the world's Great Peace amongst men."

Unwittingly, blissfully unaware of their God-directed Source, and impelled by the unifying forces of life which Bahá'u'lláh had released into the world as part of this rising *Kingdom of God on earth*, mankind twice tried to respond to that Call.

First, they raised up the League of Nations. Now, in this day, the *United Nations*.

Ignorant of the Winds of God that were driving them on to their destiny, the leaders of men, battered by two world wars, gathered at San Francisco where the Charter and Flag of the United Nations were born. Read the Charter, then compare it with the Teachings of Bahá'u'lláh, and you will suspect Him of having ghost-written the document.

Nearly half a century earlier, the Successor of Bahá'u'lláh, 'Abdu'l-Bahá, while in the shadow of San Francisco at the capital city of California, declared that State worthy to raise the first flag of international Peace.

It happened. The blue and white interlinked Flag of the United Nations was born there, and the Charter itself written.

While in New York City in 1912, 'Abdu'l-Bahá designated that city "the City of the Covenant" of Bahá'u'lláh. It was the Covenant that was destined to establish the unity of all nations, races, religions and peoples. This all took place in New York City where the world Headquarters of the United Nations was later to be established.

Bahá'u'lláh had already written special Messages to the leaders of four of those countries who were years later to become four of the five nations who made up the permanent members of the Security Council of that same United Nations: Great Britain, Russia, France and the United States. Bahá'u'lláh gave those leaders the guidance and vision needed for the future welfare of all mankind. They were all deaf and blind, as foretold.

How astonishing! How wonderful! How tragic. That the "great work" and "wonder" was still not "believed" even when it was being "told" to the world in such a dramatic, planetary fashion.

Following the First World War, 'Abdu'l-Bahá replied to a message from the Executive Committee of the Hague Peace Conference. 'Abdu'l-Bahá despatched a special delegation to bring His Document to them. It pointed out the needs of the time and how mankind had failed to live up to the Teachings for Peace which Bahá'u'lláh had given to the leaders of men so long ago. 'Abdu'l-Bahá repeated the urgent need for a World Body for the peace and welfare of mankind. He even labelled it a "Union of Nations".

My proof-reader, Marguerite, at this point put her foot down. She said that I had far exceeded the time allotted to me for the "great work". So, I shall stop here. Besides, every door I throw open uncovers even more astonishing wonders. This is true of every facet of the Bahá'í Faith, as your own study will reveal.

There is no escaping the Kingdom of God. The Writings of the Bahá'í Faith say to each and every one of its believers:

> "Strive that your high ideals may be
> realized in the Kingdom of God on earth,
> as they will be in Heaven."

Christ said:

> ". . . there is nothing covered, that
> shall not be revealed; neither hid, that
> shall not be known." Luke 12:2

Bahá'u'lláh said:

> "Never since the beginning of the
> world hath the Message been so
> openly proclaimed."

And again:

> "We, verily, have not fallen short of
> Our duty to exhort men, and to deliver
> that whereunto I was bidden by God,
> the Almighty, the All-Praised."

And finally:

> "Is there any excuse left for anyone
> in this Revelation? No, by God, the Lord
> of the Mighty Throne! My signs have
> encompassed the earth, and My power
> enveloped all mankind."

I rest my case.

Now, if any Christian, or seeker from any other denomination or Religion, should say to you: "If this Faith is so significant and so important to the world, why haven't I heard about it before?", you know exactly where to place the blame.

You might even quote Habakkuk once again:

> "Behold . . . and regard, and wonder
> marvellously: for I will work a work in

your days, which ye will not believe,
though it be told you." Habakkuk 1:5

And add the Words of Christ:

"Take ye heed, watch and pray: for ye
know nôt when the time is . . . Watch
ye therefore . . Lest coming suddenly
he find you sleeping. And what I say
unto you, I say unto all, Watch."

Mark 13:33–7

℞ : Formula for Success

51

We can now return with a new and perhaps more compassionate understanding to our underlying theme: The individual and personal lives of our new neighbours, those Bahá'í Pioneers and Teachers, who are struggling every day to lead an exemplary life of service and fellowship. Only in this way can they demonstrate that Bahá'u'lláh had not come in vain, but that He has indeed already transformed the lives of those He depends upon to raise up this better world, this *Kingdom of God on earth*.

No one promised them a rose-garden, as the song says. Or, if they did, they forgot to mention the thorns which all Bahá'ís are busily engaged in pulling out of their slowly improving lives.

You can't help liking them though, can you? For trying. And for making it the paramount purpose in life: To become a better person, a finer human being; and then help others to achieve this goal of being numbered among the *Elect* and the *Chosen* foretold by both Isaiah and Christ; for the "last days", those "worthy" souls for whose sake the entire world would not be destroyed.

The love and devotion which Bahá'í pioneers show for their newly adopted homeland can best be seen by their determination to stay at their pioneering posts on a permanent basis wherever it is possible so they can make a lasting and valuable contribution to that part of the world. They nourish the flames they have kindled. They try to make a solid useful contribution to that new country which has now become their country. They try to learn the language, the customs, the culture, and adapt themselves to it.

They sink their roots of love and co-operation deep into the soil of their new homeland. They love the people without preference, without prejudice, and without exception. Bahá'í pioneers must always encourage themselves to think of their pioneering post as home, and not as some temporary goal they are achieving and holding until they return to where they came from.

A true pioneer will never leave his or her pioneering post unless an insurmountable obstacle intervenes; and, even then, the Writings of their Faith say, they should not leave until they have found someone who is a suitable, qualified replacement to come and take their place, so the atmosphere of love and service they have created will not be dissipated and lost.

The pioneers who can, will put down deep roots, and will stay and enrich the country in which they now reside. These Bahá'í pioneers must do their work far more by the lives they lead than by the words they speak. They are "doers" not "talkers". The world has had far too much advice and not nearly enough example. They know they must win the hearts of their new neighbours by deeds, not words. By action. Not by an occasional spontaneous good deed, but by living good lives and displaying good character day after day without fail.

The friendship and fellowship of their new neighbours must be *earned* by the pioneers, by the way they live and work among the people of their new-found home. Not by their high-sounding phrases, or by their new, wonderful and noble Bahá'í principles and teachings—those, too, of course, because they *are* wonderful— but mainly by an every-day Bahá'í example of good deeds, service to all, spontaneous friendliness; and above all by the never-failing good character and good nature they display in this hard-to-live-in, hard-to-get-along-in world. The Bahá'í pioneer must be as constant, as loving, and as warming as the rays of the rising sun.

Not off and on, but always. Every day.

Bahá'í pioneers are completely open and trustworthy in all their relationships with the peoples and authorities in their newly-adopted homelands. Whenever they arrive in a new village, however remote, they always present themselves to the local authorities, Chief, Mayor, Council, so that everyone will know who they are and the purpose of their coming. Bahá'ís are loyal to the governments of the countries in which they reside. It is an explicit instruction of the Founder of their Faith, Bahá'u'lláh. It is not optional, it is obligatory.

Loyalty to Government is a fundamental principle of the Bahá'í Faith. There are available to all Bahá'í communities the specific teachings on LOYALTY TO GOVERNMENT which explain this vital and basic Bahá'í belief in a manner which can remove any doubts, misunderstandings or suspicions which their new neighbours might have because of a lack of knowledge. It will also assure those in authority that the Bahá'ís are law-abiding, peace-loving, non-violent members of whatever community in whatever country they may reside. There are no exceptions to this. None whatsoever. Bahá'ís can always be depended upon to help advance, not retard or delay, the welfare of their newly-adopted homeland.

This glimpse of the integrity and trustworthiness of all Bahá'ís toward their individual friends and the community in which they live, will give you an idea why countries, islands, provinces, states, regions, cities, towns, villages and reserves, wherever they have learned these truths about the Bahá'í Faith, and what that Faith really stands for, by being eyewitnesses themselves to the friendship, love and loyalty and dependability which the Bahá'ís generate wherever they go, are eager and happy to see a Bahá'í pioneer, or a Bahá'í family, arrive on their local scene.

One thing you may like best of all. The Bahá'í Faith will never be forced upon you. When you do hear about it, you will be delighted to find that it is also the Faith of Moses, Christ, and all the great Religions of the past. It is not something strange or new. It is not a new Religion, but Religion renewed, a fresh springtime in this dark world of winter.

No matter how beautiful and big the Bahá'í Faith appears to the pioneer or teacher, you will never be under any compulsion to hear about it if you are unwilling.

You can either take it or leave it, as you yourself choose. Whether you are interested in becoming a Bahá'í or not, it will never diminish the love the Bahá'í pioneers feel for you and your family, not one iota. They hope every one of you will want to become Bahá'ís sooner or later, once you learn about the wonderful warm spirit of the Faith and its Message of love, unity and planetary peace; but whether you do or not, the Bahá'í pioneer (every Bahá'í pioneer and teacher everywhere) will still be your good friend, your loving dependable neighbour, unchanged and unchanging.

Do you know anywhere else you can find that kind of love today?

Bahá'u'lláh has told His followers to attract the heart, not to enforce the mind. This is not a suggestion. It is an instruction to be obeyed, implicitly. People will want to become Bahá'ís only when they see these qualities of love, integrity, trustworthiness and sincerity expressed in the daily lives of their new Bahá'í neighbours.

Once they become eyewitnesses to the very qualities so desperately needed by the world around them; once they see these virtues demonstrated every day in the lives of their new Bahá'í neighbours; then, perhaps, they will begin to show an interest in the Faith itself.

This type of example of Bahá'í behaviour is the most important thing the pioneer has to share. This is what is meant by being "made in the image and likeness of God". When people see it demonstrated, they will want to emulate it. They will recognize its worth.

Then, and only then, will they begin to think of becoming Bahá'ís themselves.

The formula is quite simple.

The Bahá'í pioneer must first teach and improve himself, and only then teach and improve the world.

That is the way it should be.

"Sound the trumpets!"

52

The more you learn about your new Bahá'í neighbours, the more you will know that you are among reliable friends, people with whom you can confidently leave your children and not worry about them because you know your children are in safe hands. You know that your children are among trustworthy friends from whom your children will learn only good things, and will return home better than they left it.

It is impossible to put a value on such protection and trust for our young ones in these days. Mothers and fathers worry constantly, every day of their lives, about their children and their future. What will happen to them in school? In the corridors? On the playground? On the streets? In the alleys? On the bus going to and from school?

"What can I tell my children," father and mother ask, "so they will understand the lack of goodness, kindness and purity they see in the world around them? How can I teach them to distrust those they should trust? To be careful of people they should love with an open and sinless heart?"

"How can I protect that sweet, precious, lovable quality of innocence?"

Parents long desperately for secure surroundings for their children. They yearn for their children to live among, and play with, safe, wholesome companions.

It should, therefore, be comforting to parents when they hear that a new Bahá'í family with children has moved in next door. Parents will be pleased by the good news that their son or daughter has now met a young Bahá'í, and has found a new friend. The arrival of Bahá'í children with their parents should be good news for all children and all parents everywhere. A breath of fresh air in a world of pollution.

It is not the entire solution to such problems, but it can be an island fortress in time of need. Especially during these days of crisis when the world is fighting against a terrifying increase in child abuse, both sexual and brutal; battling valiantly to diminish an ever-advancing onslaught of drug abuse, sexual misbehaviour, excessive and inordinate use of alcohol, even at such tender ages at the very beginning of their education for life, in schools which should be a tower of strength instead of a trap of terrible temptations and conditions that victimize uncorrupted little children, and unwary adults as well, in this horrendously decadent age; and torment their souls, destroy their bodies, and open the doorway to future ruin in their precious innocent lives.

Understated. Every word!

Take heart. There is help on the way. Even now it is being exerted against such an ungodly world. These helpers may, even as you read these words, be alighting from the passenger train at the depot downtown in your city.

They are called Bahá'ís. These pioneers and teachers stand for exactly the opposite of all the dreadful characteristics referred to above. They are the "spiritual mutants" you might say, although the expression is, of course, not scientifically accurate. But the point is unmistakably clear. Their entire lives are devoted to changing all those foul things this dark world cherishes and promotes so ruthlessly for its own material gain and personal abandoned physical pleasure.

These Bahá'í pioneers and teachers have come carrying aloft the banner of Bahá'u'lláh, the Supreme Redeemer of men; and the banner of Christ and all the other pure and stainless Mirrors and Messengers of God. They will never haul the banners down!

They have come to comfort, change and transform the world wherever they find a "hearing ear" and a "seeing eye". They come armed with the powers of Heaven, and will never retreat until they have destroyed hate with love, corruption with decency, and removed the "despoilers".

They have come to fight against everything abhorrent to God and man.

Sound the trumpets!

"The decency virus!"

53

We have tried to play fair with you throughout this entire book. Therefore, it is not enough to say: "Sound the trumpets!" unless we, ourselves, hear the music of those trumpets.

Again, what we share with you here is but one tree for the forest of Bahá'u'lláh's guidance, but surely it will suffice.

THE TRUMPETS

Bahá'u'lláh, the Promised One of all Religions, declares of these Pioneers and Teachers:

> "The companions of God are, in this day, the
> lump that must leaven the peoples of the world.
> They must show forth such trustworthiness,
> such truthfulness and perseverance, such deeds
> and character that all mankind may profit by
> their example."

Bahá'u'lláh has commanded this spiritual Army of His in more than a hundred thousand places all over the planet—more perhaps since you started this book, to:

> "Be pure, O people of God, be pure; be right-
> eous, be righteous . . . Say: O people of God!
> That which can ensure the victory of Him Who
> is the eternal Truth, His hosts and helpers on
> earth, have been set down in the sacred Books
> and Scriptures, and are as clear and manifest as
> the sun. These hosts are such righteous deeds,
> such conduct and character, as are acceptable
> in His sight."

Every one of those pioneers and teachers knows deep in his or her heart these Words of Bahá'u'lláh, and guides their life by them:

> "Whoso ariseth, in this Day, to aid our Cause,
> and summoneth to his assistance the hosts of a
> praiseworthy character and upright conduct,
> the influence from such an action will, most
> certainly be diffused throughout the whole
> world."

The Writings of Bahá'u'lláh's Faith instruct every soldier in Bahá'u'lláh's radiant spiritual Army how to behave whenever they enter any city, town, village or reserve, anywhere on the face of the earth. Again, this guidance is not a suggestion, it is an order. It is not optional, it is obligatory. (Where have I heard that before?)

If you want to know who that Bahá'í pioneer is that has newly arrived in your town, and what he or she is like, nothing says it better than these Words from the Bahá'í Writings:

> "O army of God! . . . ye must conduct yourselves in
> such a manner that ye may stand out distinguished
> and brilliant as the sun among other souls. Should
> any one of you enter a city, he should become a
> centre of attraction by reason of his sincerity, his
> faithfulness and love, his honesty and fidelity, his
> truthfulness and loving-kindness towards all the
> peoples of the world, so that the people of that city
> may cry out and say: 'This man is unquestionably a
> Bahá'í, for his manners, his behaviour, his conduct,
> his morals, his nature, and disposition reflect the
> attributes of the Bahá'ís.'"

It is not optional, it is obligatory. The quotation closes with these Words:

> "Not until ye attain this station can ye be said to
> have been faithful to the Covenant and Testament
> of God."

Isn't that the type of neighbour and friend everyone would like to have living next door? Wouldn't all of us feel more comfortable and secure if we knew our family and children were associating with people who tried their best to live up to such high standards in both their personal and professional lives?

The *trumpets* continue.

Ask yourself, will the world, your city, your town, and your family gain or lose by the lives of such people in your midst? People who, without question, with enthusiasm and joy, arise to fulfil the meaning of the following Words in their lives:

> "You will be servants of God, who are dwel-
> ling near to Him, His divine helpers in the
> service, ministering to all Humanity. *All*
> Humanity! Every human being! *never*
> *forget this*!"

Our final *trumpet* is a symphony. It is a clarion call to all human-ity. This glorious outpouring of love taken from the sacred Writ-ings of the Bahá'í Faith, summarizes all we have said. The Words are a mandate to every Bahá'í. No sincere believer in Bahá'u'lláh would ever permit himself to be exempt from this inspiring, soul-stirring challenge. It is how every true Bahá'í begins each day so that you and all mankind may reap the benefit:

> O peoples of the world!
>
> 1
>
> "The Sun of Truth hath risen to illumine the
> whole earth, and to spiritualize the community of
> man. Laudable are the results and the fruits there-
> of, abundant the holy evidences deriving from this
> grace . . .
>
> The Faith of the Blessed Beauty [Bahá'u'lláh] is
> summoning mankind to safety and love, to amity
> and peace; it hath raised up its tabernacle on the
> heights of the earth, and directeth its call to all
> nations. Wherefore, O ye who are God's lovers,
> know ye the value of this precious Faith, obey
> its teachings, walk in this road that is drawn
> straight, and show ye this way to the people."
>
> 2
>
> "Lift up your voices and sing out the song of the
> Kingdom. Spread far and wide the precepts and
> counsels of the loving Lord, so that this world will
> change into another world, and this darksome earth
> will be flooded with light, and the dead body of
> mankind will arise and live; so that every soul will

ask for immortality, through the holy breaths of God."

3

"Soon will your swiftly-passing days be over, and the fame and riches, the comforts, the joys provided by this rubbish-heap, the world, will be gone without a trace. Summon ye then, the people to God, and invite humanity to follow the example of the Company on high. Be ye loving fathers to the orphan, and a refuge to the helpless, and a treasury for the poor, and a cure for the ailing. Be ye the helpers of every victim of oppression, the patrons of the disadvantaged."

The closing sentence of that outpouring of love, is the heartbeat of the Bahá'í World Community. It tells a sceptical world that this Kingdom of God is a reality, that it is a living and a growing thing, a reason to be alive.

"Think ye at all times of rendering some service to every member of the human race."

When you have heard that, you have heard it all.

Every Bahá'í you meet in every part of the world will encircle you with that same tender loving warmth. That special love you feel for the Bahá'í family you admire so greatly, and have become so fond of, since they moved in next door to you, is not unique in any way. Sweet as it is. That warm unconditioned love and sincere friendship you feel for them, and they feel for you, is not an accident. Nor is it a special individual case found only between you and your new Bahá'í neighbour. Not at all. It is found everywhere in the world, wherever there are Bahá'ís.

Perhaps you yourself can now better understand why.

Every Bahá'í man, woman and child is part of a raging planetary epidemic called:

Bahá'í Love.

Beware!

It is catching.

I call it the "decency virus".

"Move over, Marco Polo!"

54

All Flags Flying! still has the obligation to demonstrate the close and loving link between Christ and Bahá'u'lláh so frequently referred to when speaking of the Christ-promised *Kingdom of God on earth.*

Christ announced it. Bahá'u'lláh proclaimed it.

Christ foretold its coming in His Lord's Prayer. The Writings of Bahá'u'lláh's Faith explained to the world that the Lord's Prayer was more than a prayer, it was a prophecy. Bahá'u'lláh announced the fulfilment of this prophecy in several of His more than one hundred volumes written to assure the betterment of mankind, and to prepare human society for the coming of this great future Day.

Bahá'u'lláh proclaimed to the world, and in particular to the Christian world, that indeed that long-heralded Day had already begun, and that all of the promises revealed in the holy Books of the past concerning it had been fulfilled.

Bahá'u'lláh sent His pioneers and teachers out into the world to launch the earliest beginnings of this wondrous Day of God. They are busily engaged everywhere in obeying His command.

Christ, using this same method, had sent out His own spiritual Army of pioneers, instructing them to "Go . . . and teach all nations." The Apostles, and after them those they brought into the Faith, won the great victories for Christ and Christianity. Has the Christian world forgotten?

Christ said:

> "Verily I say unto you, There is no man
> that hath left house, or brethren, or sisters, or
> father, or mother, or wife, or children, or
> lands, for my sake, and the gospel's but he shall

receive an hundredfold now in this time,
. . . and in the world to come eternal life."
Mark 10:29–30

How intriguing that both Christ, the *Son*, and Bahá'u'lláh, the *Father*, would promise their followers rewards in both this world and the next because of the sacrifices these pioneers, men and women alike, have willingly made on behalf of their Faith. Even life itself when necessary.

The Writings of Bahá'u'lláh's Faith pay tribute to this marvellous act of service and sacrifice, saying:

> "Such a reward, it should be noted, is not
> to be regarded as purely an abstract blessing
> confined to the future life, but also as a tan-
> gible benefit which such courage, faith and
> perseverance can alone confer in this material
> world."

On this very theme, George Townshend, sometime Canon of St Patrick's Cathedral in Dublin, Ireland and former Archdeacon of Clonfert, points out in his book *The Heart of the Gospel*, that the history of the world needs an entirely new interpretation. It has dwelt almost exclusively on a catalogue of wars and disasters, overlooking the true underlying interpretation, a spiritual interpretation, as mankind struggles on the planet to develop those virtues and attributes that make him or her "in the image" and "likeness" of God. That struggle, Townshend says, is the real interpretation of history.

After a careful study of the Teachings of Bahá'u'lláh, Townshend left his high position in the Church, and became a follower of the Bahá'í Faith. He wrote a special document which he sent out to all his fellow-clergymen everywhere in the world to inform them of his great discovery, and to invite them to join him in fulfilling the promise of this newly-launched *Kingdom of God on earth*.

This story could easily have been part of the "great work" already described for you, since the appeal was made world-wide. But as Isaiah, Habakkuk and St Paul warned, it would not be "believed" even when it was being "told".

This illustrious former member of the Christian religious hierar-

219

chy also announced the truth to the peoples of the world through his books.*

It has been reserved for this chapter since Townshend makes such a beautiful, tender picture of the relationship of Christ and Bahá'u'lláh, outlining Their common struggle toward a common goal: the *Kingdom of God on earth.* This is the underlying theme of his most important book, *Christ and Bahá'u'lláh.*

No *dialogue* in religious history was ever more revealing and more tender than the dialogue between Christ, the *Son* and Bahá-'u'lláh, the *Father*; between *Christianity* and the *Bahá'í Faith.* These Words taken from the Teachings of Christ and Bahá'u'lláh, and placed side by side, open to our eyes the true nature of this greatest *Drama of the Kingdom* of which we have been speaking. These brief examples are, of course, but a lightning-flash, a fleeting glimpse of that astonishing, soul-stirring, world-healing story.†

CHRIST

"Nevertheless I tell you the truth . . . if I go
not away, the Comforter will not come unto you;
but if I depart, I will send him unto you."

John 16:7

BAHÁ'U'LLÁH

"The Comforter Whose advent all the scriptures have promised is now come that He
may reveal unto you all knowledge and
wisdom."

CHRIST

"I have yet many things to say unto you,
but ye cannot bear them now."

John 16:12

* See *Christ and Bahá'u'lláh, The Heart of the Gospel, The Promise of All Ages,* and *The Mission of Bahá'u'lláh,* all published by George Ronald.

† See *Dialogues of Deliverance,* same author (to appear). Over one hundred pages of the Words of Christ and Bahá'u'lláh, as the Son speaks and the Father answers. The original Actors, Christ and Bahá'u'lláh, each play an eternal "key role" in the welfare and salvation of all mankind in the one "grand redemptive scheme" of God for man.

BAHÁ'U'LLÁH

"This is the Word which the Son [Jesus]
veiled when He said to those around Him that
at that time they could not bear it . . ."

CHRIST

"Howbeit when he, the Spirit of truth is
come, he will guide you into all truth . . ."
John 16:13

BAHÁ'U'LLÁH

"Verily the Spirit of Truth is come to
guide you unto all truth . . ."

CHRIST

"He shall glorify me . . . he shall take of
mine, and shall shew it unto you."
John 16:14–15

BAHÁ'U'LLÁH

"He is the One Who Glorified the Son and
exalted His Cause . . ."
"'This is that which the Son [Jesus] hath
decreed.' And whatsoever hath proceeded out
of His blameless, His truth-speaking, trustworthy mouth, can never be altered."

CHRIST

". . . he shall testify of me."
John 15:26

BAHÁ'U'LLÁH

"Say, Lo! The Father is come, and that which
ye were promised in the Kingdom is fulfilled!
. . . He hath testified of Me, and I do testify
of Him."

BAHÁ'U'LLÁH

"We testify that when He [Christ] came
into the world, He shed the splendour of His
glory upon all created things . . . Through

221

His power, born of Almighty God, the eyes
of the blind were opened, and the soul of
the sinner sanctified.

. . . He [Christ] it is Who purified the
world. Blessed is the man who, with a face
beaming with light, hath turned towards
Him."

In one single Bahá'í book alone, *The Promulgation of Universal Peace*,
the honour and greatness of Christ are extolled, and His Name and
station "glorified" and "testified" to, in over two hundred special
loving references directed to the peoples of all religions.

There has never been, nor will there ever be again, a Love-story
such as that found in the *Announcement*, the *Proclamation*, and the
Fulfilment of the *Christ-promised Kingdom of God on earth*.

Christ told His followers that when He, the "Comforter" came,
the "Spirit of Truth" Who would lead mankind into "all truth",
He would "speak" of Him, Christ. He would fulfil all that He,
Christ, had promised. Bahá'u'lláh reminded the Christian world
of these promises, saying:

". . . O followers of the Spirit [Jesus], . . .
Open the doors of your hearts. He Who is the
Spirit [Jesus] verily, standeth before them. . . .
We, in truth, have opened unto you the gates
of the Kingdom. . . . Will ye bar the doors of
your houses in My face?

We, verily, have come for your sakes, and
have borne the misfortunes of the world for your
salvation."

All Flags Flying! should be a clarion call to all of Christianity.
Although Bahá'u'lláh directed His Message to all religions and
peoples, He gave a strong emphasis to the Christians of the world. I
myself was a Christian when I first heard the "sweet music" of
Bahá'u'lláh's voice, and I realized for the first time how wonderful
and glorious Christ really was. I always hear these Words of Bahá-
'u'lláh ringing in my ears:

"O concourse of Christians!"
"Followers of the Gospel!"
"O Pope!"

"O concourse of patriarchs!"
"O concourse of archbishops!"
"O concourse of bishops!"
"O concourse of priests!"
"O concourse of monks!"
"O Bethlehem!"
"O people of the Gospel!"

Each salutation was accompanied by a special Message of love and appeal, urging them to arise and to fulfil, while there was yet time, the purpose of their lives on earth.

This, in essence, is the Message which the Bahá'í pioneers and teachers have come to bring to your part of the world. That is what makes each one of them so precious and unique in the annals of human history.

Bahá'u'lláh calls out to you through them:

"The time foreordained unto the peoples and
kindreds of the earth is now come. The promises
of God, as recorded in the holy Scriptures, have
all been fulfilled . . .
. . . This is the Day which the Pen of the
Most High hath glorified in all the holy Scriptures.
There is no verse in them that doth not declare
the glory of His holy Name, and no Book that doth
not testify unto the loftiness of this most exalted
theme. Were We to make mention of all that hath
been revealed in these heavenly Books and holy
Scriptures concerning this Revelation, this Tablet
would assume impossible dimensions."

I myself have been guilty of dwelling too long on this exalted theme. Yet, the potential is so great and glorious that almost any receptive heart could be carried away in ecstasy.

The trumpet-call for the spiritual conquest of the hearts of men resounds on all sides. Bahá'u'lláh's spiritual battalions are moving into position. The following quotation from the Writings of the Bahá'í Faith inspired the title for this chapter, "Move over, Marco Polo!" You will readily see why.

The radiant spiritual Army of Bahá'u'lláh is on the move everywhere. Their eyes are fixed upon the banners that proclaim their goal and the "great work" they are doing everywhere, including among the underprivileged and forgotten peoples of the planet. God created them all; God wants them all. The onward-marching legions of *the glory of the Lord* are, as promised in Scripture, covering the earth "as the waters cover the sea."

"Under whatever conditions the dearly-loved, the divinely sustained, the onward marching legions of the army of Bahá'u'lláh may be labouring, in whatever theatre they may operate, in whatever climes they may struggle, whether in the cold and inhospitable territories beyond the Arctic Circle, or in the torrid zones of both the Eastern and Western Hemispheres; on the borders of the jungles of Burma, Malaya and India; on the fringes of the deserts of Africa and of the Arabian Peninsula; in the lonely, far-away, backward and sparsely populated islands dotting the Atlantic, the Pacific and the Indian Oceans and the North Sea; amidst the diversified tribes of . . . Africa, the Eskimos and the Lapps of the Arctic regions, the Mongolians of East and South East Asia, the Polynesians of the South Pacific Islands, the reservations of the Red Indians in both American continents, the Maoris of New Zealand, and the aborigines of Australia; within the time-honoured strongholds of both Christianity and Islám, whether it be in Mecca, Rome, Cairo, Najaf or Karbilá; or in towns and cities whose inhabitants are either immersed in crass materialism, or breathe the fetid air of an aggressive racialism, or find themselves bound by the chains and fetters of a haughty intellectualism, or have fallen a prey to the forces of a blind and militant nationalism, or are steeped in the atmosphere of a narrow and intolerant ecclesiasticism—to them all, as well as to those who, as the fortunes of this fate-laden Crusade prosper, will be called upon to unfurl the standard of an all-conquering Faith in the . . . jungles of the Amazon, scale the mountain-fastnesses of Tibet, establish direct contact with the teeming and hapless multitudes in the interior of China, Mongolia and Japan, sit with the leprous, consort with the outcasts in their penal colonies, traverse the steppes of Russia or scatter throughout the wastes of Siberia, I direct my impassioned appeal to obey, as befits His [Bahá'u'lláh's] warriors, the summons of the Lord of Hosts, and prepare for that Day of Days when His victorious battalions will . . . celebrate the hour of final victory."

Be happy. Be confident.

The Bahá'í Faith has no conquest in mind except the hearts of humanity. Its Message of love and unity can only improve every country in which these soldiers of love and unity appear. With their coming, there can be little doubt that it is, indeed, the beginning of that much heralded, long-awaited, and deeply yearned-for *Christ-promised Kingdom of God on earth.*

"Shout out: Hurray!"

55

We have come to the final chapter of "O Pioneer!".

So great, so important, so vital to the welfare of all mankind, and to the future destiny of the entire human race, is the spread of this planetary epidemic of love, and the work of these pioneers and teachers who are building this Christ-promised *Kingdom of God on earth*, that they will be remembered forever down through the ages to come. This is a promise in the sacred Writings of their Faith.

Bahá'u'lláh, the Promised One of all Ages and Religions, praised unstintingly these heroes and heroines of God who "have forsaken their country" for the purpose of teaching His Faith, saying:

> "By My life! No act, however great,
> can compare with it . . . Such a service is
> indeed the prince of all goodly deeds . . ."

The praise and love bestowed upon these pioneers and teachers which at the beginning of *All Flags Flying!* amazed us when we contemplated these humble, simple souls who arrived so unostentatiously and so unpretentiously in our midst, now do not seem at all excessive in the light of what we have learned about them; what it is they are doing, and what depends upon their sacrifice and selfless service.

The Writings of the Bahá'í Faith have made their place in history unmistakably clear.

> "To the band of pioneers, . . . who have
> forsaken their homes, who have scattered far
> and wide, who have willingly sacrificed
> their comfort, their health and even their
> lives . . . future generations . . . will no
> doubt pay adequate tribute."

226

It is far more than that. No wonder the Bahá'ís are enlisting under the banners of Bahá'u'lláh as pioneers and teachers and speeding out into all corners of the earth. How can they not be thrilled?

The Bahá'í Writings state further that through the heroic and courageous actions of these pioneers

> "the throne of the Kingdom of God will,
> in the plenitude of its majesty and glory,
> be firmly established."

There are no words that can praise them enough. Their teaching work has been exalted to that of the station of a martyr to the Faith. Bahá'u'lláh said so, 'Abdu'l-Bahá said so, and their beloved Guardian said so. Of that there can be no doubt.

Shoghi Effendi declared:

> "To live to teach in the present day is
> like being martyred in those early days."

That teaching, he makes clear, must be done in the same consecrated spirit as that shown by the martyrs. The pioneers and teachers must be willing to sacrifice their all and become teaching-martyrs. Not as a skyrocket that explodes in the sky and spills its treasures to the night in one glorious burst of colour, that is martyrdom; but, as a candle that weeps away its life in drops, giving forth a never-failing flame of light to illumine this dark world until it becomes bright again.

That is a teaching-martyr.

Bahá'u'lláh Himself called for these same self-sacrificing teaching-martyrs. He too, foretold their astonishing reward:

> "They that have forsaken their country in
> the path of God and subsequently ascended
> unto His presence, such souls shall be
> blessed by the Concourse on High and their
> names recorded by the Pen of Glory among
> such as have laid down their lives as martyrs
> in the path of God, . . ."

In yet another ringing passage, Bahá'u'lláh foretells the future and points out the love and prestige that will surround these pioneers in the future. He extols all pioneers and teachers who, in His

Words, have "journeyed through the countries in His name and
for His praise." He states clearly that those of us who are fortunate
enough to meet in person such selfless, heroic pioneers, will ourselves be blessed merely by coming into their presence.

Imagine!

Small wonder that I should wish to try and write a book about
them, however inadequate. So unimaginably great, so utterly urgent is the service of these pioneers to the present and future welfare of every human being walking the face of the earth today, that
Bahá'u'lláh Himself promises:

> "Whoso hath attained their presence
> will glory in their meeting, and all that
> dwell in every land will be illumined
> by their memory."

If the peoples of the earth truly knew who these pioneer-teachers
were, the towns and villages in your part of the world would empty
out when they heard the good news of the arrival of a Bahá'í pioneer or family. Everybody, you among them, would rush to the
airport, the bus depot, the train station and the harbour. You
would stand in line to shout aloud:

"Hurray! Welcome! It's about time! Where have you been?
What kept you?"

If this book, *All Flags Flying!* teaches the world only this one
thing about their new Bahá'í neighbours, it will be a blessing for
both.

Whenever I try to share this great theme with anyone, I am overcome with the realization of my own inadequacy. Whatever I have
told you here is merely "ashes" compared to the truth.

One final glimpse into the wonder of the task these pioneers and
teachers are trying to accomplish throughout the world, in the face
of indifference, antagonism, even hostility—as foretold in Scripture—will clearly demonstrate why this theme was so enthralling,
and led to the writing of this book, *All Flags Flying!*

These words from the Writings of Bahá'u'lláh's Faith hold the
key to the fate and future of mankind:

> "The inscrutable wisdom of God has so decreed
> that we, who are the chosen bearers of the world's

greatest Message to suffering humanity, should
toil and promote our work under the most trying
conditions of life, amidst unhelpful surroundings, and in the face of unprecedented trials, and
without means, influence or support, achieve,
steadily and surely, the conquest and regeneration
of human hearts."

Perhaps you will now, yourself, want to lend your share of support and help to this "regeneration of human hearts" which is the
very foundation of the Christ-promised *Kingdom of God on earth*. It is
your chance, perhaps the last for all mankind, to be numbered
among the Elect; not among the "many" who are "called", but
among the "few" who are "chosen".

The Bahá'í Writings accentuate those long-ago words from Isaiah and Habakkuk about a world that remains both deaf and blind
to the "great work" that is being carried out in their midst, a
"work" that they refuse to "believe" even when it is "told" to
them. Thus, they have impeded rather than hastened the Kingdom of God.

The Bahá'í Writings say unmistakably:

". . . True, the progress of our work, when compared to the sensational rise and development of an
earthly cause, has been painful and slow, yet we
firmly believe and shall never doubt that the great
spiritual Revolution which the Almighty is causing to
be accomplished, through us, in the hearts of men is
destined to achieve, steadily and surely, the complete
regeneration of all mankind."

This "work" and "wonder" and "marvellous" story should no
longer be a surprise to those who have read Scripture, nor to those
who have read *All Flags Flying!* up to this point.

Especially in view of these incomparable Words of Bahá'u'lláh:

"I testify before God to the greatness, the
inconceivable greatness of this Revelation."
"That which hath been made manifest in
this pre-eminent, this most exalted Revelation,
stands unparalleled in the annals of the
past, nor will future ages witness its like."

". . . the Cause We have proclaimed is
such as no pen can ever describe, nor any
mind conceive its greatness."

What chance does a sportscaster from Philadelphia have when brought face to face with even a glimpse of His crimson, all-encompassing Light? Only time and your own study will reveal to you the true beauty and glory of these wondrous pearls, these "gems of heavenly knowledge", that still lie hidden in the depths of Bahá'u'lláh's mighty and everlasting ocean. All we have shared with you here in *All Flags Flying!* has been but one drop from that eternal surging sea.

In view of this, and the more than one hundred volumes Bahá'u'lláh has written for the welfare and guidance of the world, you must forgive me if every now and then I get carried away as I did here on "O Pioneer!" and throw in a hatful of "golden rule salvos" and a bucket or two of "Love thy neighbour" more than you love yourself.

Sorry about that.

From now on, it's all downhill as promised with three laughs and a tear.

THE
ZOO
CREW

56

Our African West Winds farm had really become a ranch, housing a baby elephant, a camel, an impala, a secretary bird, a squirrel, the Honourable Mr Glow-Worm, Crock O'Dile, the Irish crocodile and his little one-legged friend, the "Out-of-Luck" Duck.

Some of the most light-hearted and laughter-filled moments of our pioneering lives came when we developed these animal puppets for my radio programme called *That Man Sears*.

Bahá'í pioneers are not missionaries. They earn their own living wherever they go, working at whatever work they can find. If they can't find it, they invent it, as Marguerite and I did for SABC–Springbok Radio.

Bahá'í pioneers are doctors, lawyers, educators, engineers, merchants, secretaries, mechanics, all working at their own professions. If none of these professions is open to them at first, they work as handymen, maids, waitresses, ditch-diggers, day-labourers, accepting whatever work they can find until they can eventually place themselves properly in their own line of work.

On occasion their transportation expenses are paid to get them to their pioneering posts and to support them in the early days, but it's only a loan. They are expected to repay it as soon as possible. These Bahá'í pioneers want to offer their Faith as a gift to the peoples of the world, a "free gift" as it says in the Scriptures. It is their gift to mankind from all of the Bahá'ís everywhere.*

Marguerite and I were fortunate to be living in our part of the pioneering world. So many of the people spoke English. The country also had radio stations with programmes in English. I worked on Springbok Radio in South Africa. Once again I had a

* The principle of "voluntary giving" is unique to the Bahá'í Faith and is very moving and beautiful. Ask any Bahá'í about it. You'll love it.

coast-to-coast programme. Only this time, it was from the Atlantic to the Indian Ocean. Don't laugh. My programmes went from Cape Town to Lourenço Marques (now called Maputo) in Mozambique.

The Springbok network required that we prepare the programmes weeks in advance so they could be reviewed for content. The farther ahead the better they liked it. This was perfect for my work as a Bahá'í Auxiliary Board Member and later as one of the Hands of the Faith. Hands in the symbolic sense that they, the Hands, carry out the work and guidance from the head and heart of the Faith in its World Centre in the Holy Land.

In order to assist me in doing my share of that world-healing work, my son Bill would write my humorous radio programmes for me while I was away on my travels. When I returned he would have another three months of programmes waiting for me to record. The programmes were always delightful, as Bill, by nature, is wittier and more amusing than his father. I would record them all, and take off again in a cloud of smoke for another three months of teaching in every corner of Africa.

Once again, I received most of the credit for whatever happened on those teaching trips, but it was Bill, writing up a storm while I was away, who deserved the real pioneering credit. Without his help I could never have left home.

Of course, when I returned, I took time to hug and kiss Marguerite. Unless she hadn't returned from her own teaching trip yet. Occasionally, we embraced and greeted each other in foreign airports even outside Africa.*

In order to liven things up on my radio show, and for use in public appearances to fatten the "kitty" for air fares, I designed with the help of Marguerite and Bill Jr., the hand-puppets already mentioned, and introduced them on my regular radio programme. All four of us worked on and perfected amusing and odd-sounding voices to intrigue and charm the listeners and viewers.

These puppets are not imaginary characters which I created merely for this book. These were real, live, money-earning puppets. They, too, were pioneers and travel teachers in the finest sense. True, they were inanimate but they helped support us during those early, thread-bare beginning days in a far-off strange land.

* See *God Loves Laughter*, pp 180–1.

They played an important role in making it a real home for us all.

On occasion, the puppets also taught the Faith. Very effectively. Especially, when they used the story of the *Sun and the Mirrors* with the children. They were good at it. Better sometimes than we were.

Through the kindness and skill of our co-pilot and collaborator on *All Flags Flying!*, our illustrator, Robert Reedy, you can now have a glimpse at what each member of this private Sears' zoo looked like.

Even now, looking back after all that time, whenever I see a drawing or a photograph of those mischief-making, heart-touching puppet faces, I still get a lump in my throat the size of the Koh-i-noor diamond, and it always feels just as precious.

The patsy

57

Since you are about to make a journey into Africa with them, a journey called "White Witch-Doctor Exposed!", you should really know a little more about them. In case of emergency.

First of all, there was Fitz, the squirrel.

FITZ

Fitz lived in a large jacaranda tree on the campus of Witwatersrand University in Johannesburg. He could hear the professors and students talking each day as they walked past the hole in his tree. Unfortunately, all he ever heard was the *middle* of what they were saying. He never heard the beginning nor the end of anything.

Fitz could sing the middle of all the current popular songs including the National Anthem. He could solve the middle of every mathematical problem. Being the educated one, Fitz was known among the other animals by his more formal name, Fitzgerald. Sometimes Fitz was referred to by his friends as "Professor" or "Prof." Fitz made it clear to everyone that while he was generally known as a squirrel among men, to a scientist he was in truth an outstanding example of *Sciurus hudsonicus*!

If you asked Fitz how he felt, he would answer, "Middling." He could give the lie to that trite old phrase, "You don't know the half of it." He did. Unfortunately, only the middle half.

This is why Fitz decided to take his "doctorate" at Wits (Witwatersrand University) in "bits and middles".

235

IMP

His friend, Imp, the Impala, was always on top of the world. Imp, unlike Fitz, knew it all: the beginning, the middle *and* the end of everything. Or thought he did. Usually mistakenly. Especially if it had to do with loving your neighbour as yourself.

If you asked Imp how *he* felt, he would cheerfully say, "Great! Just great!", even while he was sneezing with a severe head cold and suffering from arthritic pains. Imp was the original "Cockeyed Optimist".

He had huge brown eyes that would suddenly stick way out in front when he became excited, which was often. Especially when he heard about another animal in trouble.

Imp was always kind, gentle, loving and helpful. He was a true friend. He trusted everybody. Imp believed that everyone was innocent *even* when they were proved guilty. Imp also believed there was a little good in everybody.

He was always willing to give every scoundrel a second chance. And a third. And a fourth.

Consequently, he was a "patsy" for everyone, and didn't even know it. You couldn't help liking him even while you were shaking your head.

Hillary, the Secretary Bird on the other hand, was quite unlovable. Hillary was a roughneck, and a genuine crook. Charming, sly, slippery and cunning. He was so untrustworthy you could depend on it.

Hillary spent most of his time watching the toteboard, and moving in disguise among the bookies at Turffontein, Germiston, Newmarket and the Vaal, and other famous race courses such as Milnerton, Kenilworth and Greyville. Hillary spent considerable time in "die tronk", the "slammer" to you. But he was always released for lack of evidence. He swallowed it.

Hillary could give you the latest odds on anything, although he "shaved" them in favour of the "house". He, Hillary, of course, was the House.

His deplorable, but ingratiating character was not Hillary's fault. Not really. Hillary found a job, but he lost it the first day. His boss unfortunately asked him, as a Secretary Bird, to "take a letter". Hillary was very literal-minded, and he took a letter with ten pounds, seventeen shillings and a "tickey" in it.

That was his first crime.

He was released for lack of evidence. He swallowed it. The paper money was easy, but the "tickey" and silver change required surgery. By his own doctor, of course. Recently struck off the rolls.

HILLARY

From that time on, Hillary went downhill in a hand-basket (one usually filled with his own pilferings). Hillary descended rapidly. He kept crashing into bigger and better fraudulent schemes, and thus wound up as a self-made Con-man's Con-man. His patter, learned outside the main Post Office on Jeppe Street, was perfect for capturing "suckers".

"Pssssst! Step over here, soul-mate, and take a peek at these genuine, diamond-crusted wrist-watches, laden with sapphires, emeralds and rubies."

Imp was the one who usually "stepped over".

58

GREAT BIG SAM

Just when Hillary, the hood-winker, made you fed up with all animals, especially African animals, you were lucky if you bumped into Great Big Sam, the Baby Elephant.

Sam was the pick of the litter.

He was by far the most endearing of all. Not as clever as Hillary. Nor as wise as Fitz, or as zany as Imp, but much sweeter than all of them put together.

Great Big Sam wasn't really BIG at all. He was quite small, being a baby elephant. But what there was of Sam between the trunk and the tail was all heart.

Great Big Sam could join his tail and his trunk over the top of his back to form a picture frame in the shape of a heart for the tourist photographers, especially those who might be riding him at the time.

Sam had huge African elephant ears, not the puny Indian elephant kind. When Great Big Sam flapped his ears, it emptied the first two rows of theatre seats. Having caught their attention, Great Big Sam would stick his long trunk down deep into a large glass of milk and swallow it all down in a gulp accompanied by noisy suction sounds as the milk disappeared whoosh! right in front of your very eyes!

All backstage magic was courtesy of Bill and Michael, of course.

Great Big Sam's good points were legendary. Everybody knew that. There were far too many to list here. Suffice it to say that on all dossiers describing Great Big Sam, the baby Elephant, opposite his name it said: "A darling boy!"

Camille, the Camel, was the love-interest. She was the ultimate glamour ingredient in any group. Camille had large blue eyes with lovely long lashes which she could lower and raise at will, and did constantly. Coyly, of course. Camille would slowly close her eyes, leaving the curtain down long enough for you to observe the length and beauty of her ebony black lashes and the magnificent blending of her magenta eyelid mascara, in order to prepare you

CAMILLE

for the impact of that moment when she would very slowly raise them again, thus releasing the full voltage of her oh-so-blue eyes. While you were thus entranced, Camille would lean forward to touch noses and stare directly into your own eyes.

Murder!

Camille's nose was soft, tender, and a delight to rub. She could lift either side of her long wheat-coloured lips independently, or both sides together, revealing her perfect even white teeth. Camille could also sneer with marvellous disdain by curling her lips on either side and rotating her head so that the entire audience would realize that they, too, were included in her contempt.

Camille always wore a lorgnette so that she could look down that intimidating nose at Hillary and *all* others she considered inferior and beneath her. This included everyone.

Camille wore a large diamond choker around her throat, accompanied by huge brilliant diamond tear-drop ear-rings. On occasion, Camille, out of sympathy for those unable to bear direct contact with her unique beauty and "over-kill" personality, would cover her ravishing face with luminous, translucent veils fashion-designed in every brilliant colour imaginable.

Camille was really something else. Besides a camel, that is. In fact, she preferred to be called Cam-*ell*, not *cam*el. Accent on the last syllable, not the first.

True to tradition, Camille, the Cam-*ell*, could go eight days without water. However, she could not go a single hour without a compliment.

These much-loved inanimate animal friends became very dear to us. They were far more than wood, plastic, fake-fur, paint and ping-pong balls.

When I first started carving, sawing, pasting and painting the various puppets, I would lay them out in state on our bed. Marguerite would object at "nap" time. Our bed looked like a third-class passenger car on the way to Kisumu. I knew, because Bill van Zoest and I had travelled to a Bahá'í Convention in Western Province that way. Marguerite couldn't find room on the bed with all those unfinished puppets, and called over her shoulder as she went out to sleep on the lawn chair: "I'm not superstitious, but I don't like to sleep thirteen in a bed."

We all fell in love with our Zoo Crew when they were all finished. They helped us earn our living and enabled us to stay at our pioneering post. They even helped us save up a little reserve money so we could make valuable teaching trips to other nearby countries.

Sometimes, when we used the animal voices on our radio programmes, they would tell our Bahá'í friends who were listening in from the nearby countries exactly where we were going to travel the following weekend.

One of the animals would ask, "Where are you going Saturday, Bill?"

Fitz always answered for me.

"This darling, soft-hearted, bald-headed, Master of the wooden zoo, is driving to Swaziland Saturday, to Mbabane in the Dusenberry Special."

And everybody in Swaziland would be waiting for us.

"Where are you going for the Christmas holidays, Bill?"

I would say, "Well—" and Fitz would take over.

"This lovable, good-natured, lover of God and his fellow man, is hopping into the old Dusenberry Special this weekend to drive with his beautiful wife to Rustenburg. He's expecting all his African friends to be on hand to greet him. Right, Bill?"

"Amen."

"And", the Impala concluded, "we're all going along."

"Now wait just a darn minute!" I objected.

Great Big Sam ended the debate with his generous heart. "I", he said "am paying for the petrol and the roasted peanuts."

The *Dusenberry Special* became a key word to Marguerite and myself. It meant whichever car we were currently driving. It also meant that Bill and Marguerite Sears and family would be on the road, rushing to meet their Bahá'í friends somewhere. The Dusenberry Special became quite famous even when it was transformed by the magic of money successively into a Vauxhall, a Borgward, a Peugeot and a Corsair. All cars are still the Dusenberry Special to Marguerite and myself. They always will be.

The original Dusenberry Special was a powder-blue Buick Special Sedan sent over to us in Africa by Marguerite's father, Charlie Reimer, to help with our teaching trips.

Now that you've met the family, we can "put the show on the road" as they say.

White witch-doctor exposed!

59

One weekend after Marguerite and I and the puppets had returned from a very rewarding weekend Conference on the *Sun and
the Mirrors* and Progressive Revelation, we received a very special
invitation.

We packed up our famous blue footlocker with the shooting stars
plastered all over the cover and the printed names of our talented
puppet performers who were travelling inside. We had just freed
them from jail, when we had to repack them and head for Mbabane, the capital of Swaziland. We had been asked to appear in
person at Matapa School in Bremersdorp.* The Swaziland children were eager to see our entire cast of characters and to witness
their comic performance.

This, remember, was over thirty years ago. None of those young
African children were familiar with television. They had never met
such clever and human-like performers as Fitz, Imp, Hillary, Camille and Great Big Sam.

John and Val Allen arranged the entire performance. They, too,
were dear friends. They rank high on the list of those to whom we
owe a long and lasting debt of gratitude. Val and John became
Knights of Bahá'u'lláh for their pioneering work in Swaziland.

In fact, shortly after our arrival in Africa, John gave me a belt
with a magnificent American Indian silver buckle, studded with
turquoise.

"Wear it in good health", he told me. "It's for emergencies."

When I took the belt off at home that night, I discovered it was a
money-belt. It had five crisp one hundred dollar bills folded up
inside the zipper. That secret cache helped me meet many emergencies and to teach in many new African areas. It was refilled

* Since renamed Matsapa High School. Bremersdorp is now called Manzini.

several times over the years by John. He would regularly check the mileage when I returned from my longest teaching trips.

Val and John Allen had been friends with Bill and Marguerite Sears ever since the California days. The Allens were those same dear souls who came to our aid way back when we lived in a fog-bound 50c house on Lake View Avenue outside San Francisco.

Our entire family came down with the measles in one week, all except Michael. He had suffered his attack the year before. Now, Michael was taking good care of all three of us. All by himself, until the Allens came to his rescue.

I can still see Michael trudging up that steep Ingleside hill, lugging a bag of groceries nearly as tall as he was, half hidden behind it.

The Allens arrived and Michael began to make lunch for them. "That's it!" they said.

They retired Michael, made lunch, cleaned the house, laid in a supply of food, and over the next few weeks, nursed us all back to health.

Now, a quarter of a century later, here we were, fellow-pioneers in adjoining countries in Southern Africa. It's a small Bahá'í world, as they say, with Bahá'u'lláh's gallant warriors flooding out into every remote corner.

In the old days in Boston, they used to say, "You can't spit without hitting an Irishman." In today's Bahá'í pioneering world, these heroes and heroines of God are everywhere. If your plane lands in an emergency, just cry out the Name of Bahá'u'lláh, and a fellow-Bahá'í will come on the run, or send friends, like John and Val Allen.

Marguerite, young Bill and I practised the animal voices for our puppet play as we drove down into Ezulwini Valley from Mbabane. John and Val must have felt they were caught up in the middle of the Kruger National Park as they listened to our animal chatter back and forth.

The Headmaster was a Bahá'í. He was worried about us, feeling certain that the severe thunderstorm and cloudbursts must have delayed our arrival. It was so late, the programme was about to be cancelled, and the disappointed children sent back to their homes for the night.

Then to the joy and applause of all, the Sears troop escorted by the Allens, appeared out of the storm. We were all soaked to the skin by the downpour as we rushed to the stage entrance of the auditorium.

Quickly we set up our puppet theatre. Everybody helped. Because of the late hour, we had to begin the show without introducing the animals to the children. Everything was rushed. In a few minutes the curtain lifted, and we began.

Usually, Marguerite, Bill and I step out in front of the curtain with a puppet on each arm. I introduce the animals to the children, one at a time. I tell them the names of the puppets and each one of them says something humorous to the audience in their own entertaining voices. Marguerite tells the crowd what each animal does, and the puppets do a few of their special tricks for the children in order to make friends with them. Fitz and Imp tell a few amusing stories with my help. One by one the children get to meet the animals and learn their names. Marguerite, Bill and I demonstrate their magical powers during this "warm-up". This prevents any disbelief later once they begin their astonishing antics.*

Our play itself usually begins with a loud rooster crow. The curtain slowly rises. The rooster crows once more telling us it is morning.

Fitz comes out of his little house wearing ear-muffs, a fur hat and mittens. It is obviously winter and very cold. This itself was a delight in such a hot climate. Fitz skates around doing figures of eight. He returns carrying an armload of wood. Fitz slips, falls, cries out, and ice-shavings fly up. We see Fitz hanging from the wall by his tiny ice-skates, head out of sight. Great Big Sam, the baby elephant skates in and unhooks Fitz' skates. When Fitz is upright again, and has gathered up all the wood, Great Big Sam says, "I wish you'd stop falling like that."

Sam gives Fitz a wallop with his trunk, spilling all the wood, and skates off. Fitz picks up the armload of firewood and skates into his cottage.

Soon we see smoke rising from the red brick chimney of his house. The two shuttered windows swing wide open. Fitz sticks his

---

* Michael would have been there to help us, but he was off pioneering all by himself in South West Africa/Namibia at Windhoek. We missed him, both his talent and his help. I may have told you that. He was "perfectly innocent" doing far more important pioneering work.

head out. Over his shoulder, against the far wall, we can see Fitz'
portrait hanging on the wall.

Fitz calls out loudly across the valley.

"Good morning, old man of the mountain!"

A voice replies from behind the audience in deep sepulchral
tones, on "echo-chamber" from a loudspeaker hidden in the huge
bouquet of flowers at the back of the auditorium:

"GOOD MORNING, FITZ, THE SQUIRREL!"

The startled audience looks back over their shoulders. They
turn back to look at Fitz once again, when they hear him answer.
The giggles begin, and never stop until the show has ended.

Fitz does a brief "echo" routine with the old man of the
mountain.

"I am Fitzgerald, the genius!"

ECHO: "I am Fitzgerald, the genius!"

FITZ: "It is I, not the Lion, who is King of Beasts and leader of
the jungle!"

ECHO: "In a pig's eye!"

SOUND EFFECTS: [*Lion's roar*]

Fitz is interrupted as an excited hen begins to cackle, louder and
louder with increasing high-pitched intensity and excitement, until it approaches the dramatic climax of the moment of actual egg-
laying which ends with a loud triumphant cry.

Fitz disappears inside, and rushes back immediately to the window, frying pan in hand. He looks up toward the roof. Suddenly,
down a circular outside runway, built in a descending spiral,
comes rolling the freshly-laid egg. The egg spins around several
times coming down the ramp to gay, cheerful egg-laying music
before it finally goes plunk right into Fitz' frying pan.

Fitz cries out:

"Breakfast!"

The echo comes back: "Breakfast!"

Fitz slams the window shut, and our play begins.

That's what usually happened.

On the night of the thunderstorm and cloudburst, we had to
begin without any of these preliminaries. Those dear, unsuspecting
children knew nothing at all about what they were about to see or
what was going to happen.

It surely must have seemed like magic.

60

Our "warm-up" was always quite elaborate. It made the story more believable and made friends forever with the children.

The front of our stage was designed by Bill Jr. It was painted to resemble an old weather-beaten fence standing in front of Fitz' house. The middle board of the fence was made of transparent plastic. Thanks to Bill's artistic skill, it resembled all the other wooden boards.

There were shrill cries of delight and laughter from the children when suddenly a bright light would appear at the bottom of that middle board of the fence, illuminating a big number 10. The light would slowly begin to move up the fence like an ascending elevator, with appropriate "ascending" music on our hidden tape recorder.

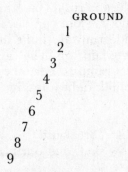

GROUND
1
2
3
4
5
6
7
8
9

Two trapdoors would flap open, and a beautiful golden cage would rise magically. A flashing bejewelled door would swing open, and out of the shining golden cage would step the magnificent Honourable, Mr Glow-Worm.

Mr Glow-Worm had a pale green belly and dozens of bright and fuzzy yellow feet. Hidden lights inside his tummy made his body pulsate with the phosphorescent glow of a firefly. Mr Glow-Worm had a wonderful dark green head with two tall glistening orange antennae. Each antenna was topped by a tiny round glittering diamond-like zircon that glistened in brilliant changing colours reflected from the stage lights. Mr Glow-Worm's large nose was a small round light-bulb painted bright red. His nose flashed on and off whenever Mr Glow-Worm talked.

Mr Glow-Worm's nose would pulsate rapidly as he discussed the exciting underground news of the day with Fitz. Mr Glow-Worm's voice was a high-pitched radio-bug. You've heard the sound on shortwave radio. It goes:

"Beep, beep, beepity beep, beep!"

Fitz, of course, being educated, was the only one of the animals who understood Mr Glow-Worm's language and could converse with him. This was important because Mr Glow-Worm was the head of the secret Underground Movement. He knew all the gossip from everywhere. He loved sharing it with Fitz, so that Fitz could share it with his friends and neighbours.

Mr Glow-Worm would say: "Beep, Beep, *Beep*! Beepbeep."

Fitz would be shocked at the news and say: "No!"

"Beep! Beep!" Mr Glow-Worm insisted.

"That's terrible!"

All the other animals, impatient to hear what was happening, and to know what was so terrible, would scream at Fitz to translate and tell them the news.

"What's happening?" they shouted, annoyed.

Mr Glow-Worm told them, "Beep!"

"Is that so?" Fitz cried out, shocked. He looked at the others and said, unable to believe it, "Did you hear that?" He covered his eyes with his little furry hands. "I can't believe it!"

"Beep! Beep! Beep!"

"Horrible", Fitz shouted. "Horrible! I just can't believe it."

"Can't believe *what*?" the other animals demanded. They were becoming more outraged by the second.

"You heard it", Fitz answered them.

"Beep! Beep! Beep!"

"Isn't that terrible?"

"What's terrible?" Hillary hollered.

"That last dreadful 'Beep!'" Fitz explained.

When the animals began pounding Fitz with the broom, mop,

hockey stick, and started throwing snowballs at him, Mr Glow-Worm made his escape into the elevator.

The golden cage descended, the trapdoors flapped shut, and on the front of the fence as the elevator descended, we saw:

GROUND

1

2

3

4

5

6

7

8

9

10

BOTTOM!

All lights out!

"Musa ukuhleka! Don't laugh!"

61

All of this which took only a few seconds was too much for the children. They would scream with laughter. Immediately all of them began to choose their favourite character. They would shout encouragement to whichever animal they loved the most. They were no longer puppets to the children.

In the night of the great cloudburst, however, Fitz began the programme at the Matapa School by coming cheerfully out of his little house with his pork-pie hat on, carrying a large bunch of colourful flowers. It was the first time any of the children had seen him. The flowers were a gift for the Headmaster of the Matapa School. Fitz was singing:

"I'm the smartest boy in Matapa School. With sneezing flowers for the Headmaster."

The children shouted and clapped with delight. Any joke on the Headmaster was fair game.

Fitz turned around, looked out at the children, and pointed his finger at them. Fitz said in Zulu: "Musa ukuhleka! Don't laugh!"

The children gasped.

They were shocked that a wooden squirrel could speak Zulu. Since Fitz had told them not to laugh, and in their own language at that, they never laughed again. Not once throughout the entire performance. Not even one single little encouraging laugh. For the rest of the night.

The more silent the children became, the funnier Marguerite, Bill and I tried to become. It was a challenge. We had to make them laugh. Children had always laughed before. Our performance was to us hilarious, but the children at Matapa School remained absolutely silent. We didn't yet know why, so behind the scenes we pulled out all the stops. We tried everything we knew in our repertoire to make them laugh.

They wouldn't.

Fitz, the squirrel had told them not to. In Zulu.

The children were frightened. They kept their hands over their mouths ever since the moment Fitz said, "Musa ukuhleka! Don't laugh!" They were still in shock over a Zulu-speaking funny-looking little wooden squirrel.

Only a white witch-doctor could do that.

"Don't laugh!" were the only Zulu words I knew. I had memorized them only for this special occasion thinking they would be a big hit. Unfortunately, I didn't know how to say in Zulu: "It's only a joke, children. Go ahead and laugh."

When the programme was over, one of the teachers, speaking on behalf of the restless children said to the audience: "Many of us will not sleep tonight."

It was customary for the children to come up to the front after a programme such as ours, to meet the performers on stage. The children refused to do it. They had already seen enough of me as the squirrel, or Bill as Great Big Sam, and Marguerite as Camille, the cam-*ell*.

The children suspected that all three of us were white witch-doctors. We had to be if we could make a cloth elephant drink milk and a carved piece of wood speak Zulu, and a fluffy big-eyed camel sing, and a secretary bird blow smoke rings out of his nostrils, and a bug come up out of the earth. The children wanted no part of it. They slipped quietly out the side doors. They were glad to escape back to their rooms.

We learned all of this later that night from our Bahá'í friend, the Headmaster. He was highly amused by it all. He considered it a most successful evening.

"However," he said, "you have no other choice but to return and do it right. Come out with a puppet on each arm and give the children the entire explanation the way you had originally planned for tonight. They deserve it, and will reward you with such happy laughter as you have never heard before."

We doubted it, but we did come back. A month later.

This time, to their delight and ours, the screams of laughter were loud, long and spontaneous. The thing they laughed at most of all, shrieked really, was the moment when Fitz said to them: "Musa ukuhleka!"

Bedlam!

They hollered it right back at Fitz in a loud shouting chorus: "Musa ukuhleka!"

I don't ever remember a more appreciative and charming audience. This time the children gladly came up on the stage afterward. Enthusiastically they shook hands with the animals. They took some by the paw, some by the nose, the ear, the trunk, or whatever part was most available or appealing. They pulled, twisted and hugged and giggled to their hearts' content and whispered: "Musa ukuhleka!" There were bubbles of laughter everywhere.

One little girl kissed Fitz on the cheek and said, "I love you."

Fitz not being any better at Zulu than myself asked what it was she had said. When told, Fitz answered back and said, "I love you, too," and gave her the Headmaster's sneezing flowers for her very own, and kissed her on the end of her nose. She ran away screaming with laughter, "Musa ukuhleka!" A dozen children raced after her, trying to steal her flowers.

Will there ever be such days of innocence, delight and wonder ever again?

BRAVO! ENCORE!
HURRAY!
WELL DONE! ¡OLÉ!
APPLAUSE!
CURTAIN CALL

62

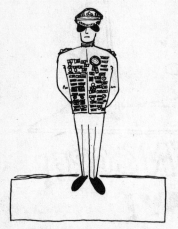

I remember the story of the famous General who attended the Military Ball. His splendid gold-braided uniform was festooned with impressive medals of every kind. A beautiful damsel was dancing with him, and very taken with his medals, said:

"General, how fascinating! How did you ever have time to win all those glorious medals?"

"Easy", the General said. He pointed to the biggest medal. "You see this huge gold medal here in the centre?"

"Yes, General."

"Well, I received that medal by mistake, and I was given all the other medals because of that one."

So it has been with many of my own journeys and apparent successes, however limited.

Many times Marguerite and I have been told, in both letter and in person, how marvellous it was that we came to such a far-off remote place like Frobisher Bay off Baffin Island, where no Hand of the Cause of God had been before. In truth, we had been heading for Labrador *en route* to Greenland and Iceland. The winds of God and weather conditions blew us to Frobisher Bay as the alternate stop.

As Mr Faizi once jokingly said to me, under similar conditions, "Bahá'u'lláh sometimes is very stubborn. He likes to do it His way." Could there be any other?

Besides, it wasn't marvellous of us at all. We were carried there by the love and generosity of a friend, David Hadden. Without his kindness and help, we would never have arrived in time for the big Youth Conference in Iceland. I would still have been back at my desk in solitary comfort watching the Canadian geese land upon the glossy surface of our beautiful nearby pond while I was enjoying the Grey Cup final.

Back to that "big medal" of the General. Every book I have ever written in the past several years has been typed, rewritten, re-typed, rewritten and typed again by Merle Cates. She is tireless, tender, helpful and forgiving. I have truly stood on her shoulders during many a hectic, wild day of deadlines. In six weeks together we wrote *Cry from the Heart!*, all 1 500 pages. Rewrote it to 1 200 pages, to 1 000 and on down to 700, 500 and finally to the 395 pages which formed the basis for the final edited copy. The final copy was edited brilliantly by David and Marion Hofman of George Ronald, the Publishers that have edited so many of my books, and have always made me appear more skilful and better than I really am. It is the story of my life.

Merle is more than a secretary. She is my Research Department, my Duplicating Division, and my fountain of good cheer. She is still typing manuscripts for me today even though we are both older than the flagship of Eric, the Red.

In the early days of Africa, when *Release the Sun* and *Thief in the Night* were written, I stood upon the tireless shoulders of Knight of Bahá'u'lláh, Doris Ballard.

In these twilight hours of three score years and ten, it is the smiling, ever-willing, never-tiring, extremely capable shoulders of Transkei pioneer, Margaret Pemberton-Pigott, that support, encourage and cheer me on.

Actually on *All Flags Flying!* I have had more secretaries than the United Nations, and in almost as many continents.

I have been showered with such blessings, throughout my entire Bahá'í life. Some of the things I did on my own with original ideas and projects, but frequently, with the BIG ONES, a veritable army of co-workers would rise up on all sides to help me carry out the plans and bring them to a triumphant conclusion.

They were the *Big Medal*. All I had to do was stand in the wings, come out, and take my bows before the applauding audience.

I confess, I did like the hurrays! bravos! olés! and author-authors! Consequently, I didn't always honestly admit that I was just a stranger passing by.

I had decided to introduce all of these heroes and heroines who had so enriched my life, but I soon learned it couldn't be done. I tried putting down the names of all those dear friends to whom I should pay tribute, but no matter how many names I wrote down, a dozen more came to mind, each more lovable than the last. These were personal, deeply-loved friends. I wanted to thank each one of them for their lifetime of help and kindness.

I thought of saying that they were just too dear and precious to put in a book, or too illustrious. It was true, but it didn't have the ring of sincerity.

They know who they are, of course, and I'm sure, right now they are nodding their heads. They know how much I love them and how grateful I am to each one of them without identifying them by name.

If I try, I can already hear the chorus from on High and from here below crying out: "What about me? Remember the time—"

I remember. You were the best. Unfortunately, I have just run out of ink.*

Perhaps I can deal properly with this problem in a later, fatter book called: Friends! It will be as thick as the Los Angeles Telephone book and have no plot whatsoever.

In spite of my many "Cameo" performances over the years, God is only too well aware of who it was that smoothed the path for Marguerite and myself, and made most of those victories possible.

For my many Bahá'í friends who are saying, "Baloney!" (I do have friends who talk that way. I'm not sure they deserve to be on the list, actually.) Or, worse, those who say: "Isn't it sweet to hear the Hand of the Cause be so modest? And humble?"

To them, especially, I reply with humility and dignity:

"In a pig's eye!"

What I have said here is the absolute and utter truth, and I'm glad to get it off my conscience. So swallow it. There's more to come.

---

* Marguerite when she proof-read this chapter said, "What about Bahá'u'-lláh's statement that truth is the foundation of all virtues?" "It's just a little Irish whimsy", I explained. (The rest is censored.) I'm getting a new proof-reader.

The bitter truth is that only we, ourselves, know what we're like inside. You can hoodwink your friends, maybe even your family, but never the Chairman of the Board on High. I know that borders on the sacrilegious, but it's easier to joke about it than to face up to the reality.

When Hand of the Cause, Mr A Q Faizi and myself worked together in the Holy Land, I came across one of his old identity cards (credentials) that was out of date. I asked him if I could have it. He said, "Yes." I carried it for years, and he never asked me why. I carried it just in case that during one of my intermittent malaria, liver hepatitis, or heart attacks I might need it. I planned to use it in the next world. I figured I could be there for months before they found out who I really was.

My second line of defence which I counted on even more, was Ethel Revell. Ethel worked for years as a secretary for the Hands of the Bahá'í Faith in the Holy Land, including the years I was serving there.

Ethel had met the Master, 'Abdu'l-Bahá, when He was in Philadelphia. Marguerite and I were on the Local Assembly of Philadelphia with Ethel for years.

Ethel Revell was a saint.

Everybody said so. Except Ethel.

One day I polled the people I was with, asking them, "How many of you agree with me that Ethel Revell is a saint?"

Only one person disagreed. We were all shocked.

"Why do you think she's not a saint?" I demanded, peeved.

"Ethel is so special", he answered, "that I think we can come up with something far better and more lofty than calling her a saint."

It was because of Ethel Revell that I developed my famous "SAINT" theory. Famous in small Bahá'í circles. Simply put, you will find that the most important letter of the word "Saint" is the first, the letter "S". It stands for:

*S*elfless
*S*teadfast
*S*acrifice
*S*erenity

I remember once when I was explaining my theory using a huge feltboard in the Los Angeles Convention Centre, someone hollered out from the back of the hall: "It also stands for *Scarce*."

Isn't that the truth!

The point is, if you think you are a saint, and you haven't developed those "s" virtues that make you "selfless", no matter how sincerely you think you are a

SAINT,
without the"S", you
AINT.

Sorry about that, too, but don't blame me, blame Ethel Revell. She started it. All I know is that from the moment I met Ethel, I kept telling her, "Ethel, I'm going to ride into heaven on your coat-tails."

Ethel was also witty.

"I'm dragging no dead wood into the Kingdom of God", she warned me. "Take it where they can burn it."

I said: "You're no saint."

"I never said I was. You keep saying it."

One night during those fragrant soul-healing years that Marguerite and I spent serving in that "snow-white Spot", "God's holy mountain", "the nest of all the Prophets", I had a dream. About Ethel Revell. I died and went to the next world. When they checked my credentials, I couldn't find Faizi's former identification card anywhere. I was frantic, and finally reduced to giving my own identity.

"I'm Bill Sears."

"Bill who?"

I was in a cold sweat.

Everybody figures that being a Hand of the Cause greases the skids for you, and that you can slip in merely by mentioning your name. Forget it, my friend. I've lived with Sears, William, for nearly three quarters of a century, and there's more than meets the eye—all except the eye of the Man Upstairs. I knew I would be in trouble, and I was. So I did the next best thing. I said, "I'm also a very good friend of Ethel Revell."

It made all the difference.

The heavenly gatekeeper broke into a big smile. He whipped out his huge golden key and joyfully unlocked the gates.

"Why didn't you say so in the first place?" he cried. He threw wide those golden, ruby, emerald and diamond gates. "Go right into the Kingdom, young man", he said. "Any friend of Ethel Revell's is a friend of God's."

I woke up feeling marvellous. I promised myself I'd try to be better. I've been trying, but the things that give me the greatest hope are Faizi's identity and Ethel Revell's friendship.

They're my hole cards.

"Canadian friends: with zeal and unity"

63

The many journeys Marguerite and I have made in nearly half a century have taken us the equivalent of twenty times around the world. I know I said ten times in *God Loves Laughter*, but that was ages ago. Much water has gone by in the wake of steamboats, under the wheels of trains, buses and cars, not to mention below the wings of our high-flying domestic and overseas flights since those early days. Especially beneath the wings of that constantly flying two-motored yellow, brown and golden bird of David Hadden, CF-WZU.

CF-WZU was the Canadian registration for David's plane. It was identified by the various Canadian Control Towers by the code words of *W-Zed-U*: "Whiskey, Zulu, Uniform". This was standard procedure for both take-off and landing.

In no time, the Bahá'í friends were awaiting the arrival of David's plane at Thunder Bay, Winnipeg, Regina, Saskatoon, Calgary, Nelson, Kelowna, Whitehorse, Anchorage, Halifax, St. John's in Newfoundland, Fredricton in New Brunswick, and Charlottetown on Prince Edward Island.

Yes, we visited them all. And then some. That was merely the warm-up.

"Whiskey, Zulu, Uniform" was discarded by the Bahá'ís as an identification. The alert Canadian Bahá'ís soon changed the meaning of the call-letters of David's plane. They dubbed David's beautiful Bahá'í bird of passage as: *CF* ("Canadian Friends"), *WZU* ("With Zeal and Unity").

That humming-bird scarcely had time to cool down, except for stringent safety check-ups. David was always a stickler for that. David didn't believe in safety first. He believed in safety first, last and always. I liked it.

David's plane carried various travelling Bahá'ís to the tropics, and Marguerite and myself to the frozen north. In fact, *Canadian Friends: With Zeal and Unity* carried me off to every Province and Territory in Canada. We flew past the great glaciers beyond Mount McKinley *en route* to the Alaskan Conference. At Anchorage we saw the beautiful blue flag of Alaska emblazoned with the silver stars of the Great Dipper as we landed at the Anchorage airport.

All of this was the least of our many happy journeys together.

Our golden bird landed twice in Greenland *en route* to and from Iceland and the Faeroe Islands. The first time we touched down, it was on a landing strip that from the air appeared about as long as Pinocchio's nose. It was surrounded by high, snow-capped, threatening mountains.

"Hey, David," I said, "do you see that five-cent postage stamp landing-strip down below?"

"I not only see it," David replied, "I'm heading for it."

I swallowed and said: "Could you drop me off at the Château Frontenac *en route?*"

When we landed in the middle of that midget icy nowhere, we were not only surrounded by snow-capped mountains, but by a ring of small icebergs.

"Marguerite," I suggested, as I unfastened my lap-strap, "let's disembark and hunt up the coffee shop and lounge."

Hysterical laughter from the cockpit. We were informed that the only restaurant and coffee shop available was in our own thermos. It was passed around enthusiastically.

A pick-up truck appeared out of nowhere loaded down with oil drums. Our fuel. Once refuelled, we were quickly airborne for Reykjavik, Iceland and the International Youth Conference. Marguerite leaned across the aisle toward me as the plane took off. She giggled as she took my hand, squeezed it, and pointed at the departing airstrip. She whispered to me: "I'm not coming back next year."

On a visit to Western Canada in David's plane, we commemorated the Martyrdom of the Báb twice. The first time was at high noon, ten thousand feet above Saskatchewan approaching Regina. The second time was immediately after we landed. We found ourselves in a different time zone. We were just in time to join our Bahá'í friends for a second observation of that same historic Holy Day.

David, with a twinkle in his eye, suggested that if we were flying West into the sunset at next Riḍván in a Lear Jet, we could try for three Commemorations.

David made a far more remarkable teaching trip across Canada than ours, astonishing as it was. David flew 'Amatu'l-Bahá, Rúḥíyyih <u>Kh</u>ánum to all those places we went, plus many others. His plane was like a honey-bee, pollinating Bahá'í communities everywhere. His illustrious passenger, 'Amatu'l-Bahá, Rúḥíyyih <u>Kh</u>ánum, brought new life to them all.

Each time I planned to make a record-breaking teaching trip of my own on any continent, she broke it. I found that 'Amatu'l-Bahá, Rúḥíyyih <u>Kh</u>ánum, had made a better one—longer, more intense, and far more effective.

When I wrote a book, she wrote a better one. When I gave a talk at one of the International Conferences, she gave a more exciting one. I am sometimes tempted to say: "Doggone it!" But when I think of her, I can only spontaneously applaud: "Bravo!"

Quietly, behind the scenes

64

We have referred to Nancy and David Hadden several times throughout this book. This chapter puts their kindness and generosity all into one capsule. Therapeutic. If Marguerite and I were to tell you in how many different ways Nancy and David Hadden have made it possible for us to serve the Bahá'í Faith more effectively from our Gardener's Cottage on their property Batterwood, high above the waterfall at the Old Mill on the Ganaraska River, you would think we were electioneering for them. Not for them to become members of the National or Local Assemblies or any special committee. Bahá'ís don't do that. It's forbidden.

Like all other things about the Bahá'í Faith, the Administrative Procedure (elections included), while enlivened by dramatic unimpeded consultative "give-and-take" sessions, still keeps the democratic process at a very high, wholesome level of participation by all.

No, we were thinking of nominating David and Nancy for the Supreme Concourse. At least as alternates.*

David turns white, then red, whenever I say things like this. Which is quite often. His pallor is particularly effective. The flush you don't notice as much, as his face is frequently highly coloured from hard work.

"Can't you take a spiritual joke?" I ask him, knowing that he can't.

Or, take Nancy Hadden. Her delightfully creative graphics and posters for the GATHERINGS aided by her daughter Kelly Hadden's colourful feltboard titles, made those sessions, in my opinion, unique, pictorial, cheerful, and the equal of any such Bahá'í Con-

* This is an inside Bahá'í joke, but if you'd like to sign your Declaration Card and join in, I'd be happy to explain it to you. . . . Where did everybody go?

ferences anywhere. Nancy master-minding each step along the way. Quietly and behind the scenes.

Marguerite and I asked Nancy if she could design a special card for the coming New Year's Day (Naw-Rúz). She did. It was sensational. A huge replica still hangs on the front wall at The Hall where so many popular GATHERINGS were held. Testimony to the accuracy of these words.

The New Year's Day card was a cut-out of all the Bahá'í Houses of Worship current in the world, in the order of their completion, in their exact relative proportion to each other, and all in vivid, varied dignified blending colours. As you turn the pages of the card, you first see the Bahá'í House of Worship in Wilmette, Illinois, and you read the inspiring words of 'Abdu'l-Bahá Who Himself dedicated that Temple and called it "The Silent Teacher". When that House of Worship was dedicated to public worship in 1953, it marked, as foretold in the Bahá'í Writings, the "inception" of that *Kingdom of God on earth* we have been talking about throughout this book.

What a New Year's Day card that was!

Marguerite and I signed the card along with Nancy and David. We sent it out all over the world as a gift, and as a reminder to all of our dear friends that the Temple which dominated all the other Houses of Worship was the one that stood beside Lake Michigan in Wilmette, Illinois; the one described as the "holiest House of Worship" that would ever "be reared by the followers of Bahá'u'lláh".

It was the "Mother Temple of the West". In front of it, in silhouette, stood some of her illustrious children already born in other parts of the world. They were all there on Nancy's card.

Marguerite and I refused to sign Nancy's later creations. It would have been akin to doing a finger-painting yourself, and then standing beside a truly masterful painting and taking bows for your thumb prints.

As soon as that first New Year's Day card was mailed out, I said to Nancy:

"Okay, what's your marvellous idea for next year?"

I have been saying the same thing to Nancy every year since. Ask her.

If Marguerite and I were to recount all of the creative things that were done for us in connection with our part in those GATH-ERINGS—feltboards, titles, easels, rostrums, rear screen, charts, graphs, props, illumined maps, sound effects—I think Nancy's name would lead all the rest; or at least be competing for that front-running spot with her husband David.*

When Marguerite and I say things like this about Nancy and David, it embarrasses the Haddens extremely, but it makes both of us feel so good!

* Nancy can become quite "shirty" about all this praise. To say she loathed it would not be too strong. She forgave me, but only because in mentioning Abou ben Adhem, I had not quoted the rest of the poem: "May . . . [her] tribe increase."

65

Marguerite and I returned home to North America from one of our assignments in Africa, but our largest footlocker containing most of our valuable possessions never caught up with us. It followed us faithfully by sea, air and train from continent to continent, always just missing. At least, that's what the shippers told us.

"The truth is," I told Marguerite, "that footlocker is fed up with our life-style and has gone off on its own teaching trip."

Marguerite, with a hopeful gleam in her eye, said, "The day that trunk finally does catch up with us will be the day we are asked to return to Africa."

We were meeting with the British Columbia Victory Committee in 1966 in West Vancouver when the bill of lading arrived for the trunk. It had been found on the docks of San Francisco next stop Tokyo. It had been rescued and was now being shipped to our address in Southern California which we had just permanently vacated.

The very last letter in that same large stack of mail was from the World Centre of the Bahá'í Faith asking us to return to Africa.

All of this concerns Roger White and William van Zoest, two extremely active and loving Bahá'í friends of ours. Both Canadians.

Roger White was a Secretary *par excellence* in all phases of Bahá'í and business life. He was at one time the Assistant Editor of *Hansard*, the official report of the Canadian House of Commons.

I always felt that Roger could meet in Olympic Competition the most formidable and top-flight Executive Secretaries from anywhere on earth in face to face and open combat at thirty paces. An International "type-off", "dictation-off", or "idea-off" and win the battle with one hand tied behind his back. That, of course, was before I met Margaret Pemberton-Pigott in Transkei. Now, I think it would be:

"Sohrab and Rustem!"

Or, spiritually speaking, even: Ivan Skavitsky Skivar meets Abdulla Bulbul Ameer.

Kismet!

Roger volunteered to come to Africa to help me with the Bahá'í work. The decision was the result of a consultation with his friend Bill van Zoest. Marguerite and I were living during the British Columbia Victory Campaign in Bill's apartment in West Van. We could see the ocean liners arrive and leave along the Burrard Inlet. Off toward the sunset, we could see the shadowy outline of Vancouver Island.

Bill volunteered to assist with some of the financial help Roger might need in Africa with Roger himself doing the rest. It was a gift from heaven. That's a stupid thing to say really, isn't it? Because we all know that's *exactly* what it was. Bill and Roger both came up one midnight, knocked on our door, and overwhelmed us with their generous offer. It was a smashing success from the moment we landed in Nairobi.

Roger and I worked together for years, both in Africa and later in North America, with Bill van Zoest always helping out.

BILL VAN ZOEST

Bill van Zoest was a self-made successful business man. I call him a modern Horatio Algar type who, with imagination, courage, inventiveness, business acumen and plenty of "derring-do!", rose like cream to the top.

Bill came to Canada from Holland with little more than what he was wearing. He worked his way up until he owned the stamp company where he was employed. He developed it, sold it, and used the resources to fulfil a very deep longing in his heart.

You guessed it. Pioneering.

Bill was always one to go wherever the need was greatest. He has never varied from that principle. When there was an urgent call that year for the frozen north, he put on his newly-acquired mukluks.

It's really not all that frozen, if you can get out before winter. Bill couldn't. Why would he suspect that winter came in August?

Bill van Zoest bought a trading store in Whitehorse, Yukon. The winters were so severe, and the icy winds blowing through the cracks in the door so fierce, that Bill would hose down the cracks and let the ice freeze to make a seal to keep out Old Man Winter.

I have a Canadian friend who loves everything within spitting distance of the 401 (Highway) and the Trans-Canada, but anything north of that he calls "Dominion on the rocks".*

---

* Irish whimsy. There are thousands and thousands of hardy souls who love only the far North. I know that. However, I still feel that this truth is best appreciated below the Mason–Dixon Line.

Bill van Zoest came to visit us in Palm Desert, California. The change from below zero to ninety-five above (Fahrenheit) was too great and too sudden. Bill spent his holiday, which he cut short, in the middle of Merle Cates' swimming pool totally submerged. He kept crying out:

"This weather is vicious! Vicious!"

He longed for the deep-freeze of his beloved North.

I made Bill famous for a week or so (maybe infamous is a better word). I wrote a parody on The Cremation of Sam McGee. It expressed admiration for Bill's faithfulness and steadfastness in the Indian–Eskimo teaching work. Besides, Sam McGee's cabin was in plain sight in downtown Whitehorse and so was Bill's CPA office. It seemed a natural, and it was very funny. I called it: "The Roost of Bill van Zoest". Now you know how to pronounce his name.

However, out of respect for Bill van Zoest, and since I *do* want to go back to Whitehorse, I will not show you a copy of the parody. It might cause Robert W Service to spin in his grave, and I know it already has caused Bill van Zoest to whirl in his CPA suit. Besides, it is not fair to a fellow pioneer, no matter how loving, how tender, and how extremely hilarious and amusing my stroke of genius might have been. Furthermore, I understand that all copies of the parody have been destroyed. Burned. And the ashes buried deep on the "marge of Lake Lebarge".*

Bill van Zoest became a CPA—not "Canadian Pioneer Anywhere!"—but *Certified Public Accountant*. The difficulties he overcame for other folks, the fantastic cases he handled made it clear to him why accountants were called "certified". My joke, not his. None of it mattered, as long as he was pioneering and teaching for the Faith.

I wish we all could be in the room with Bill van Zoest when he reads these words for the first time. He is a blond Hollander from Amsterdam, shy, humble and sensitive. His blush of discomfort will go both up into his hairline and down into his collar.

I lose a lot of friends this way, but they usually return. Love has a way of doing that. I wish I could find a friend who likes to be

---

* Isn't it odd, or was it prophetic? As I wrote the first pages of this chapter on the Yukon, I was also writing and recording a "Greeting" to all the Canadian Bahá'ís who were gathered that very weekend to dedicate the new Yukon Indian Bahá'í Institute. Where do you think it is? On the "marge of Lake Lebarge"! Everybody rise and remove their hats, please.

praised and lauded for his or her good qualities, so I could scratch them off my list.

ROGER WHITE

A darling African girl, quite young but very eager and determined to learn English, would always volunteer to read a prayer at all meetings and Feasts. The first one she tried was the prayer for unity so often recited by the Bahá'í friends everywhere throughout the world: "O my God! O my God! Unite the hearts of Thy servants and reveal to them Thy great purpose."

She was quite creative. She read aloud:

"O my God! O my God! You *knit* the hearts of Thy servants."

Nothing could be sweeter or more accurate than that. It was on the next phrase that she went off the rails.

"And review for them Thy great porpoise."

It became an important slogan for Roger White and myself. Whenever the troubles became too many, and the burden heavy, or if either of us fell into the doldrums, Roger would come out of his apartment and say:

"Bill. The time has come for us to review the great Porpoise."

I haven't told Roger yet, but the last time I was in Africa, I heard that same lovely young lady, now a graduate student, recite the Tablet of Aḥmad eloquently, flawlessly and brilliantly. As she was leaving the building later, she whispered as she passed me, "I no longer review the great Porpoise."

"Pity", I told her. "I still do myself. With the tenderest love."

There is no need to tell my Bahá'í friends about the Irish genius of Roger White. They have read his books and delighted in both the satire and the deep wisdom. *Another Song Another Season* is my favourite, although I am very taken with the single poem: "It Takes All Kinds to Make a Kingdom". It says in a few lines what has taken me this entire book not to be able to say.

In fact, I have an entire notebook full of Roger's poems accompanied by my own comments about their significance and the teachings of the Faith which they illumine so brightly, wittily and movingly. I use them on special occasions at Fireside Meetings or small gatherings. I call the evening: "Bill Sears reads Roger White."

270

One summer as Marguerite and I were packing and about to start on another series of journeys, all three of us consulted together. As a result, Roger decided to offer his services to the World Centre in the Holy Land for the six-month period Marguerite and I would be gone.

"Goodbye, Roger", I said. "You'll never come back."

"Why do you say that?"

"You'll be too valuable a jewel for the World Centre ever to relinquish."

It was prophetic.

Every time I went to the Holy Land after that, the friends would look at me suspiciously, and say with trepidation: "You haven't come to ask for Roger back, have you?"

It was useless. I knew it in my heart.

I won't say Roger's going left a hole in my life of service, but if you have ever seen the open pit mines of Utah, you'll understand my feelings at the mention of his name.

66

I've already mentioned several names, but those are only a few leaves from all the remaining forests of trees. It shows you the vastness of my problem when I try to demonstrate for you who the real heroes and heroines of *All Flags Flying!* really are. I shall give you two more brief but confirming examples of the impossibility of my task in paying proper tribute to those who deserve it.

ONE:

I have become everybody's grandfather! Because of the Ayyám-i-Há record, a fun-loving musical "New Year's Day" party for the children. The Bahá'í children all think of me as their grandfather. To be honest, I don't discourage them.

It happened by accident when we were recording the musical party. During a break in rehearsal, a little boy came racing after a little girl, threatening her with his fist doubled up. She was fleeing for her life. She hid behind me, I stopped the mayhem before the danger point, taking each one by the hand to hold them apart.

"What's the problem?" I asked.

The little boy was livid.

"Do Bahá'ís believe in the equality of men and women or not?"

"Completely", I assured him.

"Well then?"

"Well then, what?"

"She hit me in the nose, and if there's any equality, I should be able to punch her back. A good one!"

"I believe the principle goes deeper than that."

The little girl stuck out her tongue.

"My grandfather won't let you hit me."

The little boy scoffed. "He's not *your* grandfather."

"He is, too!"

"He is not!"

I broke it up saying, "I'm everybody's grandfather. There's plenty of me to go around."

"See!" she said.

The producers thought it was cute and suggested we keep it in the programme. We did. It proved to be a very unwise decision. It resulted in one of the greatest mail disasters of my life. Oh, I love the children. I'm happy to be their grandfather. The thing is, letters and postcards started flowing in from all parts of the English-speaking world. Wherever they played the tape, children wrote. "Dear grandfather" was interspersed with an "Abuelito" or two.

There was no end to the mail.

I only wish there were time to share the delight of the children's letters and the incredible things they said. I'm writing a small booklet about it called: *Everybody's Grandfather!*

Once again, I, personally, did nothing (other than break up a small-scale studio war), but I became a planetary grandfather and the author of another book, one of the funniest yet, from material supplied by newly inherited small-fry relatives.

For my part as the narrator of another record and tape recording called *The Lote Tree*, a touching portrait of the important Figures of the Bahá'í Faith, I received additional honours, not really mine. The album was enriched by the inspiring background music composed by Russel Garcia. It featured the lovely songs of Jimmy Seals and Dash Crofts, as well as a beautiful song composed and sung by Walter Black.

Both of the above albums have won for me considerable praise and affection. They have endeared me to the children and to their parents wherever English is spoken. Marcia Day of DAY STUDIOS, Russ Garcia, and Seals and Crofts are the ones who should receive the lion's share of the honours. They made it all possible. I did write the original narration, but after that I merely showed up in the studio for rehearsal and read the script.

The hard work of composing, arranging, and organizing the entire production had already taken place, plus the actual recording and distribution which came later.

"Kudos" for me on earth, "Bouquets" for them On High.

Which would you prefer? Me, too.

Two:

I still receive letters of love and thanks for the *Children's Stories from the Dawn-Breakers*. Actually, Zoe Meyer wrote the book from Nabíl's Narrative and Karl Scheffler illustrated it.

What you also don't know is that Dr Amín Banání arranged for the recording date, supplied the recording equipment, and served as engineer and supervisor of the entire master tape, and brought the whole project to fruition. Even more, he introduced me as the narrator and movingly painted the scene for those historic stories. In addition, Dr Banání organized the special photograph of myself and the children which you see on the final cassette cover.

All of the fringe benefits were mine. Not only the popularity with the children around the world, but that unforgettable Persian dinner prepared by Dr Banání himself and served with such grace and elegance by his lovely wife, Sheila.

I merely showed up. After eating a Persian dinner that made the angels sorry they died, I read the script, went to bed, and left Dr Banání to assemble, edit, and finalize the tape.

Are you getting the picture?

When next you hear *The Children's Dawnbreakers* tape, stand up and applaud. Let's hear it for the real headliner, Dr Amín Banání. He may not be "everybody's grandfather", he's far too young for that, but from now on, when you hear praises for *The Children's Dawnbreakers*, see to it that the world knows who to thank.

You might, of course, mention my name in passing.

I *know*. I've already added several more names, and have forgotten so many others. No matter. The rest of you know who you are, and you know how much I love you.

I may have been the "star of the show" to my Bahá'í friends on many of these occasions, but I was only a bit-player to God.

And that's the truth.

274

THE TEAM

67

Eleven words spoken on the side of God's Holy Mountain, Carmel, in Israel, changed both of our lives forever. It bound Bob and myself together, Robert Quigley and William Sears, in a journey of service that has lasted for over thirty years.

Our team-work has carried us into all continents, into all the media; and, we hope, into the hearts of many of the dear Bahá'í friends everywhere who arose to help us with our work.

Bob and I became so inseparable in our work together over the years, that it was not uncommon for our friends to call Bill Bob, and Bob Bill. We liked it. It meant that our Bahá'í friends thought of us as a "team". That was a source of great joy to both of us. I have even called him Bill myself on occasion and he has called me Bob. We both took it as a compliment.

It all began when Bob and Keith Quigley went on pilgrimage and met our beloved Guardian, Shoghi Effendi. That began our lifetime of "team-work" because of those eleven magic words.

These soul-stirring, unforgettable eleven words were spoken to Bob Quigley while he and his wife Keith were there on the side of the Mountain of God visiting the Holy Shrines at the World Centre of the Bahá'í Faith.

When the Quigleys returned home to Westport, Connecticut, I was waiting for them eagerly at the front door of their home on Minute Man Hill. I had been finishing the rough draft of my book *Thief in the Night* while they were on pilgrimage.

In one sentence, Bob altered the course of both our lives. I said, "Tell me all about the beloved Guardian. How was he? What did he say? Don't leave anything out. Not a word!"

Bob told me after he embraced me. Keith stood looking on with tears in her eyes. The eleven life-changing words the beloved Guardian had spoken to Bob on that occasion were these:

276

"You and Bill make a good team;
you should work together."

We have never turned back from that moment. We have sought every opportunity we could find to make those words come true in our lives as a "team" for him. We were ready to undertake anything, anywhere, like fierce young Lions of the Covenant.

It is important to understand that Shoghi Effendi, the beloved Guardian, had in no way given Bob and myself any special station. He had not singled us out for a special mission. He had not assigned us to any particular task on his behalf. We were no doubt but one of many "teams" he had inspired. It was he, the Guardian of our Faith, who originated the concept of "teams" working together in the Faith: "teams" who even as you read these words, are labouring energetically in many parts of the world.

Even so, in those beginning days of the Guardian's great World Crusade, Bob and I must surely have ranked among the most enthusiastic of his spiritual warrior "teams". We both had such a deep abiding love for the Guardian of our Faith that we were set "on fire" by his every word. We knew who he was, and the greatness of his station, and we tried to tell everybody.

To Bob and myself, Shoghi Effendi was not only the Guardian of the Bahá'í Faith, he was also the great-grandson of the Supreme Redeemer of all men, Bahá'u'lláh, the Promised One of all ages. He was descended from the Herald of the Bahá'í Faith, the Báb. He was the grandson of the Centre of Bahá'u'lláh's mighty Covenant, 'Abdu'l-Bahá, the Mystery of God. It would take a volume to even begin to say properly who Shoghi Effendi really was. Even then words would fail utterly. To us, during every hour of our lives, he was indeed, the "sign of God" on earth. It was enough for us.

I eagerly awaited the return of Bob and Keith from their pilgrimage on that historic day. I was about to return to Africa to my pioneering post. I had come back to Philadelphia for three months as a summer-replacement on my own television show so I could earn enough money to keep Marguerite, the boys and myself at our pioneering post overseas for at least another year. It provided the means that enabled us to concentrate on teaching and travelling throughout Africa. We had been travelling so extensively, that we beat a path to the "Money Store" (Barclays, Chase Manhattan,

Bank of America) to pay for tickets. We used cash. "Don't leave home without it."

When Bob told me we were now a "team", and the beloved Guardian's "team" at that, I suggested we develop some way to work together by mail as I was catching the next plane to Africa.

"Sorry", I said.

Bob replied: "Sorry, my foot! I'm coming with you!"

And he did.

As soon as he could gracefully leave the successful CBS and NBC daytime television shows he was producing. I could see that Bob was already moving like Halley's comet, so I decided to wait for him, so we could go together, and land in Africa as the beloved Guardian's team.*

En route to Africa, Bob and I visited the Bahá'í summer schools in Caernarfon, Wales and Stuttgart, Germany. Not to mention trips through England, France, Italy, Greece, Egypt and Uganda.

The "team" had already opened the game.

Keith followed as soon as their daughter May was born. May, who learned to speak Zulu words almost as soon as she learned English, was named for May Bolles Maxwell, an illustrious heroine and martyr of the Bahá'í Faith whose pilgrimage to the Holy Land to visit the Master, 'Abdu'l-Bahá, had given birth to that delightful book *An Early Pilgrimage*.

'Abdu'l-Bahá said to this wonderful woman:

> "There are two visits; the first is for a blessing; then
> ye come and are blest and are sent forth to work in
> God's vineyard; the second ye come with music
> and the banners flying, like soldiers, in gladness
> and triumph to receive your reward."

As you have already guessed, it was these Words of 'Abdu'l-Bahá which inspired the title of the book you are now reading: *All Flags Flying!*

It is the hope of every band of Bahá'í pioneers that they will have the bounty of that triumphant *second visit* to the heart of their world.

---

* Keith would have come also but she was pregnant and packed for the hospital. Courageously, she pushed "the team" out of the nest and faced her ordeal alone.

278

During the year Marguerite and I went to Africa, 1953, the Bahá'í pioneers conquered one hundred countries in eleven months in every part of the world, in an unprecedented great wave of teaching. It was a pioneering outburst unequalled by any similar religious event in the past history of mankind. Those were the words of the Guardian of the Bahá'í Faith during my own pilgrimage in 1954.

When my work as one of the Chief Stewards of the Bahá'í Faith necessitated my return to North America, there was only one way the beloved Guardian's "team" could still serve together on a regular and effective basis. Bob, Keith and May, at my suggestion, followed Marguerite and myself back to the United States so we could proceed with our "team-work" on behalf of our beloved Guardian.

During my travels when I appeared on television in Pago Pago, American Samoa, or journeyed to Sydney, Brisbane, Canberra, Melbourne, Adelaide and Perth in Australia, and then on to Mauritius, South Africa, Nairobi, and all points of the African compass, it was always Bill Sears who was "on stage" and received the love and plaudits of the friends. In reality it was the other half of the "team", Bob Quigley, working quietly and energetically at home, on daytime and night-time television shows for CBS, NBC and ABC, who made most of those trips possible by his kindness and generosity. It was part of our team-work.

"If you're ever in trouble," Bob would say to me, time and again, "and need anything, cable or phone, and I'll send it."

He has. Many times.

"What if I need *you*?" I countered.

"I'll leave immediately."

He has. Many times.

Even apart we were a "team".

68

One look at Bob's Irish face and you think of shillelaghs, shamrocks, the rivers Shannon and Liffey, Galway Bay, County Cork, and Blarney Castle. Bob Quigley can dance an elegant Irish jig as well as a chorus-line tap-dance *à la* any Broadway Show. By launching himself into the early work of the Bahá'í Faith, Bob passed up a part in *Yellow Jack* which fell to Jimmy Stewart who was then at the start of his career. Later Bob repeated this sacrifice. He walked away from successful television shows on all three networks and jeopardized his professional career by his sacrifice in order to bring his half of the "team" to Africa to work for Bahá'u'lláh.*

There was a special charm and pleasure working with Bob, over and above his writing, performing, producing and directing. It was his original ideas. He never ran out of them. He was the best in the business. His delightful sense of humour saved many a day. Bob generated fun by his penetrating comments so rich with irony and significance but never mean. In times of conflict and trouble for the friends, Bob's remarks would often chase the boogy-man away with a particularly brilliant bit of hilarity. Humour fell spontaneously from his lips. Not wisecracks, but genuine wit that sparked your own imagination and elicited surprisingly delightful remarks from you yourself when you didn't know you had it in you.

Robert Quigley had an expertise at getting the best out of the

* You couldn't tell Bob it was a sacrifice. He said often, "No one will ever remember in the future what I did on CBS, ABC or NBC." He was right. But be sure that in the ages to come, they will remember the Guardian's "team" and the trails they tried to blaze, and the new friends and fellow-Bahá'ís they left behind. Can you really call that sacrifice?

people he interviewed for the Faith on radio and television. His personal remarks were frequently sly and full of mischief. They were often tender and always kind. Bob's manner would put his guests at ease and prompt natural, spontaneous, and often singularly entertaining and informative answers from them.

However, when Bob was aroused by a slur against his Faith, the air became crackling blue as just before the lightning strikes during a thunderstorm. Bob's observations on those occasions reminded me of the story about the two Arabs who were fighting with scimitars. One swung his big blade with a violent "Whoosh!" The other Arab laughed and said, "Ha! You missed me!" "Did I?", the scimitar-swinging Arab replied, "Just shake your head."

He did. And his head fell off.*

The Bahá'ís, of course, are peace-loving, law-abiding, gentle, non-violent people, but nothing expresses better than the above verbal sword-play what Robert Quigley was like when aroused in defence of the Bahá'í Faith, or any other Religion or Messenger of God.

To my way of thinking, Bob was a big "Whoosh!" man. He was invariably fair, funny and compassionate. You were both happy and lucky to have him on your side. Or should I say your team.

When I read the draft of this chapter to Bob, he didn't like it. I knew he wouldn't, that's why I wrote it by myself.

"Why don't you like it?" I asked.

He replied, "It's the first time anyone ever had their eulogy before they died."

"You forget", I reminded him, "that I have read your letter from the beloved Guardian in which he says you are a person of great spirit and capacity."

"Don't persecute me."

"I won't. I don't do that until the next chapter."

Bob and I had the bounty of visiting the grave of the "Immortal Lua" Getsinger beside the Nile River in Egypt. She died a martyr to the Faith in Cairo during the first World War. We were so touched by Lua's life, her eloquence, her courage, her great teaching gifts, and above all her deep love for the Master, 'Abdu'l-Bahá, that we began writing the story of her life while we were still in Egypt. We finished the first chapter while sitting on the porch of

* I've told this story before? It's worth a re-run.

the Semiramis Hotel beside the Nile. We had a perfect title for the book: *The Flame*. Lua burned with an incandescent fire that affected all who met her. It was an inner fire that had been kindled by her beloved Master. Lua has been described as a "flame of God".

While we were serving together in Africa, Bob and I made a very important journey to the Indian Ocean, to Mauritius Island, the "land of many rainbows and shooting stars". We counted sixteen rainbows in one day as we travelled through those green valleys with their rainclouds and mists.

We had been requested by the World Centre to investigate a threat which a handful of enemies were making against the Faith in an unsuccessful effort to undermine the teaching work. We were a double-team on that occasion. I went as a Hand of the Faith and Bob as a member of the Auxiliary Board. Both of us went as members of the National Spiritual Assembly of South and West Africa.

We outprayed, outwitted, and outmanœuvred the enemies. It was easy. As a very gifted teacher and scholar of the Faith, Helen Bishop, used to say: "We have all the big spiritual guns on our side, the Báb, Bahá'u'lláh, 'Abdu'l-Bahá and Shoghi Effendi." It was hard not to feel sorry for them. Until you read their dossier.

Robert Quigley was a spiritual giant that week, both as a teacher and a protector, and as an administrator as well. Through his knowledge and skill at negotiating, Bob was instrumental in helping the Mauritius friends win the first legal recognition for the Faith on that island.

"You were a tower of strength", I told him on the plane back to South Africa.

"You were there, too."

"True, but this week, you were the captain of the team."

One wouldn't think that team-work could apply even to clothes, but one weekend when we were scheduled to speak in Milwaukee, and arrived at the Billy Mitchell Airport, we discovered that all my baggage had gone on to New York. I spoke at the banquet in Bob's shorts, shirt, necktie, Oxford-grey slacks, and his best black cashmere jacket.

"What did you think of the talk?" I asked Bob later as we were going up in the elevator at the Schroeder Hotel to our room.

"You can't beat that black cashmere jacket and red tie."

Before leaving Milwaukee, we were invited to appear on a Sunday religious television show. No script, no rehearsal.

"Wing it", the producer said.

We did.

About a year later, we received word that we had won a special award as the year's outstanding religious programme in its category. We both laughed, quite pleased.

"How about that?" Bob asked.

"You can't beat that black cashmere jacket and red tie", I said.

It was another "first" for the team.

Oddly enough, the two best public talks I have ever delivered, in my opinion, were at that banquet in Milwaukee, and at the Royal Albert Hall in London. Both times, I was wearing someone else's suit.

The London talk took place in 1963, on the one hundredth anniversary of Bahá'u'lláh's Declaration, His Announcement to the world that all of the promises of the sacred Scriptures had now been fulfilled and the Day of the "one fold, and one shepherd" had arrived at last. It was a very great occasion, and I was one of those lucky enough to participate from the platform.

A London newspaper described the event as one of the greatest ecumenical gatherings ever held in the world. Bahá'ís were there from every part of the planet. Some seven thousand of them from all the races of mankind and every previous religious conviction, including atheists, agnostics and sceptics.

It was another first for the Bahá'ís.

On that historic occasion, I was wearing the best suit of clothes owned by a truly unique Bahá'í author, administrator and scholar, Mr Horace Holley. Horace had recently passed away. He was one of those rare original thinkers who always opened up new vistas to his listeners and readers.

His wife, Doris, gave me Horace's favourite black pin-stripe suit.

"Wear it in London", she said.

I told Marguerite: "I can't wear Horace's suit."

"Don't worry", she said. "We'll let it out a little."

"I wasn't thinking about the size, I was worried about not being worthy."

Marguerite assured me that Horace, in the next world, was urging me to wear his suit. I finally gave in.

"Okay", I agreed, reluctantly. "I'll wear it. I need all the help I can get."

"That's exactly what Horace is saying."

The rest of our discussion is private.

Incidentally, the "team" of Quigley and Sears was together in London on that historic occasion. Bob and I stayed on at the request of the World Centre to make a condensed master recording of all the highlights of those week-long magic hours.

We finally compressed the entire week into two hours of superb highlights, each moment filled with excitement, joy and rapture. Even so, we still wept for every minute we had to leave out. The original tapes, of course, are in the archives. Perhaps some day you will hear them all, as well as the two-hour edited version.

It was a splendid "first" for the Guardian's team. Something for posterity. We were truly thankful.

"A Religion with a sense of humour"

69

Bob and I have attended Bahá'í summer schools from Caernarfon, Wales to Mauritius Island in the Indian Ocean, from Stuttgart, Germany, to Buenos Aires in Argentina, from Eliot, Maine to Santa Monica, California, from Louhelen, Michigan to the Bosch School in Santa Cruz, California.

Long before football and basketball teams inspired their cheer leaders and their fans to begin holding up one finger to show the world on television that they were "number one", Bob and Bill had been giving each other that same one-finger sign. Every time we won another "first" for the Guardian and the Faith, we held up our index-finger and made a check-mark √ in the air, meaning: "One more for the Guardian's team!"

We scooped the American sports world by at least a full decade.

Bob and I were always eager to achieve one of those "firsts" which were so greatly prized by the beloved Guardian. Shoghi Effendi longed to hear the news of the first Navajo Indian believer, the first African tribe, the first new island, the first translation of one of Bahá'u'lláh's books, or the first Bahá'í prayer translated into a new language—Eskimo, Iroquois, Latvian, Urdu, Zulu, whatever.

Marguerite, Michael and I had the bounty of participating in the first Bahá'í summer school south of the Sahara in Teso, Uganda. We, too, were always on the look-out on behalf of the "team" for a "first", knowing all too well that the day would soon come when there would be no more "firsts" to conquer and that the Bahá'ís had better hurry because already the "knowledge of the glory of the Lord [Bahá'u'lláh]" was beginning to cover the earth "as the waters cover the sea."*

*Habakkuk 2:14

285

David Hadden designed and constructed two huge identical rostrums, each with its own telephone and bell, so Bob and I could do a special "talk-back-and-forth" at one of the GATHERINGS. Bob and I were speaking on our new book, *The Flame*. We used this two-rostrums technique on other occasions as well, talking spontaneously back and forth to each other. Sometimes even by phone. We spoke simultaneously. Not at the same time, but interrupting each other to emphasize certain points, and to remind each other of any important dramatic highlights we might have overlooked. It added charm, informality and a light-hearted touch to the evening. It is always easier to make people cry if first you make them laugh. This two-rostrums technique was definitely another "first" in delivering Bahá'í talks, and it took a team of two to handle it.

Since we were both in the business, Bob and I decided to try and win a "first" for the beloved Guardian in the media, however humble the beginning. We achieved this personal goal with the help and guidance of the National Spiritual Assembly of the United States.

Our first prototype radio series dates way back to 1945–1946, and was called: *Mr Justice*.

Many of the actors who took part in that early radio series following the second World War went on to stardom in radio, television and the films. The series was transcribed, as they called it then, so it might be made available for use everywhere in the English-speaking world. Later Bob arranged for some of the most popular of the programmes in the series to be translated into Spanish. He hired Spanish-speaking actors so the programme could be used in Latin America as well.

Another first.

One brief sample, tremendously abridged, will convey to you the spirit of the first prototype Bahá'í radio series, *Mr Justice*. The National Spiritual Assembly of the United States urged us on.

The entire series was aimed directly at those deep-seated prejudices so common in America at that time. The opening programme was called: "Send them back where they came from."

The prejudiced souls who called for such immediate action forgot entirely that if their wish were actually granted, and everybody went "back where they came from", they, too, would have to go.

Only the American Indian would be left. A prospect no doubt, quite pleasing to the American Indian.

Mr Justice took a hand to show the utter absurdity of such prejudices of nation, race, religion and class. Mr Justice emphasized the irony of his lesson by actually sending them "back where they came from". He focused on one large apartment house on Eighty-Third Street in New York City.

It is a February morning. A cold, biting mid-winter blizzard rages across Manhattan. The Apartment at 843 Eighty-Third Street is in an icy cold grip because the janitor, Gunderson, has gone back to Oslo, Norway. There is no morning milk for the hot coffee because the milkman, Pacelli, has gone back to Milan.

There is no bread for the toast. The bakery driver, Van Leden, has left for Amsterdam. There is no electricity to toast it, because O'Toole, who replaces the fuses, is off to Dublin.

On and on it goes, the story becoming both more tragic, more ironically pathetic and more amusing as the disaster deepens.

There are no lights even when the fuse is replaced. No electricity of any kind. No gas. No water. All utilities are shut off. Completely. All the relevant people at the power plants and public utility control centres have gone "back where they came from": To Belgium, England, Spain, Greece, Yugoslavia, wherever.

No need to deal with the taxis, buses, subways, and the commuting trains, although the actual drama does, of course. The operators, have all gone back where *they* came from, too. To Wales, Luxemburg, Syria, Argentina and India.

No one can untangle the snarled and snarling traffic on the George Washington and Triborough bridges. The toll gates are shut down. Bedekian, MacGregor and Boleslawski have gone back to Syria, Scotland and Poland.

Okay.

Enough is enough.

The owner of the apartment house where the heart of our drama takes place, a certain Mr Krasny, is poring over an atlas and various maps in his study. He is energetically using a magnifying glass, micrometer, and slide-rule. Krasny doesn't know what to do, or where he can go. The country where Krasny was born and raised no longer exists. Poor soul! He has no place to go back to.

The biggest loser of all, of course, is Mr Hubert Goldeagle, the very person who started all the trouble in the first place. He couldn't bear seeing all these foreigners moving into his one hundred percent pure American neighbourhood.

During the closing moments of the drama, Mr Justice, who takes Hubert Goldeagle on a personal tour of the tragedies he has engendered by his foolish ideas, finally sends Hubert home. Mr Justice calls our attention to the ambulance sirens screaming up Lexington Avenue. They are *en route* to the Goldeagle residence. Brakes squealing, tyres skidding, the ambulance roars to a screeching halt in front of Hubert's apartment house. Running footsteps mount the stairs. Doctors, paramedics, assistants, nurses, stretcher-bearers, all rush wildly into the house. Time is of the essence.

They have come for Hubert Goldeagle!

Quickly they cover the long kitchen table with a white sheet. They lay out all the needed instruments. Two huge attendants seize a startled Hubert Goldeagle and slam him onto the table and fasten him down.

Goldeagle, you see, on his father's side, is German, Swiss, French and Danish. On his mother's side he is Irish, Scots and Greek.

There is only *one* way to send Hubert Goldeagle back where *he* came from:

Surgery!

Of course it's ridiculous!

But along the way, telling points are made on the fundamental oneness of the human race. The Bahá'í "remedy" of love and unity for a disunited world is gently offered. There is only *one* race, the human race.

This, remember, was nearly half a century ago when there were still outcries from those who wanted to see only "one hundred percent Americans" in America.

Fat chance! The radio series helped these absurd, blind, unthinking people learn that the decimal system (one hundred percent) came from the Greeks, and the homeland they were claiming as their own, America, was named after Amerigo Vespucci, an Italian geographer. That, of course, was only the beginning of their folly, and the start of the fun we, the Bahá'ís, had of exposing it.

The more Bob and I studied and deepened our knowledge of the Bahá'í Faith, the more we realized how far in the forefront of all

288

advanced thinking were the Teachings of Bahá'u'lláh. It was the material of which "firsts" were made in every area of human life.

Whenever some grave new problem arose to afflict our troubled world, such as drug abuse, excessive use of alcohol, dissolving marriages, divorce, the shattering of family life; whatever it was, we would share what Bahá'u'lláh and the Writings of His Faith had to say on the subject. In many instances nearly a century before the trouble started. Almost inevitably we would hear our friends say: "Why didn't you tell us this before? This is the answer!"

Of course we did tell them before. Until we were blue in the face. All about the Christ-promised Kingdom of God on earth. But, as it says in Scripture, no matter how "wondrous" the story, or how "great" the "work", the "strange sleep" in which the present materialistic world is held enthralled prevents them from "believing" the story even when it is being "told" to them, and is happening dramatically and unmistakably right before their very eyes.

That's Scripture.

So great is the Power and Source of these Teachings, so rewarding and comforting are the Teachings offered, so germane to the needs of this day, that the Writings of Bahá'u'lláh's Faith promise:

> "If you read the utterances of Bahá'u'lláh
> and 'Abdu'l-Bahá with selflessness and
> care and concentrate upon them, you
> will discover truths unknown to you before
> and will obtain an insight into the prob-
> lems that have baffled the great thinkers of
> the world."

You can, therefore, imagine the impact which that first Bahá'í radio series had on the listeners nearly half a century ago. It ripped the shutters off from those closed-up rooms of the human mind and let in the pure fresh air and sunlight of truth for a change, and things were never the same again. Not for those who heard and understood.

Our prototype radio series did it all with tongue in cheek, with satire, with laughter, and above all with love.

You name the prejudices, and in that early Bahá'í radio series, our star, Mr Justice, went after them all. No challenge too great.

No punches pulled. Wham! Right into the gizzard. It was indeed a "first". Not only a "first", but a first far ahead of its time.

Variety Magazine, the so-called Bible of Show Business, reviewed our Bahá'í radio series, and said:

"Here at last, thank God, is a Religion with a sense of humour."

70

This "first" in radio was followed sometime later by an even more exciting first in television. It was not the first Bahá'í television programme by any means, but it was the first Bahá'í television series using the same crew, same cast, same musical chorus, and special guest stars. A unified series in the true sense.

It was called *The New World*. It was the first prototype series of thirteen Bahá'í television programmes, and it originated in Honolulu, Hawaii.

When the first Bahá'í TV series was completed, the Guardian's "team" had scored one more goal on his behalf. To say it was the team that scored would be wrong. They never could have done it without the loving, enthusiastic and dedicated help of every member of the National Spiritual Assembly of the Bahá'ís of Hawaii.

They were magnificent. The greatest share of the success for that entire television series belongs to them. It was a miracle that the series was ever completed. Through their love and unity an "all-out effort" was mounted, and the series was accomplished for an average cost of around $800-00 for a thirty-minute segment. Most television programmes spend that much per show in just sending out for coffee and doughnuts, but we completed thirteen episodes on half a shoe-string.

Repeat: It was a miracle of love and co-operation. Teamwork all the way.

The entire Honolulu Bahá'í Community expended unstintingly of its time, energies, and resources, coupled with their never-failing friendliness and fellowship. All, without exception, the chorus, the players, the stage-crew, the technicians, the artists, the musicians, everyone associated with the programme.

Almost all of these television programmes were produced, rehearsed, and filmed from midnight to six in the morning with a huge, hilarious breakfast at the Ala Moana Hotel to follow, frequently hosted by Robert Quigley.

It was a perfect demonstration of "universal participation". Team-work, all the way.

This one was a "sweep". Not only a *first*, but a first, second, third and fourth. Everybody deserved an award! Especially the Hawaii friends.

Mahalo!

In fairness to the Team-Managers, Marguerite Sears and Keith Quigley, I have to admit that it was not always *Bob* Quigley who came to my rescue.

There was also Keith. When she was not hosting a special party for the Bahá'í youth and their friends, she was thinking of ways to make my stay in California more pleasant and productive. Her generosity always competed with Bob's in everything, including an unlimited use of her automobile which was another one of my favourite places to be when not working.

It was a dream car! A beige Cadillac Seville. Keith had owned the car almost forever but, like the Koh-i-noor diamond, it improved with age. When I entered that beige beauty, I talked to myself.

"*Varoom!* Look out, Marguerite Grand Prix Sears! Here comes Barney Oldfield, the old man! *Varoom!*"

Okay, I've got that out of my system. Why should Marguerite have all the fun?

I remember the day Sid Bulkin, another dear friend, came to the Quigley's residence to play the master tape of *The Lote Tree* for me. He wanted me to hear it before taking off for Wilmette and Africa. The sound was so perfect I said, "That's sensational. I'll have to own one of those someday myself."

Shortly after my arrival at the Bahá'í Convention in Chicago, one of those same big beautiful top-of-the-line Sony machines arrived at my hotel room. It was wrapped up as a gift, with an accompanying note.

"Love, Keith."

She had overheard me talking to Sid from the kitchen, and felt that if some day a Hand of the Cause of God wanted a machine like that, there was no day like today. I immediately made copies of my

Convention talk and sent them off to the pioneers and teachers in different parts of the world. I've been keeping that darling machine busy ever since.

Do something every day for the Faith, the beloved Guardian said. Something to advance the work of teaching. Influence the world if you can. Or a hemisphere, a continent, a country. The larger the area you can motivate, and set on fire with the Teachings, the better. Never let a day go by without doing something—however great, however small. Do all in your power to bring at least one soul closer to his or her heart's desire. My words, the beloved Guardian's ideas and concepts.

They were always the theme of his team.

The Quigleys have an African Room filled with carvings, carpets, and arts and crafts from the Sahara to Cape Town, and from all those places they visited while pioneering in Africa. That amazing African Room would make a splendid six-page spread in any magazine. It keeps our hearts close to a part of the world we all love.

We often go into the African Room for prayers before turning in at night. Sometimes we pray at the dining-room table, sometimes in my room. Wherever it is, we're always seeking special guidance on some future project. Hopefully, another "first".

Bob and Keith have prepared a special self-contained apartment for me in their home. A refuge whenever I fly in and out of California. I have been using it for years, have written many radio and TV scripts there, and parts of various books and study classes, while seated at my very own round table.

Keith has arranged a private delicatessen for me just eighteen feet away from my bed, a huge refrigerator stocked and restocked with my favourites: apples, colby cheese, yoghurt, Perrier water, oranges, grapefruit, Hormel's hot chili, pizza, and other wonders to delight an austere religious palate at midnight. Or during a late replay of the Southern California–Notre Dame football game at the Coliseum.

When I try to thank Keith, she, with an airy wave of the hand, says: "What are friends for?"

This is usually just after she has added peanuts, pop-corn and Baskin-Robbins double-decker Butter Pecan and Cherry Burgundy ice-cream cones to the Trojan-Irish crisis menu.

71

One of the most delightful experiences ever enjoyed by the "Team" took place in the Continent of their choice, Africa.

Bob Quigley of Hollywood Squares fame, and William Sears, broadcaster of Eagle's football in the NFL, found themselves in another world entirely one lazy autumn afternoon on the streets of Mohale's Hoek, Basutoland (now Lesotho) in Southern Africa.

Bob and Bill were parked out in front of a country store along one of the main streets. It was a perfect African day. A cloudless sky except for one or two cirro-cumulus white sheep which were making their way across the heavens toward Teyateyaneng ("TY"). On the distant horizon stood several of those magnificent umbrella trees with their lace fans opened against the sky. There wasn't a sound in all the countryside even in downtown Mohale's Hoek, except for the singing of the African birds, and the clop, clop, clop of the horses' hooves as three shepherds, wrapped in colourful Basuto blankets and wearing their famous conical-shaped hats, made their way out of town, driving their flock before them.

It was a quiet pastoral scene. It was a Reg Turvey watercolour, all serenity and peace.

All of a sudden it became chaotic, a turmoil. Loud, boisterous, strident.

It began slowly.

Two African men passing by, saw Bob and I putting our groceries into the back end of the car. They also saw the hand-puppets lying in living colour in their open carrying cases.

"What are those animals doing in the back end of your car?" they asked.

"They're part of our family", Bob replied.

I lifted out the Secretary Bird, "Hillary", along with the Impala, "Imp", to demonstrate. One of the men put two fingers into his mouth and whistled loudly. He waved his arms in a manner that said, "Come over here and see this."

A crowd began to gather.

I slipped Hillary up over my sweater sleeve, and Bob did the same with the Impala. We began talking to the people on the street in the "dishy" voices of the two animal puppets.

The Impala looked at the Secretary Bird and said, "We'd better cut down on the charisma and charm or we may start a riot in the street."

The animals were an instant unqualified success.

We told our rapidly growing African audience what a wonderful country Basutoland was. Imp and Hillary turned face to face, and began arguing loudly with each other, insisting which one of them thought the country was better. They admitted how lucky they both were to be staying, even for a few days, in such a beautiful place as Mohale's Hoek.

We had to wait while those who understood English translated for those who didn't.

"I'd rather go to America", one of the young African boys told Imp, the Impala.

"No, you wouldn't", the Impala replied. "You're far better off right here."

"Right!" Hillary, the Secretary Bird agreed. "Look how they spoiled me in America", he said.

Hillary demonstrated how dissolute his character had become by blowing smoke-rings out of this throat. Additional smoke came first out of his left nostril, then more smoke out of his right. As a finale, Hillary blew smoke out of all three at once.

The Africans applauded appreciatively.

Imp, the Impala, had eyes that would suddenly stick way out of their sockets when he became excited. He did so now, causing spontaneous laughter. Imp put his nose right up against the cute little nose of one of the smallest African children, and said, "Domella, Ntate." (Good morning, father.) Everybody was delighted, except the child, who punched Imp gently on the end of his own nose.

"I'm a girl", she objected. "A Mme not an Ntate."

Imp, with pretended horror, drew back, stuck out his huge brown eyes, and brought the house down. Or should I say brought the street down, as it was now five deep with people around the entire car. They may have missed some of the English words, but none of the pantomime. They were hungry to laugh at anything.

Imp kissed the little girl on the cheek and warned her, "Watch that nose-punching, short stuff!"

More hilarious laughter.

"But you are a very beautiful little girl", he added. "I knew you were a girl all the time." Imp kissed her on the end of her nose, and she shyly retreated behind the back of a friend.

Most of the audience didn't understand what "short stuff" meant, but they loved the visual humour. They revelled in the strange appearance of the puppets, especially the eyes of the Impala when they would stick out inches at a time. Every time Imp shot his eyes out, everyone clapped their hands merrily and laughed enthusiastically.

They kept asking for more, crying out: "Eyes! Eyes!" "Mahlo! Mahlo!"

A tall sombre person with a reversed collar, who had been following Bob and myself around town for most of the day in his red pick-up truck, stepped forward and tried to get the attention of the crowd. He obviously was keeping a sharp eye on us because he knew we were Bahá'ís. When he was asked, "Who are they?" meaning us, "and why are they here?" he replied:

"They're a couple of missionary blokes from the United States who have come to Basutoland to deceive and corrupt the innocent children with their fancy toy puppets and their smart American tricks."

Both the Secretary Bird and the Impala overheard these false and slurring remarks. They turned, aghast and shocked (one of their best "takes"), and went for his throat—verbally. They weren't about to take these insults lying down, and they certainly didn't intend to let themselves be belittled in front of the children.

"We're not missionary blokes", the Impala objected.

"What's more important," Hillary added, "if you can corrupt children with love and friendship, with kindness and fellowship, we're guilty. Hang us!"

Bob and I picked up the other animal puppets from the back end of the car. Great Big Sam, the baby elephant; Fitz, the squirrel; Camille, the cam-*ell*; and the Honourable Mr Glow-Worm. The real missionary bloke began to object, but was drowned out in the deafening applause and laughter that greeted these new characters.

The Impala looked out at the crowd, wiggled his nose, and stuck those huge eyes way out. Applause and laughter. Imp turned his head, pointed his nose toward his missionary accuser and said:

"*He's* the real missionary bloke. We don't get a cent for doing this. We do it because we love it. We came here because we love the country and all the people in it."

Hillary, too, was incensed at the unnecessary attack. His big yellow mouth opened wide, and his little red tongue began flapping.

"Obviously what this missionary bloke knows about the Bahá'í Faith, you can stick in your lunch-box and still have room for two apples and a sandwich. So play that on your piano!"

These comments received a big laugh and a warm welcome from everyone except the real missionary bloke. He stomped off down the street in search of the authorities, religious or civil, who could support him. He made threatening noises over his shoulder.

"I'm going to put a stop to this—this—this—"

He couldn't think of a name for it, so Imp, the Impala, helped him out.

"This public love-affair?" he suggested.

The missionary bloke scoffed angrily and left the scene.

Some of the children hollered at him as he left. I don't understand Southern Sotho, but I told Bob that I *did* understand intonations.

"So?"

"So, what I think they said, was 'Go soak your head!'"

Our drama had scarcely begun.

"Hip! Hip! Hip! Hip!"

72

Close your eyes for a moment and picture the following scenario.

Could anything be more unlikely?

Two television personalities, now Bahá'í pioneers to Africa set down in the middle of a delightful remote African town. Remote to us from far-off California, but part of the heartland of that lovely country Basutoland, now Lesotho.

Bob Quigley, who was the producer of some of the top daytime television programmes on NBC, CBS, and ABC; and Bill Sears, sportscaster for the Philadelphia Eagles of the National Football League, both standing on a dusty street in Mohale's Hoek. More, they were proclaiming the love and unity of the Bahá'í Faith with hand puppets. They were upholding the oneness of God, His Messengers, His Religion, and all His peoples with the help of a squirrel, a baby elephant, a camel, an impala, a secretary bird, and a glorious green and gold glow-worm.

"Now *that*", I whispered to Bob with a chuckle, "is religious education."

The curtain was going up on the second act of our street-scene comedy-drama.

Around the corner of the grocery store a company of prison convicts came marching up the street. They were all dressed up in their prison garb, red-and-white-striped uniforms. They carried picks and shovels over their shoulders and were off to work on the roads. The convicts were carefully controlled by prison guards with rifles as they marched up the street to the rhythm of: "Hip! Hip! Hip! Hip!"

Coming down the other side of the street and a little farther off, was an even larger group. They were school children decked out in their prim school uniforms. They also were marching in special rows. They were coming from the opposite direction to the prisoners and they passed each other while the children were singing at the top of their voices. Their harmony was astonishingly lovely. Both Bob and I, former singing Catholics, recognized the old familiar Protestant hymn:

> Yes, we'll gather at the river,
> The beautiful, beautiful river; . . .

The prisoners passed the children and waved their picks, shovels, and free hands at them. They liked the music. One of the prisoners called out: "Sing it loud, little chicks!"

The school children caught sight of Imp and Hillary riding so saucily on the arms of Quigley and Sears. They became enthralled. Immediately and completely they were fascinated and enraptured. Their eyes became saucers. Yelling with happy laughter, they broke ranks and raced for our automobile like Red Indians surrounding a covered wagon on the old Chisholm Trail. The teachers were frantic. They blew loudly on their whistles to try and control the student rebellion. In vain. They hurried over after the children, shouting at them, trying to restore order. Also in vain.

The guards prodded the convicts who had stopped to enjoy the scene, poking them with the muzzles of their guns, and shouting: "March! Move on!" The prisoners, like everyone else on that Mohale's Hoek street, were enchanted by the puppets. For them it was a moment of joy and happiness in an otherwise drab day and dreary life. They were "moving on" in response to jabs from the butts of the rifles, but very slowly, sideways, and with heads turned back toward that captivating pair, Imp and Hillary.

The prison guards yelled angrily at them, making severe threats. The prisoners reluctantly fell back into step. They started off down the road again. Their hearts were not in it.

"Hip! Hip! Hip! Hip!"

The teachers were blowing their referee's whistles louder and louder. Frenzied. They had been reinforced by the powerful lungs of a huge, intimidating "games mistress" waving an unstrung tennis racket. She was formidable. The children came to immediate attention when they heard her harsh voice. The "games mistress", an amazon, pointed the unstrung tennis racket threateningly toward the school. The children, cowed, fell pell-mell into rows again and went marching off up the street, bursting into protective song: "The Lord is My Shepherd".

The Lord and three teachers. You couldn't help wondering how that tennis racket became unstrung.

Even so, the children kept peeking shyly over their shoulders and grinning at their new-found friends, a secretary bird and an impala. Hillary shouted after them.

"You're wonderful children! And we love you!"

The children yelled back, punctuated by shrill whistles from their teachers.

"We love you, too!" they cried, in Sesotho with a smattering of English and a touch of Afrikaans.

Imp, the impala, stuck his big brown eyes way out to the front of his head one more time, and hollered: "We both love you. We love all little children!"

When the children saw those big brown eyes of the Impala pop way out again, they couldn't suppress their giggles. The hymn suffered considerable damage from their shrieks of laughter. More whistles, more ominous threats, more pointed fingers, and a new hymn "Jesus, lover of my soul", and all was well again. The children marched off noisily in rhythm, stumbling and bumping into each other, as they kept turning for one last look at their new friends, Imp and Hillary.

The impala and the secretary bird turned toward the fast-departing prisoners, and cried out a farewell to them as well.

"We love you, too, you rascals!"

The convicts laughed, held their picks and shovels aloft, and waved goodbye to the animals without turning. The guards, brandishing their weapons, started to chant and all prisoners wisely joined in.

"Hip! Hip! Hip! Hip!"

Imp and Hillary had the last word. They shouted encouragement to the red and white striped convicts as they turned the corner by the gas station and began to disappear out of our lives.

"Hang in there, baby!" Imp hollered.

"Look us up when you get out", Hillary hollered. "We can turn you around!"

Both convicts and animals went into gales of laughter.

The far-off "Hip! Hip! Hip! Hip!" faded away and was lost in the sound of the singing of the birds, and an occasional "Caw!" from a high-flying crow.

Bob and I were still standing beside the open back of our car, a hand-puppet on each arm. We were now all alone on the street, just the four of us, Bob, Bill, Imp and Hillary. Everyone else had vanished. The entire crowd. The street was empty and silent.

I looked at Bob, he looked at me, and Imp looked at Hillary. The Impala summed it up for all of us. He said, in that deep bass gravelly voice:

"That's all she wrote."

We carefully laid the puppets back into their carrying case and closed the lid of the trunk.

"I always hate to do that", I told Bob. "The animals always give me that baleful look."

"I don't blame you", Bob grinned. "How would you like to be a glow-worm locked up in the dark with that eye-ball-popping impala?"

Before we could climb back into the front seat, a little African boy came shooting out of the grocery store. He raced to the car to see if his two friends Imp and Hillary were still there. He looked all around, saw nothing, then slid his hand along the crack of the trunk, hoping to pry the lid open with his fingers. He bent forward and tried to peek in through the crack. Disappointed, he rubbed the palm of his small hand across the top of the closed lid and sighed.

"Can I help you?" I asked, coming back toward him.

He turned and flew up the gravel path back into the doorway of the store. He hugged his mother tightly. She tousled her son's head affectionately, and drew him into the flowing folds of her Victorian-style long dress until he disappeared completely from sight.

Bob started the car and we drove leisurely down the streets of Mohale's Hoek. Neither of us spoke for a long time, but both of us were smiling. Inside and outside. A Hollywood Network television producer and an NFL play-by-play football announcer, both bowled over completely by a streetful of happy African children. Knocked for six.

Who would ever believe it when we told the story? Money couldn't buy the warm, happy feeling that pervaded our lives. Not even American Express travellers' cheques in the largest denominations. We both had learned what priceless meant.

The entire afternoon had been like an imagined scene from some beautiful fantasy. A dream-sequence. A tender, sweet, unforgettable half-hour in our pioneering lives.

As we drove out of Mohale's Hoek into the countryside and headed toward Maseru, Bob spoke up at last.

"You were right, Bob", he said, laughing, "*That* is what I call religious education."

"I'm Bill", I told him. "You're Bob."

"Oh, then remind me to return your maroon sweater."

73

TIME: *Twenty-seven years later. Summer. 1984.*
PLACE: *African Room, the Quigley's residence, California.*
CHARACTERS: *The Team, Bob and Bill. Asleep.*

Bob and I have been haunted every day of our lives by those eleven magic words of our beloved Guardian: "You and Bill make a good team. You should work together."

We long to work together far more than we do. These past few years, I have been travelling on my own in Africa while Bob has continued to roll up more television successes and Emmys in America.

At long last, however, things are looking up for the team.

Both Bob and I have now reached what is laughingly called the age of retirement. To any Bahá'í, this merely means the fates have been kind, and let you live long enough to enjoy some late-blossoming pioneering and additional world-type travel-teaching. In other words, the time has now come for you to throw it all into "high gear"!

Bob and I probably would have written this book, *All Flags Flying!*, together, if the tip of Southern Africa wasn't such a long way from the Southern Coast of California. Right at this very moment, however, I am writing the draft of these pages in long-hand aboard Lufthansa, as once again we head back toward each other. So who knows what may still happen?

We both have reached that stage which I once attributed to my own grandfather in *God Loves Laughter*. His old body no longer seemed able to contain his youthful spirit. He was a Mack Truck motor built into a bicycle. Ditto Quigley and Sears, *circa* 1985.

We have to let the clutch out very slowly and carefully these days for fear the "power" within might explode and make a shambles of the parts. There's still a lot of good stuff in both of us, if we can keep it volatile.

I chuckle to myself when I look at the two of us stretched out sitting in our two easy-boy lounge chairs in the African Room recalling our dreams of glory. Neither one of us hears the sound of the TV set as it loudly describes the dramatic closing moments of the Yankee–Dodgers Exhibition baseball game, although Bob is a dyed-in-the-wool Yankee fan, and I am a never-say-die Dodger Blue. Our minds are miles and miles away elsewhere, decades away perhaps. Most likely in Africa.

Out of a prolonged silence, Bob finally says:

"What great new 'first' can we think of this year?"

"Before Riḍván?"

"Naturally!"

"You're right. The time is short, but the beloved Guardian said the Bahá'ís should give their all."

"That's it! What we have to do this year is give more than our all."

Another profound silence sets in. Nap time.

Awakened, a warm feeling of special love surrounds me. I look over at Bob then back to his team-partner Bill, and I recall the moving words of a sonnet by Shakespeare:

> "That time of year thou mayst in me behold
> When yellow leaves, or none, or few, do hang
> Upon those boughs which shake against the cold,
> Bare ruin'd choirs, where late the sweet birds sang."

I laugh about it. I think to myself that there was a time when people might have said about Bob and myself, "Break up the Yankees!" Now, perhaps it might be: "Who are those two distinguished very elderly looking serene old gentlemen?"

That would be a grave mistake.

We both know in our hearts that when next Robert Quigley and William Sears work together as a "team" on any project for their beloved Guardian, hopefully another "first", they will arise like the Lions of the Covenant they once were. Regardless of their age, or the state of their health—"Gung Ho!" they are spiritually armed and dangerous.

Bob and Bill will be motivated by their ever-green memories of

Shoghi Effendi, their beloved Guardian, by his voice, his flashing eyes, his tenderness, his love, his inspiration. It does something to both of them when they recall his words about Bahá'u'lláh:

> "He will come to our help if we only arise
> and become an active channel for God's grace."

No matter how sere and yellow those leaves may be that hang upon the boughs and shake against the cold, both Bob and Bill will resist every storm, and refuse to put into port until our job is done. We shall both take an intense and youthful delight in whatever new "first" it is that the beloved Guardian's "team" now has set their eyes upon. They will hear his voice, loud and clear, cheering them on their way:

> "Today the need is so great on the part
> of humanity to hear of the Divine Message,
> that the believers must plunge into the work,
> wherever and however they can, heedless
> of their own shortcomings . . ."

From the very first moment they became a "team" for him, they have always known where to put their trust. Their beloved Guardian told them clearly:

> ". . . have a perfect reliance upon God; let your heart
> burn with the desire to serve His Mission and proclaim
> His call; and you will observe how eloquence and the
> power to change human hearts will come as a matter
> of course."

It has always been so. For nearly half a century his team, Bob and Bill, have proven to themselves this truth of his words, taking comfort and strength in every one of his promises.

> ". . . the very act of striving to serve,
> however unworthy one may feel, attracts the
> blessings of God and enables one to become
> more fitted for the task."

So we try again. And again. A "team", of the Sign of God on earth never retires. It can never lose if it never quits.

That is why two of us don't mind going into overtime in order to score one more goal, and win one more "first" for him. When the whistle blows, we shall answer. We shall see his radiant face and hear his words of encouragement:

> "The firm and irrevocable Promise is given . . . The powers of heaven and earth mysteriously assist in its execution . . . Let the doubter arise and himself verify the truth of such assertions. To try, to persevere, is to insure ultimate and complete victory."

So we try. Bob and I. We arise. We persevere. We plunge head-long into the work. Heedless of our shortcomings. Our hearts burn with desire.

All his words!

And suddenly, once again, the sweet birds sing.

DOWN
MEMORY
LANE

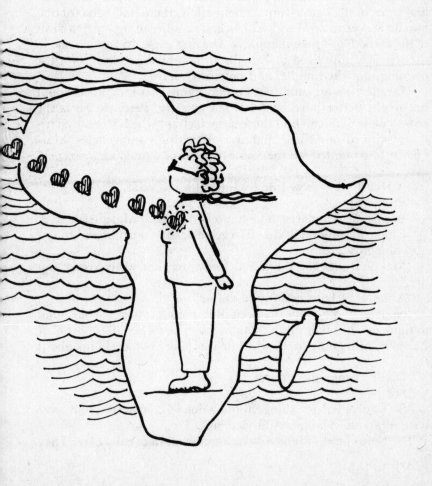

74

Marguerite and I felt we had better set the record straight before we went any further down Memory Lane. All was not honeysuckle and roses in the Sears camp. The truth is, there had been friction and flack ever since Marguerite began proof-reading the first draft of the book. No, I take that back. The first page. In fact, no one in the whole family liked it. Nor the second or third draft. Not the opening, not the middle, and not the close.

Marguerite suggested that certain items I had included about her might better have been left out entirely. Perhaps this is the reason none of us can find those large sections which were mysteriously snipped out of the manuscript leaving gaping holes. Marguerite also pointed out that some of my time sequences were cock-eyed.

"Asters do not grow side by side with daffodils."

"Pity."

"In one or two places, now happily deleted," Marguerite said, "you have southbound Canadian geese passing northbound robins and bluebirds."

"Maybe it was the robin and the goose that were wrong, not me."

"A touch of Irish whimsy perhaps?"

"No longer. You took it all out. But doesn't it boggle your mind to think of what that robin thought when he passed the goose over Lake Ontario going south while he was going north? Think about it."

"Don't change the subject."

"So?"

"So, you've written things about Michael that you should have written about William. And vice versa."

The boys couldn't remember, and they didn't really care. They were upset about other things and complained bitterly. They both agreed that several of the events associated with them had never happened that way at all.

"Both Michael and I were much funnier on those occasions than you have pictured us, Dad", Bill objected. "We had much more panache and charisma than you've given us credit for."

Mike agreed. "Far more. Not to mention pizzazz. You've slanted the book your way, Dad, instead of our way."

I accepted their criticism, feeling that a father couldn't be all bad if he had two sons who even knew such words as panache, pizzazz and charisma.

Even our close Bahá'í friends with whom Marguerite and I pioneered and served the Faith (and with whom I had mistakenly shared a few chapters) slyly hinted at the imaginary and fanciful character of *All Flags Flying!* They didn't care for my treatment at all. They admitted, when I questioned them closely, that while I had been quite kind, merciful and accurate in describing most of the Bahá'ís and the events associated with them, unfortunately, in their own case, I had failed dismally in trying to capture their true essence and worth. They volunteered to write a few helpful paragraphs for me to include in the book to improve their image.

I kept telling both my family and my friends that *All Flags Flying!* was neither an autobiography nor a biography. It was never intended to be.

"It is a novel", I told them. "Pure and simple. It was designed to show the impact of the Bahá'í Faith on one small family and, through them, upon the places they visit around the world as pioneers."

"Then why", Marguerite asked, "do you use real names, real people, real places, and real events?"

"Because I know these people and these places. I want my novel to ring true."

"You just *think* you know them", Marguerite said, coldly. She was holding in her hand, the last and what I hoped would be the final draft of the book. She shoved it violently down into her sewing basket. "I particularly loathe this chapter", she warned me, showing me one she had just detached from the manuscript.

"Which chapter is that?" I asked innocently, knowing full well that this same time bomb was the real reason Marguerite found the book offensive.

"You must be out of your mind!" she said.

The fierce nature of Marguerite's objection, of course, testifies immediately to the complete accuracy and truth of everything I had written about her. I didn't say *that* out loud. Instead, I said, placatingly, "I feel that in your case, darling—"

"Don't darling me, you viper! Until you've rewritten every word of this chapter!"

Marguerite tore it in half and threw the remnants in the fireplace. Nonchalantly I went, over, struck a match and burned them.

"Thank you for being so understanding."

I grinned, wickedly.

"I have four carbons. One for burning, one for cutting out huge holes, one for tearing into shreds, and one for miscellaneous, hiding, crumpling and stomping on."

"You won't have a wife if one of them, or any part of them is given to the printers."

"Shall we leave it to posterity to judge between us?"

"There will be no posterity for certain people unless those paragraphs about my lead foot on the gas pedal are not immediately, entirely and permanently expunged!"

"Is it true what I have written in the book about you, Mario?"

"Out!"

"I mean Mario Lanza, not Mario Andretti."

"Out!"

"Johnny Rutherford?"

"Out!"

"Crispin Pemberton-Pigott?"

"Out! O-u-t OUT!"

Whenever Marguerite Reimer Sears begins to spell out the words, it is time to head for the cyclone cellar. All families know these familiar danger signs in other members, and know when it's "soft-pedal" time in the valley.

Since you have heard so many fine outstanding things about Marguerite throughout *All Flags Flying!*—all true—it won't hurt to show that on occasion she has feet of clay, not to mention a lead foot on the gas pedal. We never thought of it as a shortcoming, but as an adventure. The boys call it "Zingo!" driving.

Marguerite refused to play my tape of her San Diego, Freeway 5, Grand Prix. I told her:

"We went by Capistrano so fast we couldn't see the swallows returning."

"It's not the time for swallows."

All ice.

"Just a tender touch of hyperbole, to make a point about your 'Zingo!' driving without being unkind."

"Or unmarried?"

"Touché! No *Zingo* is worth that."

"I hope I never hear that word again."

"Zingo!"

Old frosty-eyes stopped the car in the middle of the busy intersection at Olympic and Sepulveda, got out of the car, impervious to the blowing of horns and loudly-shouted rude remarks from stopped trucks and cars. Marguerite calmly walked round to my side. She tossed the car keys into my lap.

"You", she said, "drive."

It was perfectly true about Marguerite's San Diego, Freeway 5, Grand Prix. We were late for a Bahá'í picnic. I taped the exact words her sons, William and Michael, had shouted during the big "Zingo!"

Whenever their mother entered the Red Rabbit, the Blue Buick, the Burgundy Bobcat, the Yellow Datsun, or any other Sears current vehicle with their mother at the helm (Spelled: *Hell-em!*), the moment Marguerite turned the motor over with an unnecessarily power-laden zoom! the boys would immediately cry out their encouragements.

"Eat 'em alive!"

"You can do it, Sterling Moss!"

And together they would shout: *"Zingo!"*

I have this all on tape. In living sound with verifying Freeway traffic noises from those cars we passed ("Ffft! Ffft! Ffft!"), including approaching Highway Patrol sirens.*

Out of pure charity, and a sincere desire to preserve the beauty of our approaching golden wedding anniversary in the face of gathering threats, I agreed to rewrite the "Zingo!" chapter.

I admitted my error before witnesses and confessed that whatever I had written in *All Flags Flying!* dealing with Marguerite at

---

* This tape is now strangely missing.

the throttle of the *Old Ninety-Seven* was fictionalized, romanticized, and fantasized by me, Bill Sears, her adoring husband.

In my own longhand writing, with Marguerite looking over my shoulder, waiting to proof-read the page, I stated clearly:

"None of us, Bill, Mike, or myself has ever been 'scalded to death by the steam'." Frightened to death, perhaps. But in general, I admit that all those snide lead-foot comments, which I now totally disavow, were prompted by Irish-inspired whimsy.

"They bear no resemblance to reality. In no way, do they even faintly mirror forth my beautiful wife Marguerite's moderate, re-strained 'slow-poke' image."

Although you can't see it since my back is turned to you, my nose kept growing longer and longer and longer as I wrote the above things down on paper.

"Zingo!"

God's children don't all have wings!

75

Something good came out of "Life in the fast lane". Marguerite decided that perhaps it was salutary for me to have teased her about "Zingo!"

She suggested that I should do more of the same in other episodes of *All Flags Flying!* She suspected that I might have been too one-sided, and should show some of the failures as well as the successes of the Bahá'ís as they struggled to acquire those needed spiritual characteristics.

Marguerite had a point. Perhaps I had subconsciously favoured those with the "decency virus" while talking about my fellow-Bahá'ís. I didn't think so, but agreed that a few salty shortcomings couldn't hurt the overall picture. One thing was certain, every one of us (you included) has to battle every day of our lives to become finer human beings, even just plain ordinary nice people.

Some of us quite clearly have more on the ball than others when it comes to improving. Themselves, not others. I cite here the example of two summer schools I should never have attended. I shared both "happenings" with Marguerite to see if I was capturing the spirit of her suggestion.

The Summer School Committee urged me to go to the school a day early, on Friday instead of Saturday, the day I was expected. The friends, they said, would be overjoyed and would have a thousand things for me to do. It would be a Friday to remember, they promised, full of exciting things.

I went. It was a Friday to forget.

Nobody met my train. No reservations. I hailed a cab and, together with the cabbie, tried to run down the rented quarters of the Summer School. We found it. It was abandoned. Only a stray grey cat was living there. He had no information for me.

315

Finally, in a downtown hamburger stand, I met an old friend from my other more worldly television life. He was glad to see me. We talked sports. He was an extremely kind man and was able to bring me together with the Bahá'ís.

"My wife is a Bahá'í," he said, "and I know they moved the Summer School location at the last minute."

He knew where it was and dropped me off bags and all. The Bahá'ís were startled to see me.

"What are you doing here?" they asked. "You're not expected until tomorrow. There's not a blessed thing for you to do."

"Maybe I could go over to the cathedral and make a novena", I suggested.

Nobody heard me. Or heard me and didn't think it was funny. There's a lot of that going around.

"We'll find something for you to do", they promised.

They didn't.

I did nothing. All morning, all afternoon, and all night. I was good at that.*

I could see it was my fault. I'd come early and unexpectedly and there were no reservations. All the rooms were taken. Until tomorrow. I wondered what had happened to that old Bahá'í hospitality of sleeping on the couch, in the bath-tub, or on the floor in a borrowed sleeping-bag?

"Why don't you just hack around until the square dance tonight?" they suggested. "By then we'll have found a dozen rooms for you."

I hacked around.

No one introduced me to the friends at the school all that day. Not even during the square dance and charades that night. Perhaps they were saving me as a "Mystery Guest".

There was one highlight.

An Amazon approached me during a particularly rollicking

---

* I was always grateful for free time. I carried a manuscript with me at all times and appreciated the stolen moments when I could try to complete it. I'm the only Bahá'í author, I think, who can answer the question "Where did you write this book?" by saying: "In a railway station in Birmingham, a plane over Australia, in an African hut in Zambia, a restaurant in Tokyo, a public park in Montevideo; and, oh, yes, at home."

schottische or polka. I can never tell the difference. She held out her hand to me.

"Let's dance."

"I don't dance."

"Tonight you do", she said, convincingly.

She gripped my hand fiercely, and lifted me bodily out onto the floor with a flourish. I bounced off her sturdy bosom, and we took off on a trail of musical disaster.

"You can't dance", she complained, quite shocked.

"I told you I couldn't."

"I'll lead", she mumbled, adding, "Everybody can dance."

That solved nothing. Having sandbagged me into the dance, she now took complete charge. The schottische ended and the band immediately began "Roll Out the Barrel". There was no decent interval for me to escape. Together we completed several musical "Crack of the whips!" I suspected that this must be one of those "exciting things" the School Committee had referred to.

"Are you anyone I should know?" she asked me, between breaths.

"I'm beginning to think not."

The dance mercifully ended. My moment in the Summer School spotlight had arrived at last. The Chairman of the evening came over, patted me on the back, and said:

"This is the time for you to speak to the friends, Mr Sears. But keep it short, we don't want the ice-cream to melt."

On the way out, I heard someone say, with a surreptitious glance at me, "Who was that bald-headed guy who cut short the square dance so abruptly?"

Such is fame.

The next morning, the Summer School opened officially. Quite obviously I was expected. I was kept so busy for two whole days, morning, noon and night; and so completely surrounded by a flood of warmth, love, tenderness, respect and appreciation that I longed for the anonymity of Friday.

I met my friend the Swedish masseuse that night at dinner. She had avoided me all day, ever since our shimmy-shaking schottische. I sat down beside her.

"Shall we dance?" I asked.

She looked the other way, saying: "Miss Berenson is not in tonight."

At another Summer School, another year, another continent, I practised medicine without a licence. I had no choice.

An energetic bushy-bearded middle-aged man accosted me in the hall-way. He held up the open palm of his hand, like a traffic officer.

"Stop!"

"What did I do wrong, officer?"

"Please, do you mind if I embrace you?" he asked. "I am desperate, and in great need of immediate help!"

I can still see Bob Quigley at the airport in Tampa, Florida, trying to disperse the friends so we could board our plane.

"Bill," Bob yelled at me, "you've got to stop the hugging and kissing, the plane's leaving!"

Sometimes it was difficult. One of the friends asked if he could say a prayer. He chanted the Fire Tablet. It was his moment in the sun, and he ignored the urgent appeals of the airline guide who was motioning frantically for Bob and myself to board. He stood there with his arms folded and carried on. He was still standing there when Bob and I looked out of the window of our departing plane and sped down the runway. I always think of him as still standing there at the departure gate in Tampa.

So you can see that I am not against embracing.

At big Conferences, Conventions, I have been known to hold fellowship gatherings down in front following my talks.

Bahá'ís often say to me, "I wanted to come up and talk to you, but there were so many people around you!" They are often too shy. Or, they may say: "I didn't come up because I suspected you were tired. Besides, I was ashamed of the little amount of work I had done this year."

"You're exactly the ones I want to talk to", I tell them.

Being with the friends is one of the most happy things that can happen to me as a Hand of the Cause of God. Occasionally, when I feel that I have been over-protected, or whisked away from the friends too abruptly before I have a chance to really talk to them in person, one on one, I announce from the platform that following my talk, I am going down in front to stand there, until the sun goes down if necessary, until I have a chance to meet and greet everybody in that auditorium who wants to be greeted. There is always plenty of hugging and cheek-kissing because sometimes that may be the only chance the friends have to spend some time with a Hand of the Cause of God.

The truth is, I often feel that those moments together down in front, those hugs, handshakes and cheek-kisses, are far more important than anything I may ever say during my talk. A lot of people disagree with me, but that's what makes a ball game. If that seems too "Goody Two Shoes" for you, tough luck!

No, I haven't forgotten the fellow with the bushy beard waiting to be embraced at the Summer School. I had a feeling about him, and I wanted to mention some sweet memories down Memory Lane before I faced up to him.

O yes, I did embrace him. I was quite ashamed of myself for having hesitated. In fact, I was deeply touched.

Tears came to his eyes as he kissed me first on one cheek then on the other. He embraced me soundly a second time, and said, all choked up:

"I'm so grateful to you. I've been laid up in bed all week, with a viral 'flu, and a temperature of 103. But, I knew if I could come down to the school and embrace a Hand of the Cause, I'd be cured."

Another fast embrace. He pressed me tenderly to his 'flu-ridden body.

"Thank you! Thank you!" he cried.

Tearfully, he was gone in a black Mercedes. I was left standing there with the residual.

Four days later, after a slow decline, I myself was down with a viral 'flu and a temperature of 103. I spoke to Bob Quigley who had just joined me from far-off California.

"Bob, do you think you could get me the name of the chap with the bushy beard who embraced me?"

"I think so."

"And the names of all his local relatives?"

He said: "I won't quote you at the Convention. Your halo just fell off."

"I'm using it as a hula hoop to throw and catch my victims."

"It's nice to see you a little riled up and rotten like this."

Bob wasn't so casual and philosophical when I offered to embrace him and kiss him on both cheeks. He did, however, point out a very basic truth.

"You will be a better man for this experience."
I nodded.
"But not today."

76

Since William Sears Junior was the elder of our two sons, he was also known on official documents as William Bernard Patrick Michael Terence Sears. Both Bill and I had the same name. I was the seventh, he was the eighth William Sears. My father told me so. Both Bill and I jettisoned all of it except: Bill Sears.

We couldn't make the "moves" with all that excess baggage.*

My own father, Bill's grandfather, years ago used to take his young pal out for long walks with him on his rounds of the local and nearby grog-shops and matinée movie houses, lavishly dispensing pop, hot dogs, and penny candy. Often, both would return with a stomach-ache.

My father, reminiscing one lazy Saturday afternoon, told me that while I was *not* the seventh son of a seventh son, I was the seventh person in his family to be named William Sears. Both myself and my Irish grandfather were also named "Barney". Since my other grandfather had a horse named Barney, I suffered considerably at school until I became Bill.

My father hinted quite strongly, in a friendly way, that while I might easily qualify for the worst of the William Searses, my darling young son Bill Jr. was certainly among the very best.

I already knew that. In fact, I teased my father by reminding him that it was I, and not my son Bill, who was "born in a caul" as the Irish say.

"Your son", he replied, "doesn't need a caul."

"Touché!"

It was during the Depression when I had no job but lots of time that I, too, used to go out walking with my son, Bill. He was just above my knees at the time and was togged out in a colourful

* Michael now has a son named William. That makes him the ninth. He also has a son named Michael. I'm not sure what he's starting there.

scarlet-and-grey Ohio State warm-up suit which I had cut out and sewed up for him. His hair was blonde (now dark brown) and fuzzy all over the top of his little bald head. When his blonde hair and sparkling brown eyes didn't knock them dead on the street, his Ohio State sweat-suit did. The combination was devastating. We could have taken orders from all passing parents. We could have lived quite extravagantly by passing the hat when Bill, in his scarlet outfit would sing the Ohio State pep song: "Across the field the band starts playing, show them Ohio's here!"

Perhaps even more heads turned when Bill was wearing his black-and-gold outfit from Army, the Black Knights of the Hudson. Not to mention the kelly green of the Fighting Irish of Notre Dame.

I didn't have anything else to do, so I made him five outfits and taught him the pep songs of all five Universities. We could have been big on Broadway but we had other fish to fry right there in Milwaukee.

If you think one word of this about that incredible young child has been exaggerated, ask any of his aunts and uncles in Wisconsin. I recommend his Aunt Ella in Sussex. Watch her face light up when you ask her about little Billy Sears. Prepare to catch her when she swoons away with joy and delight at the mention of his name.

Bill was only as high as Jimmy Fox's bat, but already he was a unique and special child.

I'm not talking about IQ or genius stuff, although he had his share. I'm talking about goodness. The way he treated people. Grown-ups and children alike. If it wasn't so "icky" to say about such a manly and virile little fellow, I would have described it as "sweetness". But everybody is suspicious of sweetness in such a small fry. They get nervous.

Bill never lost it. He's still using it in his profession, by phone, by mail, and in person. And especially in dealing with young people. They're harder to handle than Russia, but he does it. Ask any of his four daughters.

When he was little, Bill Jr. was so kind, warm-hearted, friendly, thoughtful and considerate that Marguerite and I began to worry. He just kept getting better. More and more each year. We wondered. "The good die young" stuff.

However, Bill is now becoming middle-aged and has his first few grey hairs, and is still so infuriatingly decent, kind, reliable and gentle, it burns my biscuit. It appears that the "good" die old, too.

The truth is, my son William, is exactly the kind of a person I'd like to be. In fact, I've been working at it all my life. Unsuccessfully so far. I've raised up quite an attractive false front, but behind it hides a moth-eaten, relatively unimproved old man. But still gamely trying. I have to. The goal of every Bahá'í is to become a better person, a finer human being. If you've learned anything from this book, you've learned that. I realize with melancholy sadness that I myself am still a long way down the road. But that beggar Bill, is already well on his way there.

I keep backsliding, falling down and skinning my nose. Like you, I'll bet. Bill Junior, on the other hand, is a genuine, good-natured, thoughtful, first-class human being. Without trying. Doesn't that frost you? It comes naturally to him. He's even pleasant when he first wakes up in the morning. Maybe he just hides the "anguish" within. After all, he's living in the same world we are, and drives through the smog twice a day to and from work. It can't be all croissants and coffee.

Bill is the sort of person you're overjoyed to see at the airport when you arrive. He's met me there so many times, at such odd hours, even on holidays and his day off, from a long distance away, but always makes me feel that the nicest part of his life is taking place right then when he's bent over toting his father's excess luggage.

When he takes you back to the airport, it's another story. When they call your plane, you feel tears of sorrow. You realize you are leaving behind a genuinely nice, lovable human being. They're so scarce.

Half-way between Los Angeles and Toronto on Air Canada Flight 794, you're still saying to yourself, "Doggone it! Why can't I be that way? When I try so hard?"

It will really upset Bill when he reads what I have written about him in this book, so maybe we'll see a little steam and rottenness coming out of him yet, at least this one time.

But don't count on it. His boiling-point is out of sight.

Still, I've given it my best shot.*

* You may have guessed. I like the boy.

William would have been spooky to Marguerite and myself all these years, if he hadn't been so witty, comical, and full of fun. I told you he wrote all of my radio scripts in Africa when I was out of town visiting the Bahá'ís all over the continent. His scripts were always more amusing than mine, more entertaining.

Mine was a comedy programme, but Bill's style was not joke-telling. Instead, he poked fun at himself and the world and society, making them laugh at themselves, and making them like it. One day my boss at the advertising agency met me in the hall, and congratulated me.

"Hey, Sears! You're doing great work! Your scripts are getting better all the time. Keep up the good work."

"I will", I told him.

I would, too, because I was about to leave on a long trip to Morocco and Algiers, and was carrying home two reams of paper for Bill.

Both Marguerite and I feel sure that seeing the funny side of life and writing about it, saves our son William from being "taken in the night!" as a too-good-to-live child.

Of course, I have to confess that I was present the day he hit his knuckles with the monkey-wrench while repairing the old Ford Consul. Bill's instant and spontaneous remarks lost him halo-points and several wing-feathers; not to mention the astonished admiration of his father, an old sportscaster who wrote the book on spectacular phrases related to hammer-and-wrench accidents to fingers, knuckles and thumbs.

I told Marguerite, "He's safe for a long, long time!"

On the other hand, Bill made valuable character points by re-pairing that old Ford Consul one more time. He kept it running for over two hundred thousand miles, after an already illustrious ca-reer as a pioneering car for Marguerite and myself in all parts of Africa.

Bill Junior didn't have a jealous or envious bone in his body. He greatly admired, and was both pleased and delighted by the orig-inal wild things his brother Mike said and did. Bill would chuckle appreciatively and say:

"I like the kid's creative style."

He did, too.

324

Bill gave a special dimension to pioneering for his whole family, and we all saw him off on his second pioneering adventure to St Helena Island, once the lair of Napoleon I.

Bill was filling in temporarily for an absent Bahá'í pioneer. It was a warm-up for his third post when the Call came for Latin America. He sailed off to Uruguay with his friend Fred Schechter where they married sisters. Not one of the goals of the Plan, but a lifelong fringe benefit of the journey for both.

I had planned to write about my son William's death-defying, *Romeo and Juliet* love affair that rocked and baffled the two continents. However, being older and wiser, after beginning this journey *Down Memory Lane* with a proof-reader, I am withholding that engrossing story until I can tell it in more juicy detail in the new book Marguerite and I are writing together called "*Tokoloshe*", or: *I Married Eleven Dachshunds*.

Besides, I wanted to check personally with Bill about this romance before releasing it to the world.*

Bill joined us in Africa, and soon the whole Sears family were at their pioneering post together. Bahá'í family ties are deep and strong and sweet to the taste. Almost the complete opposite of what you see in the world today.

Marguerite invited Bill's young lady to join us in Africa for a visit, but both she and Bill vetoed it. Michael referred to her only once, saying:

"By the way, Romeo, how is—?"

Bill slowly turned and fastened laser-beam eyes upon his brother. This was long before we knew what laser beams were, and how powerful and dangerous they could be. Thus, the subject of Bill's romantic love affair was ended at that moment. Forever. *That* love affair anyway.

In the words of that great Irish philosopher of love, "Kissing Barney" Sears, after whom both William and I were named:

"All love must come to an end. Until next time the sweet fragrance of another darling Colleen comes wafting on the gentle breeze from Galway Bay. May it be soon."

"The Trade Winds, he means", one of us said, slyly, glancing at William Bernard Patrick Michael Terence Sears the Eighth.

There is no truth whatsoever in the rumour that *any* of us ever referred to Bill Jr. as "Kissing William".

Not in his presence anyway.

* He's not all that angelic.

325

77

I was by nature, temperament, and interest, more like my son Michael. This will probably surprise, perhaps even alarm and shock my son Michael when he reads it.

However, Marguerite confirms it.

Although, as time went by, I would be the first to admit that my son Michael left me far behind, in the smoke-trail of his after-burners.

I had considered writing a book with Michael (father and son), but never did because I felt Michael could probably do it better by himself.* We did start one, long ago, called: *A New Name Written*, but it remains unfinished. Some of the original ideas Michael contributed to it would knock you right off your chair.

Michael turned out to be one of those rare human beings, an original thinker. The only person I knew among his fellow-Bahá'ís who outstripped him in this almost unique field was that dear friend of both Marguerite and myself, Horace Holley. Michael, however, is still young and is already hot on Horace's heels and closing in. However, in knowledge, wisdom, depth of spirit and service, neither Michael nor his father can ever catch up to Horace unless we make Methuselah's age.

From his earliest days, Michael was one of our most forthright, straightforward and courageous Bahá'í teachers. The world didn't hold any fears for him at all, and certainly not the people in it. Frequently Michael would involve—embroil is perhaps a better word—both Marguerite and myself in his odd but creative teaching projects such as the one you read about earlier, dubbed by Marguerite "Holiday Bahá'í vs. Rice Christians".

Unhappily, as time went on, Michael lost his burning desire to

* I think I do shade him on the funny stuff.

326

launch an assault on the non-Bahá'í world, but as an innocent, blue-eyed, blonde-haired child with a mass of wavy curls, he was fierce and fearless when it came to teaching.

I liked it. Sometimes Marguerite, Bill or I would jokingly say: "Where's old F and F?"

Let me give you an example of his "fierce" period. It will especially please and delight those of you who know him today.

One Sunday afternoon we were taking the Ingleside streetcar to a Bahá'í meeting at the San Francisco Bahá'í Centre on Post Street. We were riding through the Twin Peaks Tunnel *en route* downtown. Michael was seated across the aisle behind two gentlemen who were talking energetically with each other. Michael liked to mingle with strangers in those days. You heard me.

He had his little blonde head pushed forward toward the seat in front of him so he could follow every word of the conversation going on. Michael's head swung from side to side, following the comments, like a spectator at a tennis match.

Finally, Michael, the first of the great streetcar teachers, could resist the temptation no longer. He thrust his child's face between the two men to put in his two cents' worth.

One of the men turned to Michael.

"What do you want, kid?"

Michael enquired of the older gentleman, the one with the beard, "Do you know what day you are living in?"

Michael, of course, was quoting the Words of 'Abdu'l-Bahá. Both men were startled. One said, lamely, picking up his San Francisco *Chronicle* and looking at the date-line on the paper:

"May 19th, Thursday."

"No! No!" Michael explained. "I mean do you know the Day of God you are living in?"

Quite obviously they didn't. Nor did they want to know. All they wanted was for this peculiar kid with his shiny face to vanish from their lives.

"Beat it, kid!" the bearded one said.

"My information is free", Michael assured them. "Free and without price, as it says in the Bible."

"Are you Billy Sunday's kid or something?" the other man asked.

"I'm a Bahá'í teacher," Michael replied, "and I'll give you the

Glad Tidings for nothing if you want to turn your seat around and listen."

They didn't.

"Old F and F is at it again", Bill whispered to his mother.

The two men had had enough. They arose and departed abruptly, getting off at the next interchange inside the tunnel. Michael hadn't finished his point yet, so he zipped right out into the aisle after them. He followed them all the way down to the exit door, speaking quite loudly.

"If you're not happy today," Michael called after them, once again quoting 'Abdu'l-Bahá, "what day are you waiting for in which to be happy?"

Obviously, it wasn't this day. Just in case Michael was some strange unexpected instrument of the Lord sent to harangue them because of their misspent lives, they were both anxious and eager for a quick exit.

The two gentlemen were not only made uneasy by Michael's old-man comments on the world, but even more so by his extreme youthfulness. Michael had so many wavy beautiful curls, it looked like a carefully designed fashion wig. Coupled with his angelic face and those saucer-sized blue eyes, it was too much. The men fled in fear the moment the car door opened.

The bearded man, fearing that Michael might pursue them out into the tunnel, yelled back over his shoulder:

"Get lost, kid! Scram! Get out of our lives!"

The streetcar door slammed closed, and Michael walked back to his mother quite put out and disappointed.

He shouldn't have been. The people in the crowded streetcar applauded his efforts as he came back up the aisle. Michael bowed as he had seen his father do on the stage, then slumped down in the seat behind his mother. He leaned over and whispered to her about the two gentlemen:

"I don't think they're ready."

Marguerite didn't want to dampen Michael's ardour, but she did point out that Bahá'ís don't force their attentions on people, but wait until they are asked.

"I could be old and dead before that happened", Michael objected. "Besides, I was perfectly innocent. When I stuck my head between them, one of them did ask. He said, 'What do you want, kid?' so I told him."

"My son! My son!" or did I say that already?

78

In his childhood days, Michael genuinely liked people, all people. When he was little, Michael found it very easy to talk to almost anyone. That knack of his open fellowship with all mankind began to disappear with time. Perhaps Michael's surprise at the constant rebuffs he received from people in that increasingly indifferent and cruel world out there discouraged him. The lack of interest and the unwillingness of people he thought were friendly to become involved in anything, eventually put Michael off. Off people.

"Nobody listens to me", he told his mother.

"The ones who are ready will", she assured him.

"I'd sure like to meet some of them."

"You will", I promised. "They'll storm your doors some day."*

"The Bahá'í Faith is so good," Michael said, sighing sadly, "I thought everybody would fall over backwards when they heard about it."

"They should," I agreed, "but Bahá'u'lláh said we have to attract the heart, not enforce the mind."

"It's how we live our lives as Bahá'ís that will win them over in the long run", Marguerite added.

"That's too slow", Michael objected.

I told Michael that we were building the Christ-promised Kingdom of God on earth, brick by brick. It was a big job, a long job, and a slow job. You can't rush it.

"It's permanent, however", I assured him. "We don't have to see it, as long as we know it's going up for the future. Always upward, never backward, no matter how slow."

"I'd like to see it right now while I'm still little", Michael insisted.

"You'll see enough of it", I promised him. "There will be many astonishing victories in your day. Be sure."

* I didn't know it was prophetic, but then I didn't know about Africa.

I noticed as the years went by that Michael's sentences became shorter and his friendly advances to strangers more rare. Eventually, when Michael was older, it took a small-arms explosion to open up a conversation. Unless Michael spontaneously opened it himself.

Once into it, however, Michael's contributions were plentiful and original, sometimes brilliant. Many of my own most useful ideas for Bahá'í projects have originated with my son, Michael. But, in conversation with strangers these days, Michael is harder to open up than a large-shell clam. If you didn't know there was so much fine tasty meat inside, you might not even bother to try.

However, I should point out that Michael is in no way a misanthropist or anti-people. He has never suffered from the slightest problem in talking to his African friends either at home or on the road. There seems to be a special rapport between them.

Marguerite, and my nephew, Art Del Moro, made that clear to me after their teaching trip to Sugar Bush in Transkei, Southern Africa.

Marguerite and Art had a wonderful time, thoroughly enjoying the meeting, and joining in on the lovely and spirited singing; and later, answering the penetrating questions.

Most intriguing of all was the welcome the Africans gave to Marguerite as the wife of one of the Chief Stewards of the Bahá'í Faith. They were pleased but not thrilled, until one of the African men asked, "Your name is Sears?"

"Yes."

"Are you by any chance related to Michael Sears?"

"I'm his mother."

Pandemonium!

First a standing ovation for Michael Sears. Then unstinted applause for his dear mother. They even threw in a little for Art Del Moro and William Sears, the father.

Michael was big in Sugar Bush. He also walks tall in a number of other African villages in other African countries.* In addition to his teaching and consultation on problems, Michael originated the "Yankee click" method for the Xhosa-speaking Bahá'ís. In those spots where the Xhosa expresses himself eloquently and explosively with the *click* (as in Miriam Makeba's popular "Click Song"), Michael would achieve that click effect by snapping his fingers in

* Including Lesotho, where he pioneered for a couple of years.

the appropriate places. It showed colossal lack of skill with the Xhosa language, but he completely won over the hearts of his Xhosa friends. Particularly the youth. His finger-snapping caught on, and swept the school sessions. In a spirit of fun, the young people would use Michael's finger-snap technique along with their own dramatic clicks. Laughter followed as Michael's finger-snapping temporarily won the day.

It's hard for me to avoid my son Michael when I am travelling in Africa. The words and music of his "Song of the Pioneer" are well known, and sung by the Bahá'ís in many parts of English-speaking Africa. Sometimes even in translation. The song begins: "Africa, Africa, come let us sing . . . Tell the people of the Message we bring."

It's a happy, rollicking call to teaching.

One of the most touching moments of my Bahá'í family life came at one of the great Bahá'í World Conventions on the side of Mount Carmel, the Mountain of God, in Israel, World Centre of the Bahá'í Faith. I was present at a session of all the members of the Continental Board of Counsellors for Africa, as well as members of the National Spiritual Assemblies of Africa. We were up on the roof garden of the Nof Hotel in Haifa, looking down on the sacred Shrine of the Báb, and the beautiful gardens that surround it.

I was introduced to the assembled guests by a member of the Universal House of Justice, a former African Pioneer himself. When I finished my brief talk, the National Spiritual Assembly members from Southern Africa began to sing Michael's song: "Africa! Africa!"

All joined in.

I remember how delighted and surprised I was a few years earlier during a special Victory Weekend campaign of teaching in the United States. The director of the California children's chorus, Mary Zemke, introduced me to the theme music. The children sang it for me.

"America! America! Rise up and sing!"

It was Michael's African *Song of the Pioneers* with American lyrics. It stirred up the "onward marching victorious legions" of Bahá'u'lláh's radiant spiritual Army. It especially stirred a father sitting in the front row.

331

I said to myself as I sat there listening, what Michael had said so long ago to those two gentlemen on the Twin Peaks Tunnel streetcar:

"Do you really know what day you're living in?"

People who take the time to know Michael are not only rewarded with a pleasant hour or two, and given some useful, frequently quite original, new slants on the teaching problems they face and how to solve them; they may also have found a lifelong friend. Caution: It won't be easy.

Another unique characteristic Michael developed in his later years, is a tendency to pace. He walks back and forth around the room as though he were looking for a quick exit, so he could seek something much better than he has found so far. Something which, if he keeps on the move, he might still capture before it is too late. Michael's constant movement back and forth has another stimulating effect. When talking with him, you don't waste time on nonessentials. You get right down to business. I do myself because I fear that Michael will be off to a more promising place before I have time to tell him how much I admire him.

I know. I know.

You're saying that all fathers talk this way about their sons, and that it's only natural for me to claim certain filial bragging rights. But I do have a unique pair in William and Michael.

Bahá'ís do not gamble, but if they did, I've got a "pair" that will beat a *full house*, *four of a kind*, or even a *royal flush*.

Anywhere.

Anytime.

79

Since William and Michael started the journey with us, we thought you ought to know how things stand with them now.

Michael is still at his pioneering post after all these years. He is married to a beautiful South African girl named Ruth. Her family originally came from the Near East. She is a member of the Bahá'í Auxiliary Board for that area, and we expect great things from her. After all, she was born on Christmas Day and her parents were named Joseph and Mary.

Where can she go but up?

Michael and Ruth have two sons, William and Michael. Both are smarter than their grandfather. They have a golden retriever named Henry. Our grandsons graciously allow Marguerite and myself to use their bedroom when we come visiting. It was at the boys' table that I began and finished several of my books, including parts of this one, and much of *A Cry from the Heart!*

William is married to a lovely Chilean girl named Mariel. They have four Spanish–English speaking daughters: Marguerite, Mariel, Julia and Marcia. Marguerite is married, the others may soon be, so I may some day become a great-grandfather.

I will, however, make no tape-recording that says I am "Everybody's Great-Grandfather!" I would have to hire at least three secretaries to handle the mail. Bahá'í children (and grandchildren) can "write up a storm".

I was lucky enough to be present at my son, William's wedding in Santiago, Chile. I missed Michael's in South Africa. Qué lástima!

I was on a prolonged teaching trip throughout Latin America the year we established 21 new National Spiritual Assemblies in the Western Hemisphere. My son, William was smart enough to be married during one of the trips that carried me to Chile.

I wanted to show off to my new Latin relatives the progress I had made in learning Spanish, so at the airport, I filled out my entry documents in that language. At Immigration, on the paper where it requests you to state your "marital status", I confidently wrote: "Cansado".

Of course, the word was "Casado" (married), and not "Cansado" (tired). No wonder it puzzled the Immigration Officer. He looked at me, at my paper, then back at me.

"Cansado?"

"Si."

He asked me once more to be sure, "Cansado?"

"Si, si", I said. "Cansado. Muchos Años. For many years. Very cansado."

He shrugged his shoulders sympathetically, being a married man himself.

"Es possible", he agreed.

I was bone weary and it was past midnight. As I walked along the reception line of those happy smiling Latin American faces, I shook hands with each person. I tried my best to be wide awake and charming.

I said, "I'm happy to see you. Pleased. Muchas gracias. Delighted. Thank you. Maravillosa. Gracias for coming." My Español finally ran out, and I fell back on Merci beaucoup. Danke Zehr. Grazie and Prego. Toda raba. Mange tak. That finished me, so I went back to Muchisimas gracias.

In a miasmal early morning fog caused by coming down from 12 000 feet to nearer sea level at Santiago, I was beginning to drift off mentally. I greeted the last handsome young man through half-closed lids, "I'm most happy to make your acquaintance", I assured him.

"You should be!" he replied. "I'm your son. You're here to see me get married."

You win some, you lose some.

The wedding, incidentally, was beautiful. My daughter-in-law was named Mariel. Her father, Señor Carlos Bulling Peterson, was described by the Guardian of the Bahá'í Faith as "the father of the Bahá'í work in Chile". Mariel's mother, Señora Julia Alvarado de Bulling, is one of our fine Spanish-speaking teachers in both South and North America. The brothers, sisters, and relatives, stretched all the way from Quilpué to Viña del Mar and back. I like and admire them all.

Both my sons, Bill and Mike, married into delightful families. What father-in-law anywhere has two more beautiful daughters than Ruth and Mariel? I chose wisely because they both make my favourite dessert: crème caramel and flan. The best in the world. It's a stand-off!

They are all Bahá'ís in both families. All active, all busy in their own way. Bill, Mike, and Mariel all serving on Assemblies. Both National and Local. The young people busy with children's classes. Sorry, they are now, of course, youth and young adults. Ruth is a member of the Auxiliary Board.

One of the rare delights of my Bahá'í life came when I was asked to attend the Convention in South West Africa/Namibia the year their new National Spiritual Assembly was to be established.

I represented the World Centre, Michael represented the Mother Assembly from which the new child was born, and Ruth represented the Continental Board of Counsellors for Africa. It all took place just a short distance from the very spot where Marguerite, Michael and I had first landed in Africa from the *African Sun* at Walvis Bay so long ago.

What memories we shared that weekend!

I remember one summer when the four of us were teaching in four different continents at one time. Michael was in Africa, Bill was in South America, Marguerite was in North America, and I was in Europe. Pity we couldn't have adopted someone to serve in Australasia.

On rare occasions, the Sears family does all meet together. The last family reunion was in California. It was the first time Michael had returned to the USA since he was seventeen. A Sears family reunion is something to behold when it happens. It is as rare as a five-headed shamrock. It begins very slowly. There is so much to say, so much news to catch up on, that at first no one knows where to begin. We just sit there and smile radiantly at each other, reminiscing.

There is always an inordinate amount of hugging and kissing that goes on. As time goes by, the news just bubbles out spontaneously. There is also quite a bit of "Remember the time in Zanzibar when the mad Arab . . ." Or: "Will you ever forget the moonlit night in Beau Bassin, Mauritius Island, after the International Conference when the whole busful saw three midnight rainbows? Moonbows?"

I don't believe that any one of the four of us would give up a single blessed moment of those bygone pioneering days.*

Marguerite and I thought you'd like to know what happened to Bill and Mike before we say goodbye. It's a popular thing in newspaper columns nowadays to ask, "Whatever happened to so-and-so?"

Now you know. And they're entitled. As we say in the sports world: "They paid their dues."

---

* This may be a slight exaggeration. Did I say that before, too? *Three or four times?* Really!

"Sala hantle: Stay well, my friends!"

80

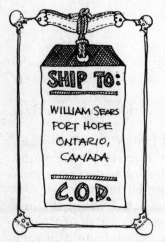

One morning several years later, we received the bills of lading for a set of trunks and footlockers we had shipped from Africa. One of them was the blue sea-chest with brilliant shooting stars, and the names of the real stars, our animal puppets, printed in the centre. They had come home to join their family in a far-off land.

I didn't want Marguerite to see the blue trunk since she was proof-reading the chapters about the "Zoo Crew!" and the Ganaraska River was already at flood-tide. The workers on the farm helped me carry the luggage up into the attic above the projection room at The Hall.

Since the advent of the Muppets, all other puppets have had to take a back seat to their genius. But in Africa, some thirty years ago, Fitz, Imp, Hillary, Great Big Sam, Camille the Cam-*ell*, Crock O'Dile, the Irish Crocodile, and his little friend the "Out-of-Luck" duck stood tall and proud.

They were extraordinary, and all stars in their own right.

In those days of delight in Africa, the Sears Zoo Crew had quite a "run". They not only appeared from time to time on *That Man Sears* on Springbok Radio, they also starred at John Orr's Department Store, Anstey's, The Milner Park Spring Show, and scored a smashing "first", at Ciro's night club, now defunct. They brought the house down as the saying goes, and received a standing ovation from that blasé night-club audience.

In the Chaucerian English of Imp, the Impala:
"We wuz a *smasheroo!* A Ringy-Dingy-Do!"
It may have been an understatement.

Our Zoo Crew was always a smash hit. Or, as Hillary, who was now carried away by his new elegant image as a famous star among night-club entertainers, was fond of saying, "We killed the people outright! Next stop Las Vegas!"

Hillary was decades ahead of his time in many of his "snappers" as he called his bright sayings. He was years in advance of those who later mimicked Hillary's own words of self-praise:

"If you've got it, flaunt!"
He did. Profusely!

Marguerite finally proof-read this particular chapter about the arrival of our friends. When I came in for afternoon tea, tears were running down her cheeks.

"That bad, eh?" I said, joking about my writing, but suspecting why she felt so sad.

"I can't stand you and your wretched Irish whimsy", she said, stamping her foot. Marguerite burst into tears, threw the manuscript at my head, and fled from the room, crying over her shoulder: "And I can't stand your eternal flash-backs either!"

"How about my flash-aheads?" I asked her. "And my flashes-where-you-are?" I laughed, trying to bring her out of her tearful mood. I knew Marguerite was lost in the wonder of an Africa she loved, had left, and could never forget.

I picked up the manuscript and finished proof-reading it. I punched the holes and fitted the pages into the final manuscript covers. I took my vitamins, my herbal tea, and a whiff of oxygen from the tank, then went out for a walk beside the waterfall.

I, too, had been carried too far down Memory Lane. It's amazing how fond you can become of a hunk of balsa wood or a hank of fake fur. Neither of us could help thinking about them. Marguerite dislikes it intensely when I personify those pieces of wood and ping-pong balls. It makes her sad. If you can't move people that way, you'll never be successful with puppets. Besides, the tears only show what Marguerite was already feeling in her heart.

Now, over a quarter of a century after their days of glory in Africa, all these dear puppet friends of ours sleep in silence beside the Ganaraska River in Canada, twelve thousand miles from their original home. They are packed away carefully inside their own much-travelled sea-chest. They are stored permanently in the attic of the famous Hall at Hadden's where so many glorious GATHER-INGS have been held in the past.

No doubt our animal friends heard everything that took place on the stage below. Like Marguerite and myself, they must have been filled with many long-ago happy memories of Africa, the Continent of Light.

Whenever I think of Great Big Sam, or Hillary, or Fitz, even after all this time, I still get a lump in my throat. I wonder what they're saying about us there in the dark. I know it doesn't make sense, but I suffer pangs of guilt when I think of such talented actors out of work, and only eighty feet away from their element, a stage. Once they were stars.

Several weeks later I was searching for one of the radio scripts I had written in Africa. I wanted to adapt it for our Television Series in Hawaii. I decided to go up in the attic at the Hall and rummage through the trunks to find it.

I began shoving boxes, footlockers and trunks aside looking for the one that said Radio Scripts, SABC. Suddenly, I felt a stab-like thrill of pure pleasure. I was looking down at a tiny brown and gold box with a name printed on the top in big gold letters: The Honourable Mr Glow-Worm. Next to him, in a corner, stood that old familiar blue sea-chest.

In the centre of the trunk, amidst a fading shower of shooting stars, I saw painted in crimson letters the names of those dearly loved old friends.

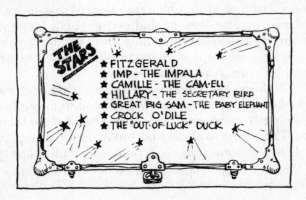

I could hear their delightful dishy voices talking to the African children in Swaziland. I could still laugh at the memory of "Musa ukuhleka!"

As I read their names on that sea-chest, a quarter of a century came rushing back. I slumped down on a nearby footlocker, and as senior citizens have a tendency to do, I withdrew from today, and revelled in my past.

Through a distant echo chamber in my mind, growing ever louder and more clear, came the sweet musical voices of other dear African Bahá'í friends: Andrew Mofokeng, Florence Marumo, William Masehla, Ephens Senne, Gilbert Tombisa, Daniel Ramoroesi, Max Seepé, May, Dorothy, Jane, Bothata, Selai, Baker, on and on went the names and faces that moved across the screen of my closed eyelids. They were all calling out to me once again, as they called that long-ago day to my departing plane: "Tsamaie hantle, Ntate. Go well, father."

I breathed my silent reply to those phantom voices, as I watched them in memory drive away from the farm. They smiled, laughed happily at all the fun we'd had together, and waved out the open windows of their car as they drove off.

"Tot siens!"

Their headlights flashed a final time through the dark pine-trees, then disappeared forever around the bend toward Muldersdrift Road. They were going back into that special world of their own that we never really knew, or fully understood.

In some far-off African township.

I found the radio scripts, and turned to leave. Something drew me back for one last look at that blue sea-chest. My wrist tingled as I saw the name Imp, the Impala, that perfect patsy. I longed to slip him on to my right arm one more time. Even without an audience. I longed to hear his raspy deep gravel-filled voice cry out: "I'm innocent, I tell you. Perfectly innocent!"*

I carefully lifted the moth-eaten Impala from the sea-chest. He still looked good to me. I slipped him on to my right arm as easily as though I had done it yesterday. I bugged out his marvellous eyes. The rotted rubber band broke, and I had to push his eyes back in with my fingers. I pulled his faded and peeling

* Quite obviously Imp, the Impala, would have been Michael's puppet if Mike had not been off pioneering in Windhoek, South West Africa/Namibia.

brown nose right up against my own until they touched. I made him say:

"Domella, Ntate. How've ya been, stranger?"

"I missed you."

"Me, too. It's mighty lonely down there in a dark trunk, you know."

"I'm sorry about that."

"Me, too. Especially when you've got a bunch of deadheads down there on your stage. You call that performing! Don't you know you've got the greatest living actors in Africa, all lying up here in trunks, stiff as a board?"

"I know. It's a pity. But it couldn't be helped."

"That's it then?"

"That's it."

"Remember me to your lovely wife. She always was the decent one in the family."

I laid the Impala gently back down beside his pal, Hillary, the Secretary Bird. I stuck my finger in Hillary's bright red mouth, and made his jaws move up and down. Bob Quigley's voice floated back to me from that far-off street in Mohale's Hoek, Lesotho.

"We love all of you children! You're beautiful! Yes, you, too, you convict rascals. Hang in there! Hip! Hip! Hip! Hip!"

I knew such days, magical days of friendship and delight, would never return, but what a bounty for Marguerite and myself to have been a part of them. I mixed my Sesotho with Swahili as I nodded to all my friends, said goodbye, then gently closed the lid of the sea chest.

"Sala hantle. Stay well, my friends."

The touch of wistfulness that filled the air in that dark attic in Ontario, Canada, vanished the moment Marguerite slipped in and sat down beside me on the footlocker.

Her face was aglow with a radiant smile. I knew she had overheard me talking to the puppets.

"Sorry", she said.

"Why?" I asked, giving her shoulders a squeeze. "Because you missed me when you threw the manuscript at me?"

"I was sorry your conversation had to end. It was beautiful."

Marguerite leaned over and kissed me on the cheek. She whispered

341

comfortingly to me, the words of an African proverb we both knew well.

"Don't be sad. Be happy. If there were no *goodbyes*, there could be no *hellos*."

81

Marguerite and I have finally settled down in one place. We live beside a waterfall, an old mill, a dam, and a private pond which Canadian geese visit in season. Right this very minute, we are surrounded by tranquil pine-trees, singing birds, and a vast green meadow where the mares and their young foals are gambolling through the clover. I have to admit that I am now in my element, and have come home at last to do nothing but write and complete all my unfinished manuscripts.

I am now three quarters of a century old, and it's nice to know that the constant journeys have ended. I can now focus with the intensity of an acetylene torch upon the writing of those many rough drafts which I abandoned when I became Miss Marco Polo's planetary travelling companion.

It was Marguerite's suggestion for me to concentrate on writing. She would confirm it herself, if only I knew where she was. She left me a note, but I can't remember where I put it. Somewhere in the dictionary, I think. Perhaps under "Anchored".

It's pleasant to realize that after such a long and unbroken period of being "on the wing" for nearly half a century, Marguerite and I can now have our mail sent to one permanent address.

It's all over but the shouting.

There are, of course, many wonderful things still to be done and many Bahá'í goals still to be won. The goals of the current Plan are always in the forefront of our minds, and we plan to help win them from our home base. Marguerite and I are consulting about these goals this very afternoon, whenever she gets back from wherever she's gone.

I think she went to a nearby Indian Reserve, Tyendenaga, which we both love dearly. She went to deliver some books. Or was it to deliver a Fireside talk on pioneering? I forget.

But I do know we are consulting on which of these exciting Homefront goals we ourselves can undertake. I'm listing them alphabetically, and pointing out to Miss Seven League Boots* which goals can be won from a prone position; which can be achieved by sitting down; and which can be conquered from just standing in one place and looking out of the window at the ducks on the pond as you compose an encouraging letter to the friends calling upon them to "arise!"

All these efforts, of course, are to be done "Largo" and not "Allegro".

I don't want you to think that writing will be any "retreat" on my part. Far from it. I still plan to attend Convention in Canada and the USA each year. I also plan to be present at many large International Gatherings, Temple dedications and Youth Conferences.

Hands of the Cause of God never retire. Instead, they "re-tyre" and start off down the road to wherever they are needed, confident that some of their best Bahá'í mileage is yet to come. But, there is no reason they can't jog in place occasionally, and think every move over carefully.

I am using a cane now, a walking-stick. It was carved especially for me in Venda, Africa and was presented to me by another dear friend, a member of the Bahá'í Auxiliary Board for that African region, Edward Budeli. It helps with my arthritis whenever I can remember which leg to limp on.

More important by far, the crook at the end of the cane is extremely useful for hooking Marguerite's arm and pulling her away from the atlas and any unfolded road maps. Also for pounding on the top of the desk whenever I find her absent-mindedly checking on steamer sailings or airline schedules. That, of course, is all over for both of us now, but old habits are hard to break.

The cane is also very handy when we are walking over the bridge spanning the dam on the Ganaraska River heading for the

---

* You'll be pleased to know that I have hidden her "boots".

Old Mill to watch the salmon come up the river to spawn. I think all that courage and effort shown by the salmon to jump the dam has unhinged Marguerite temporarily. I think the determination of those gallant old fish to get to their goal at whatever the cost, has "gunned" Marguerite's pioneering or travel-teaching motor. If I thought this were true, I would poke her with the rubber end of Edward Budeli's cane, and put her into the water with the salmon.

I haven't done that yet because I know Marguerite's frenzy is only temporary. After all, we both admit that for us, long-distance travelling is "kwisha kabisa" as they say in Swahili. Meaning "completely finished". I understand that it is bad grammar, but perfectly understandable. Whenever I notice Marguerite trembling, with her eyeballs on bright, I quickly ask her to spell geriatrics. Backwards.

I have purchased a new typewriter, ten reams of paper, a pack of carbon, three brand new all-black ribbons, and have re-upholstered my typing chair.

Marguerite will tell you all about our exciting "settling down" plans as soon as she gets back. She promised it wouldn't be long when she telephoned me from the Triple A, or was it the Passport Office?

I'm so pleased. This six months period of being in one place has done wonders for Marguerite. I've never seen anyone regain their strength and enthusiasm so quickly and so thoroughly. Quite obviously this permanent-location process is going to be very good for her. I noticed that even her singing voice was "on key" with perfect pitch as she did the dishes and hummed "Around the world in eighty days".

Excuse me.

Somebody seems to be pulling fiercely on the end of my cane. If I'm not mistaken, I think it's—

Sorry, I'll have to contact you later! We seem to have an emergency. To be honest with you, we may have to forget about my concentrating on writing and putting an end to my world-wide travels. That may have been a bit premature.

It appears that Marguerite also took my passport to the Kenya Embassy as well as her own.

Apparently, I'm still on the wing.

Guess whose?

Caramba!

JOURNEY'S END

"Kwa heri: Go in happiness!"

82

Will all the pioneers now in the field, and those potential pioneers who are still planning to arise and achieve this great blessing and immortal service, please stand up?

Bravo!

Every one of you!

Someday, all the world will know and extol the value of the work you have done and will yet do. For now, you can take comfort in the knowledge that the Writings of the Faith of Bahá'u'lláh, the Supreme Redeemer of men, honour you and proclaim your fame.

THE PIONEER

". . . they represent a force for
good, they are like a light-house of
Bahá'u'lláh shining at a strategic
point and casting its beam out into
the darkness."

To you, the stalwart pioneers and teachers of the Bahá'í Faith, each and every one, without exception, and to your children and families who journeyed with you, we dedicate this book.

You are the stars, the heroes and heroines, of every word written here. This story is your story. Even the title of the book honours you. In the face of hardships and setbacks, in spite of the loneliness which at times engulfed your lives, with unsurpassed courage, tenacity, steadfastness, and consecration, you braved every danger, faced every crisis, and kept *All Flags Flying!*

348

To whom else on the face of the earth could we possibly have dedicated this book?

Hand of the Faith, Mr A Q Faizi, a dear personal friend, said it best. Speaking to some seven thousand of his fellow-Bahá'ís in the Royal Albert Hall in London, England in 1963, on the one hundredth Anniversary of Bahá'u'lláh's Declaration to the world, Mr Faizi's praises were for you, the pioneers and teachers, both old and new. He told the Bahá'ís and the world:

"These are the people upon whose shoulders we stand."

The following honour-roll of names brings to a close the pioneering saga of one small Bahá'í family, Marguerite, Bill, William and Michael Sears. We have chosen this special way to say good-bye to all those places and people we have come to love so dearly.

True, it does not include all of them. In fact, it is only a precious few. A vast unrecorded number still waits in the shadows to arise in their turn and appear out of the mist. We have symbolized this constant movement, this spinning world of ours with the names of those cities, towns, villages and reserves where great victories have already been won by the pioneers. Victories won, not by us, but by those "upon whose shoulders we stand".

As we see these familiar and much-loved names from the past appear, stand out, then vanish, we know that in the future others will arise by the hundreds, thousands, hundreds of thousands, and millions to take their place. The song of the Kingdom will never be ended until it covers the earth "as the waters cover the sea", but the melody will linger on to enrich and beautify every single life which is touched by the Teachings of Bahá'u'lláh.

We "leave the words with those who have the heart."

Marguerite, Bill, Michael and myself shall recall each and every name, those recorded and unrecorded, with warm and tender love, for we have visited them all. Their roots are deep in our hearts.

Forever.

Hail!

But never farewell:

349

Piggs Peak
Pontypridd
Umbumbulu
Hiroshima
Prince Rupert
São Paulo
Mdantsane
Jerusalem
Kelowna
Teyateyaneng
Tenerife
Eagle River
Mexicali
Cardiff
Seoul
San Salvador
Brussels
Potchefstroom
Lagos
Portland
Dakar
Windhoek
Winnipeg
Ermelo
Berlin
Frankfurt
Venice
Pago Pago
Charlottetown
Oshawa
Khartoum
San José
Tilling
Cork
Harare
Derry
Hilo
Mohale's Hoek

Quilpué
Orlando
Casablanca
Canberra
Tokyo
Caracas
San Pierre
Little Rock
Hamburg
Westminster
Dar es Salaam
Addis Ababa
Kampala
Buenos Aires
Piet Retief
Kyoto
Devon
Ladysmith
Mbabane
East London
London
Panama City
Dublin
Frobisher Bay
Athens
Shetland Islands
Apia
Mmabatho
Tegucigalpa
Tyendenaga
Scotsville
Indio
Bethlehem
Pietersburg
Rome
York
Faeroe Islands
Davison

Thousand Oaks
Bloemfontein
Quebec City
Maputo
Osaka
Monrovia
Istanbul
Umtata
Tanzania
Minneapolis
Machakos
Aitkin
Montevideo
Window Rock
Geyserville
Wilton Manors
Johannesburg
Cape Town
Cairo
Edinburgh
Rio
Guayaquil
Simi Valley
Canton
Port Elizabeth
Victoria
Maseru
Tía Juana
Bahamas
Boston
Viña del Mar
Pietermaritzburg
Saskatoon
Denver
New York City
Gallup
Perry
San Antonio

"Kwa Heri: Go in happiness."

350